For my
happy FATHERS DAY
love Katherine
2003

W9-CQF-869

MOUNT TAMALPAIS
A History

Mt. Tamalpais is bathed in early morning light in this fine portrait taken from Red Hill, San Anselmo, circa 1907. A train coming in from Fairfax leaves a plume of smoke at lower right. (Courtesy of Charles Ford)

MOUNT TAMALPAIS
A History

Lincoln Fairley

James Heig
Picture Editor

Scottwall Associates
San Francisco, California
1987

Front Cover: *Mt. Tamalpais* circa 1938 by Percy Gray. Courtesy of James L. Coran and Walter Nelson-Rees; color photograph by Stephen Fridge
Endsheet Map: Dewey Livingston
Book Design: James Heig
Typography: Alphabetics, San Francisco

First Edition
Copyright © 1987
Scottwall Associates
95 Scott Street
San Francisco, California 94117

Grateful acknowledgement is given to The Book Club of California for permission to reprint an excerpt from *A Naval Campaign in the Californias — 1846-1849: The Journal of Lieutenant Tunis Augustus Macdonough Craven, U.S.N.,* edited by John Haskell Kemble.

No part of this book may be reproduced in any form or by any electronic or mechanical means, including information storage and retrieval systems, without permission in writing from the publisher, except by a reviewer who may quote brief passages.

Printed by Braun-Brumfield Company, Ann Arbor, Michigan.

ISBN 0-942087-00-3 (clothbound)
ISBN 0-942087-01-1 (paperback)

Acknowledgments

This book has grown out of a love of Mount Tamalpais, and I hope reflects it. My attachment has been fostered by frequent hikes, covering all the trails. I am not an old-timer; my experience covers only the last decade. But my enthusiasm and my curiosity have been eager.

As a newcomer I have been greatly dependent on the many lovers of the Mountain more knowledgeable than I. Two men in particular have been indispensable. Ben Schmidt has been a constant source of inspiration and assistance. He has hiked all over the Mountain for some sixty years, including the untouched areas away from roads and trails, and has become more than commonly expert in the Mountain's flora, its geology and its history. Another long-time hiker to whom I am deeply indebted is Fred Sandrock, the spark plug of our Mt. Tamalpais History Project. He has been exceedingly generous in sharing his vast store of information.

Many others have been helpful. Nancy Skinner has generously shared her valuable collection of historical photographs, as well as her detailed knowledge of the Mountain, accumulated over the years as the leader of hikes and as a teacher of courses about hiking and the Mountain. Bob Lethbridge, now retired after more than thirty years' service with the Marin Municipal Water District, about which he is writing a history, has contributed much historical information not only about the MMWD, but about many related matters, a great deal of it based on original research in the County newspapers.

Several librarians have helped me find the many fugitive materials necessary to my project, most particularly Thelma Percy, Head Librarian of the Mill Valley Public Library, and her research staff; and Gladys Hansen, Librarian of Special Collections, San Francisco Public Library. The staff of the Bancroft Library at UC Berkeley were most helpful to us in finding photographs and maps.

A host of others have made significant contributions, but I have space to mention only these: Dick Sasuly, who originally kindled my enthusiasm for the Mountain; Salem Rice, geologist; Marian Hayes Cain, long associated with the Mountain Plays; Ted Wurm, author of *The Crookedest Railroad in the World;* Pete Martin and Greg Jennings, Captains in the Marin County Fire Department; John Thomas Howell, botanist; Roy Farrington and Nancy Jones, generous sharers of their unsurpassed collection of photographs of paintings of Mt. Tamalpais; Jim Vitek, now retired from the MMWD, who gave me a helping hand at the outset; Bob Lucas, Dewey Livingston and Hermann Zutraun, who have been helpful in supplying photographs; Synnove Newman, who generously turned over to our History Project the visitor registers from the East Peak dating from the 1880s; the late Esmond Milsner, of the Tamalpais Conservation Club, who made available the archives of the TCC; Richard Gililland, formerly a Mt. Tamalpais State Park ranger; Randy Hogue and the other current State Park rangers; Louise Teather, Dorothy Whitnah, Jim Morley, and Mark Reese, writers about the Mountain; and Harold Gilliam, inspirational conservationist. My thanks to Margaret Greene and Nancy Skinner for reading the manuscript.

To Sara Jacobson, who typed and retyped the manuscript with great skill and accuracy, I am deeply grateful.

I owe a particular debt to James Heig of Scottwall Associates, the publisher. Through his meticulous and thoughtful editing, he has added greatly to the readability of the text. Jim is also responsible for the selection and arrangement of the photographs, as well as for the design of the book.

No matter how significant their contributions, none of these people is in any degree responsible for the accuracy of the information; for this I must take full responsibility. I should like to add, however, that I consider the book only a start in pulling together the widely scattered sources for a history of Mt. Tamalpais. New information is coming to hand constantly, adding to and correcting what has been set down here. I anticipate that my associates in the Mt. Tamalpais History Project will continue to add to our understanding and appreciation of the Mountain.

I wish to thank *California History* and *The Californians* for permission to use material originally published in their pages.

Finally, my debt to my wife, Bertha, is immeasurable. Though not herself a hiker or an *aficionada* of Mt. Tamalpais, she has actively encouraged and supported all my efforts.

San Francisco, March 1987   Lincoln Fairley

Disclaimer and Guide to Further Reading

The author makes no claim that this volume is a complete description and history of Mt. Tamalpais, nor that it does full justice to the Mountain's enchantment. It is at best a first approximation, and is, indeed, the first attempt to put together in a single volume material available, for the most part, in very scattered sources. It is hoped that others, among them other members of the Mount Tamalpais History Project, will make additional contributions.

The reader who wishes to read further will be assisted by the notes attached to each chapter. For a much more extended bibliography, the reader is referred to one prepared by the author and available at the History Room of the Mill Valley Public Library, the California Room of the Marin County Library, and the California Historical Society Library.

Preface

Mt. Tamalpais has been a magnet for huge numbers of people for well over a century. Explorers, hunters, artists, writers, botanists, tourists, hikers and runners have felt its pull. Even loggers and ranchers, who came to the Mountain to earn their livelihood, probably enjoyed it for itself. The image of the Mountain which so many revere is in large part the product of those who have loved it.

Nature, of course, began it. Physically, the Mountain is the upthrust product of the Pacific plate pushing for millions of years against the North American plate, creating the melange of rocks which we have come to see as a familiar and beloved form. The social history of the Mountain began thousands of years ago with the native peoples who thrived on its lower slopes and waterways. Their myths about the Mountain still persist. Spanish and Mexican missionaries, soldiers and settlers paid little heed to the Mountain.

As California's first straggling European and Yankee settlers were joined by the rush of gold-seekers, in the decade preceding 1852, the immigrant population increased from c. 7,000 to c. 250,000. Gradually people were drawn to the Mountain; first came hunters, then cattlemen and lumbermen, then sightseers and hikers, who began climbing on the Mountain in the 1870's. The Mountain Railway, opened in 1896, brought thousands to the East Peak to revel in the view, and to Muir Woods to admire the big trees. The Mountain Theatre has drawn thousands of visitors since its opening in 1913.

Among all these admirers, it is the hikers who have made the Mountain theirs. They have swarmed over it in the thousands, decade after decade. They have built and maintained hundreds of miles of trails. Through their organizations they have spearheaded the movement to preserve the Mountain in its natural state. Without their dedication the Mountain today would be a very different place.

What has attracted all these many people, now numbering three million each year? No one thing, obviously. But for all of them the Mountain is a source of recreation in its most literal sense, of health and beauty and peace. People come for a quiet picnic, to admire the marvelous views, to revel in the wildflowers and redwoods, to gaze in awe at the marvelous architecture of canyon and ridge and promontory. For many the experience of nature is deeply spiritual.

Sidney Lanier, the poet of the South, once described the scenery in the Appalachians in a letter to his wife:

> How necessary it is that one should occasionally place oneself in the midst of those more striking forms of nature in which God has indulged His fancy! . . . Thou canst imagine what ethereal and yet indestructible essences of new dignity, of new strength, of new patience, of new serenity, of new hope, new faith, and new love, do continually flash out of the gorges, the mountains, and the streams, into the heart, and charge it, as lightnings charge the earth, with subtle and heavenly fires.

These words show us precisely why Mt. Tamalpais is so precious to so many, and why it must be protected in the future.

ix

Dedicated to
Ben Schmidt and Fred Sandrock
my guides and mentors

Mount Tamalpais
A History

Table of Contents

An aerial view of the Marin peninsula shows the Mountain forming a sharp perpendicular to the predominant parallel ridges running northwest to southeast. This contrariness channels clouds, fog, and warm or cold air, producing radically different climates on the various slopes. Differences of 20 degrees between two flanks of the Mountain are not uncommon. Kentfield almost invariably receives the heaviest rainfall in the Bay Area each year. (Courtesy of Nancy Skinner)

CHAPTER ONE

Old Tamalpais and Table Hill

Tamalpais has always been a presence, a kind of pivot in the landscape, for people who live within sight of it. Few cities in the world have a mountaintop so conveniently close by. In its shapely rising from sea level it draws the eye from almost anywhere on the Bay, serving both as a barrier to the north and an invitation to explore the wilderness beyond. Mt. Diablo, much larger, seems remote and intimidating; Tamalpais is neighborly, intimate, accessible. The profile of the Mountain is so familiar that many people see it in dreams, or could draw it without looking. Gazing at it, one feels connected with hundreds of generations of people who have pondered its form, felt its mystery, wondered what it might be like to stand at the very top. Almost three million people each year now satisfy their curiosity by going up to the summit or down to Muir Woods.

The friends of Mt. Tamalpais refer to it sentimentally as "Old Tamalpais," and it is indeed old. Geologists date its emergence from the later Jurassic and Cretaceous era, somewhere between 150 million and 80 million years ago. One of them has described it as part of a "complex, disrupted assemblage called the Franciscan Formation" — in other words, a heap of rubble — the upthrust debris resulting from the grinding together of several tectonic plates. The rocks which compose it are of various ages and from

various layers of the earth's crust, among them the serpentine, from the lowest level of all. Mt. Tamalpais was never a volcano, although some people thought it was because of the hot springs on its ocean side.

Perhaps as long ago as 25,000 years, a people we persist in calling Indians migrated down from Alaska, presumably having crossed from Asia on the then-existing land bridge, and occupied the Bay Area. Much more recently, according to Otto J. Sadovszky, a professor of linguistics, the people we now know as Coast Miwoks arrived, perhaps by boat, having migrated over a period of centuries from the Ob River in Siberia. These latter were the natives whom Drake met somewhere in what we now call Marin. They had been here for perhaps two or three thousand years, living in much the same fashion as their predecessors. The Spaniards considered them a source of converts and of labor for the missions, causing such a radical change in their way of life that their culture was rapidly destroyed. Then the Yankees and other Europeans who followed brought diseases which within three decades virtually wiped out the Miwoks. The result is that we know very little about them.

Among other things, we don't know whether any of these early people ever climbed to the summit of Mt. Tamalpais. The Miwok story of creation, transcribed by C. Hart Merriam at the turn of the century, suggests that the Indians thought of the Mountain as the domain of their god, Coyote, and hence a holy and awesome place which they would not visit. This interpretation is given some limited credence by the often reported but never authenticated story of Jacob Leese and Chief Marin. Leese was a trader, not a surveyor as the story usually claims, one of the early settlers in San Francisco (then Yerba Buena) in the 1830s. Marin was allegedly a Miwok chief, though some scholars say he was actually a composite of several chiefs. (A dentist now living in San Francisco claims to have traced his ancestry directly to Marin.)

Leese was to lead a party of Indian assistants to establish an initial survey point at the top of the Mountain. The Indians objected strongly, saying that the summit was inhabited by spirits and that no one who went up would come down alive. One of Leese's party was Marin, "known to his people as the bravest man in the world," according to the 1880 Munro-Frazer *History of Marin County*. But even Marin was daunted by the prospect of facing the dreaded spirits, so Leese went to the top alone and placed a large limb across an old dead tree, making a cross that could be seen from the valley below, and returned to the men. Marin, unable to ignore the dare, left his terrified companions behind, scaled the mountain and left his shirt on the cross as proof of his ascent. While the chief's reputation remained unblemished, Leese reported that the other Indians were convinced that the Devil himself had robbed Marin of his clothes.

One may question whether the Leese-Marin episode actually occurred, but there can be little doubt that the Miwoks looked at the Mountain with awe and reverence. So do we.

Our ignorance persists into the Spanish era. Records of voyages along the coast date as far back as 1542, when Don Juan Rodrigues Cabrillo made the first reported reconnaissance of the west coast, but there is no verifiable record that any of these voyagers specifically identified Mt. Tamalpais, much less went ashore to climb it.

George Davidson, geographer for the first United States survey of the Pacific Coast, says that Cabrillo in the *San Salvador* and his chief pilot, Bartolome Ferrer (Ferrelo) in the *Victoria,* were "the first Europeans to see the hills of San Francisco and the islands of the Farallones." Davidson might, with equal truth, have said that they saw Mt. Tamalpais in 1542, since the Mountain is easily the most visible feature of the landscape the Spaniards observed.

Sir Francis Drake, a generation later, could not have missed seeing Mt. Tamalpais if he careened the *Golden Hinde* in San Francisco Bay, as some people contend. From Drake's Bay, the more likely site of his landing, the Mountain is less of a landmark, but nevertheless could hardly have been missed.

Spanish galleons, returning to Mexico from the Philippines, usually approached the California coast somewhere north of the Farallones. Though the first of these voyages was made in 1566, the first close encounter with the Marin coast occurred in 1595, when Sebastian Rodriguez Cermeno in the *San Agustin* was shipwrecked in Drake's Bay. In a remarkable voyage, the captain and some of the crew made it to Mexico in small boats, while others of the crew reached Mexico by land, according to one dubious account. Both groups of survivors, especially those going overland, can hardly have missed seeing the Mountain.

A few years later, in 1602, the Spanish authorities sent General Sebastian Viscaino to look for the *San Agustin* in order to recover from the wreck the porcelain and the beeswax for church candles, part of its precious cargo. He found nothing of the wreck, but gave Point Reyes the name "La Punta de las Barrancas Blancas," the point of the white cliffs, a designation which some consider a confirmation that this was where Drake careened the *Golden Hinde.* And Volanos (or Bolanos), who had been the pilot of the *San Agustin,* is remembered, according to Davidson, in the name "Bolinas." Viscaino made a chart of the coast which shows the Farallones, but neither the Golden Gate nor Mt. Tamalpais. Yet he, too, must have seen it.

Nearly two hundred years later, Spanish explorers discovered and named San Francisco Bay. Juan Crespi, whose diary recounts the land expeditions of 1769 and 1772 from Mexico City up the California coast, refers to a mountain he called "Nuestro Padre San Francisco," which some believe may have been Tamalpais, though the identification is very unclear. The Portola party of 1769, of which Crespi was a member, is believed to have climbed from Pacifica to the top of Sweeney Ridge, the point from which their sighting of San Francisco Bay is alleged to have been made. From the monument there which commemorates the event, one can see a portion of Mt. Tamalpais, but Crespi would have had a much better view of it from the east side of the Bay, which the second Portola expedition explored in 1772. If it was Tamalpais he saw, "Nuestro Padre San Francisco" is the first name of which there is any record.

More dependable is the record left by the Ayala expedition which sailed through the Golden Gate in 1775. Father Vicente Santa Maria drew a map of the Bay, adding to the rough sketch which Crespi had drawn an indication of a mountain in the location of Tamalpais, to which he attached the name "Sierras de San Francisco." Jose Canizares, Ayala's sailing master, made a quite superior map which identified a range on the north shore of the Bay as "Cerro de San Francisco."

The British explorer, Captain George Vancouver, sent out by the British government to survey the west coast, sailed by in 1792. On a chart of the coast between 30 degrees and 38 degrees 30 minutes north latitude, Vancouver drew a profile of the "Entrance of Port of San Francisco," looking northeast from outside the Gate, which clearly shows the profile of Mt. Tamalpais. This is the first unmistakably clear record of a sighting of the Mountain and the first representation of its appearance, but he does not give it a name.

The very next year an overland expedition of ten soldiers, led by Lt. Don Felipe de Goycoechea, was sent by the Spanish governor in San Francisco "to explore the mainland from the Puerto de San Francisco to that of Bodega." (The Spaniards were concerned over Vancouver's visit, as well they might have been; California was almost ripe for plucking.) The party must have gone over some part of Mt. Tamalpais, and may thus have been the first to climb the Mountain. The Lieutenant, in his report, says that after crossing the Bay, "I ascended the highest part of the sierra, distant from the port about four leagues." His identification of Bolinas Lagoon, where the party spent the first night, is quite exact, so it would seem certain that the men crossed Bolinas Ridge, the northern spur of the Mountain. "The highest part of the sierra" suggests that they climbed to the peak, but this is unlikely. In any case, Goycoechea's party of 1793 must be accorded the distinction of being the first Europeans to cross over

the Mountain, though probably not to reach the summit.

A few years later, according to the story in Gertrude Atherton's book, *My San Francisco, A Wayward Biography,* a Spanish-Russian pair climbed the mountain. She writes of the romance between His Excellency, Nicolai Petrovich Rezanov, a Russian baron who visited San Francisco in 1806 in the bark *Juno* to purchase food for his half-starved workmen in Sitka, and Dona Concha Arguello, daughter of the commandante of the Presidio of San Francisco:

> There were picnics *(meriendas)* on the islands, which, during long walks with Concha, he investigated thoroughly. They crossed the Bay in the *Juno* and climbed Mount Tamalpais, from whose crest he had a fine view of the surrounding country with its forests of redwoods, pines, and oak trees, its ranchos with their herds of cattle and abundant harvests . . . A principality! A kingdom! An empire! He saw himself as overlord of all this.

Atherton gives no source for this story. Rezanov visited San Francisco all right, but one may wonder whether he and Dona Concha ever climbed Mt. Tamalpais. No such expedition is noted in Rezanov's report to his superiors in Moscow. There are no other known or alleged climbs by the Spaniards. A rather scornful entry made by Count Rezanov in the *Juno's* log shows the Spaniards' lack of interest in Marin:

> The Spaniards, as fanatics, are not interested in industries; they do not even have a rowboat, and the frigates which deliver their supplies are not interested in the north shore (of the Bay).

One of the first non-Spanish Europeans to visit the Bay Area was David Douglas, a famous botanist for whom the Douglas Fir *(Pseudotsuga menziesii)* is named, and who, according to John Thomas Howell, in his authoritative *Marin Flora,* may have climbed the Mountain:

> According to a memoir by F.R.S. Balfour, Douglas climbed Mount Tamalpais in the fall of 1833, but this record of what may be the first ascent seems doubtful unless further information substantiates it.

Another account of a climb appears in the recently published *Pictorial History of Tiburon* (1984). John Reed, the pioneer whose mill, still standing in Mill Valley, has been made a national landmark,

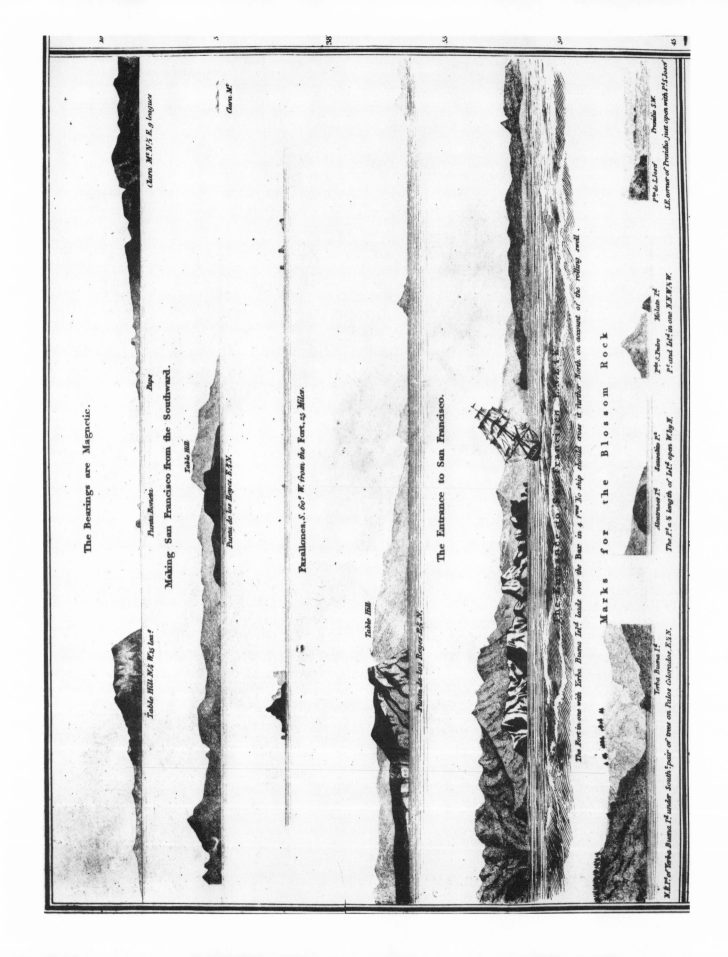

The Bearings are Magnetic.

Making San Francisco from the Southward.

Parallones, S. 60° W. from the Fort, 25 Miles.

The Entrance to San Francisco.

Marks for the Blossom Rock

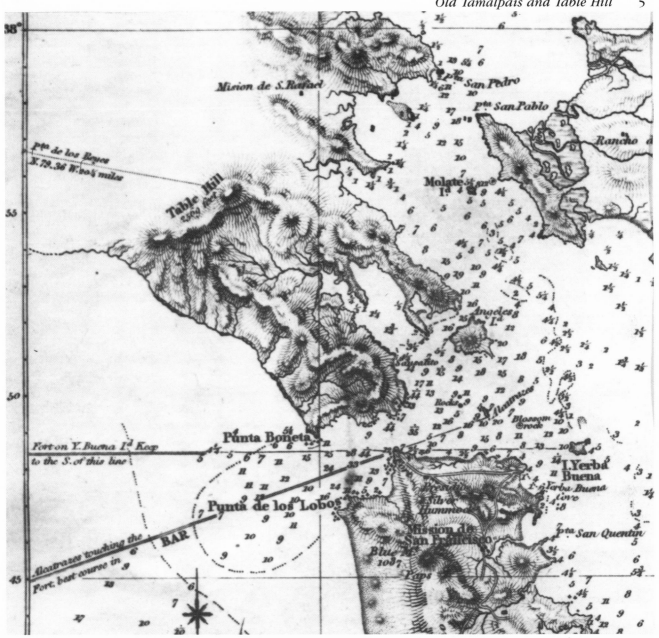

Above: Detail from the 1826 Beechey map shows "Table Hill" with a bearing based on true north, which suggests that someone must have climbed to the top of the Mountain with surveying instruments. The accuracy of this map is amazing, considering the time at which it was made. Blossom Rock, named for Beechey's ship, is just above Yerba Buena Island. A trail leads from Yerba Buena Cove (now Montgomery Street) to the Presidio, and another to Mission de San Francisco (Mission Dolores). "Silver Hummock" is today's Lone Mountain, and "Blue Mountain" is Twin Peaks. Punta Boneta and Punta de los Lobos retain their Spanish names. Sausalito, surprisingly, is spelled as it is today. Beechey must have asked the soldiers or the missionaries how to spell the Spanish names; those which were hopelessly foreign to English ears were then translated into English.

Opposite: This drawing shows how the Golden Gate looked from a ship approaching from the southwest. Table Hill, in all three drawings, is Mt. Tamalpais. Beechey instructs navigators how to enter the harbor safely: "The Fort (the Presidio, now Fort Point) in one (in line) with Yerba Buena Isld. leads over the Bar in 4 fms. No ship should cross it further North on account of the rolling swell." Blossom Rock, a submerged hazard which was dynamited out of existence in 1870, is located by lining up "The N.E. Pt. of Yerba Buena Id. under South(ernmost) pair of trees on Palos Colorados, E. ¼ N." The Palos Colorados we call the Berkeley Hills. (Courtesy of the Presidio Army Museum)

is said to have climbed to the summit of Mt. Tamalpais to erect a wooden cross, which "could be seen all the way to the Farallones." For Reed, a devout Catholic, a cross must have seemed an appropriate way to celebrate the birth of his first son, John Joseph, born July 16, 1837. Though the visibility of the cross from the Farallones is clearly an exaggeration of enthusiasm, one Marin resident, a direct descendant of John Reed, recalls her mother telling her the story when she was a child.

Another instance of Mt. Tamalpais' being used for a celebratory announcement occurred 74 years later, in 1911, when California women won the right to vote. After passage of a statewide referendum (125,037 for, 121,450 against, carried by Los Angeles, with San Francisco and Alameda voting no), feminists proclaimed their victory by flying yellow suffrage pennants from the peak of the Mountain.

A few years after Reed's ascent, in 1841, Lt. Charles Wilkes made an overland trip from San Francisco to Fort Ross; of necessity he traveled over some part of Mt. Tamalpais. Wilkes, who was visiting the Bay Area as head of the United States Exploring Expedition, was invited to Fort Ross by Governor Alexander Rotcheff of the Russian-American Fur Co., The Governor sent down a number of his finest horses for the use of Wilkes and his party. The visit was no doubt in the interest of both parties — to the Russians, who wanted to know what Wilkes had been up to in the northwest where he had just been exploring, and to Wilkes, who had been dispatched to find out what other nations had in mind for California. He explained his purpose to people here in San Francisco by saying that the U.S. Government had expressly commissioned him to keep an eye on British vessels, but Washington was concerned about the Russians as well.

To the uncertainties about who first climbed the Mountain was added about this time an uncertainty about its name. Not only is the origin of "Tamalpais" still in serious question, but for many years the name used in official federal and state publications was not Tamalpais, but "Table Hill" or "Table Mountain."

This name was bestowed by Captain Frederick Beechey of the British Navy, who arrived here in his ship *Blossom* in 1826. As he sailed toward the entrance to San Francisco Bay he noted a mountain range on the north side whose appearance suggested to him the name "Table Hill," which is the name he put on his excellent chart of San Francisco Bay. His chart, reproduced here, became the basis for the first United States charts of the Bay.

Beechey's chart is of special interest in other respects as well. The accompanying illustrations show that as he sailed by Point Reyes he took two bearings on Mt. Tamalpais, indicating its direction from Point Reyes as E¼ N or E½ N. These were compass bearings, based on magnetic north. The chart itself has another range between the two points, showing the bearing from Mt. Tamalpais to Point Reyes to be N 79.36 W. This bearing is relative to true north, and must have been taken by sextant or theodolite at the summit. The two kinds of bearings agree almost exactly if account is taken of compass deviation from true north. We can only infer that Beechey or one of his officers must have made the first climb to the top of Mt. Tamalpais in 1826-1828. A search of British naval archives has turned up no record of who made the climb or on what date.

The name "Table Hill" was adopted by Charles Wilkes, of the U.S. Exploring Expedition, in 1841. But Wilkes, for no reason he ever assigned, also called the Mountain "Palermo," a name that didn't stick. "Table Hill" and "Table Mountain" did. This name persisted into the 1880s, and for a time was the official name used in the *Coast Pilot,* the U. S. Government's guide for mariners on the Pacific Coast. The early (1860s) editions were written by George Davidson, who carried on the field work, including a number of climbs of the Mountain (perhaps first in 1854) for purposes of triangulation. Davidson says in a footnote that "Table Mountain" was the current name, but that "old Californians called it 'Tamal Pais'." He does not identify the "old Californians" or cite any source. In 1889, when the fourth edition of the *Coast Pilot* was issued, both names were used to introduce the description of the mountain.

Meanwhile, prior to the federal coast survey, the state of California had conducted what is known as the Geological Survey, though in fact the field work included many disciplines besides geology. The state legislature, in an early fit of stinginess, refused publication money for anything but the geological report. The lawmakers' interest was almost exclusively in what the survey had found in the way of minerals; the gleam of gold blinded them to other findings.

Josiah Dwight Whitney, director of the survey, writing in that section of the report headed "North of the Bay of San Francisco" (1865), continues the confusion over the name:

> The culminating point of the county is Tamalpais, which rises to the height of 2,597 feet, forming a portion of a ridge which extends across the peninsula in a nearly east and west direction; in this ridge are three summits of nearly equal height, all being over 2,550 feet. One of these points is a Coast Survey Station, and is called "Table Mountain."

This apparent differentiation between "Mt. Tamalpais" as the whole range, and "Table Mountain" as one peak (West Peak), is new and perhaps explains the continued use of both names. This seems to be the last reference in offical reports to "Table Mountain"; all subsequent reports and maps call it "Tamalpais."

But to this day there is no final agreement on where the name "Tamalpais" came from. Did the Spanish use one of the names given by Santa Maria, Crespi, and Canizares, or did they coin "Tamalpais"? Or was it of Indian origin adopted by the Spaniards or their European successors? Some experts believe that it is a combination of two Miwok words, "Tamal" and "Pais" or "Piis." But what was the meaning of the words? Until very recently the origins were obscure. The problem was compounded by the fact that various tribes and even subdivisions of tribes had different languages or dialects, so that meanings were far from uniform.

The mystery seems to be cleared up by Catherine A. Callaghan, professor of linguistics at Ohio State University, who has compiled a dictionary (not yet published) of the language used by that branch of the Coast Miwoks who lived in Marin, south of Bodega Bay. She translates "pais" as "hill" or "mountain," but finds "Tamal" more ambiguous because the Miwoks did not think precisely as we do. The word meant "coast" or "west" or "coast people" or "west people." (Tomales Bay, sometimes called Tamales Bay, probably has the same origin.) Thus "Tamalpais" would mean "West Mountain" or "Coast Mountain."

But we still don't know who was the first to climb the Mountain. I like to think that some young Yankee sailor from one of the several New England whaling vessels which Beechey reported seeing in Richardson Bay in 1826 couldn't resist rushing up to the top on a day when he was sent ashore for water. Maybe some day a whaler's log, long hidden away in a New Bedford attic, will tell the story.

We do have an excellent account of the first climb recorded in print by the men who were there. William H. Brewer, second in command of the California Geological Survey, climbed to the top of the Mountain in 1862. He called the Mountain "Tamalpais" without equivocation. Brewer and Charles F. Hoffman, also of the survey staff, started from San Rafael on a blustery March day and climbed to the summit. His story appears, not in the Survey's report, but in Brewer's own book *Up and Down California, 1860-1864.*

> The whole region between the bay and the sea is thrown up into rough and very steep ridges, 1,000 to 1,600 feet high, culminating in a steep, sharp, rocky peak about four or five miles southwest of San Rafael, over 2,600 feet high, called Tamalpais. On this was once a Coast Survey station, an important point.
>
> On March 28 we were up early and were off to climb this peak. A trail led through the chaparral on the north side. We reached the summit of the ridge, got bearings from one peak, and started along the crest of the ridge to the sharp rocky crest or peak. The wind was high and cold, fog closed in, and then snow, enveloping everything. We were in a bad fix — cold, no landmark could be seen — to be caught thus and have to stay all night would be impossible. We waited behind some rocks for half an hour, when it stopped snowing and the fog grew less dense; we caught glimpses of the peak and started for it.
>
> The last ascent was very steep. We climbed up the rocks, and just as we reached the highest crag the fog began to clear away. Then came glimpses of the beautiful landscape through the fog. It was most grand, more like some views in the Alps than anything I have seen before — those glimpses of the landscape beneath through foggy curtains. But now the fog and clouds rolled away and we had a glorious view indeed — the ocean on the west, the bay around, the green hills beneath with lovely valleys between them.

Vol. 2 No. 2   Cortemadera, California   October, 1902

List of 42 prominent objects, visible from the Eastern Peak of Tamalpais Mountain, extracted by permission, for "The Golden Hinde" from an extended paper prepared by Prof. George Davidson, for the Geographical Society of the Pacific, and not yet printed.

All distances are in statute miles; all bearings are by compass.

October 11th. 1902.

1 Eastern Peak of Tamalpais Mt. 2580 feet above the Sea. It is 13.5 miles N.59° W. from the City Hall of San Francisco. The distance of the sea horizon is 67 miles.

Tamalpais Mt. is the "Beechey Hill" of Captain Beechey, 1826; "Mt. Palermo" of the Wilkes Expl. Expd. of 1849; the "Table Hill" of Ringgold 1850; and the "Table Mountain" of the U.S. Coast Survey & since 1854, Tamalpais Mt.

2 Pt. Reyes Light House; distance 24¾ miles: bearing S 86° W.

3 Point Reyes Head; 597 feet above sea; nearly same bearing & distance as preceding.

4 Drakes Bay, distance 21½ miles; bearing North 86° W. and marked by the "white cliffs" of Drake; they reach three hundred & twenty feet above the Bay and face Southeast.

5 Bodega Head; distance 37½ miles, bearing N.61° W. 241 feet above sea.

6 Salt Point and Gerstle Cove; the farthest part of the coast line visible: distance, 61 miles: bearing N. 59° W. Height 35 feet.

7 Fort Ross; distance 56 miles; bearing N.56° W. About 60 feet above sea.

8 Ross Mountain; distance 60 miles: bearing N.52° W. Two Thousand Two Hundred Five feet above sea

9 Sulphur Peak; High peak in Clear Lake region; distance Sixty miles; bearing N.30½° W. Height 3460 ft.

10 Uncle Sam; Another high peak overlooking Clear Lake; distance 74 miles; bearing N.25° W. Height not determined.

11 Snow Mt. East; seen as a small peak close under left flank of Mt. Helena; distance, One Hundred Two miles; bearing N.22½° W. Height, 7040 feet.

12 Mount Helena; distance, 51⅓ miles and bearing twenty and two thirds degrees West of North; height 4338 feet.

13 Sonoma Mountain; distance, twenty seven and one half miles; bearing N.16° W. Twenty two hundred and ninety three feet high.

14 Monticello; in Coast Range over looking Sacramento Valley; distance fifty five and one half miles; bearing N.6° E. Height three thousand and fifty nine feet.

15 Vaca Mountain in same range; distance forty one and one half miles N.24° E. Height two thousand three hundred and ninety four feet

16 Capitol at Sacramento; Dome visible under favorable weather conditions; distance seventy five miles; bearing N.35¼° E. Height two hundred and sixty three feet above sea.

17 Light House, Mare Island; distance twenty & two thirds miles; bearing N.43° E. Height seventy four feet.

18 The Sierra Nevada. First observed by Prof. Davidson from Tamalpais in 1858. Range visible from Mt. Lola to Round Top through fifty six miles.

19 Mt. Lola; distance one hundred & fifty eight miles; bearing North 32° E. Height Nine thousand one hundred forty three feet.

20 Castle Peak or Mt. Stanford; Nine thousand one hundred thirty nine feet.

21 The Needles, eight thousand nine hundred twenty feet. Mt. McKinstry, seven thousand nine hundred eighteen feet.

22 Mt. Tallac; nine thousand seven en hundred and eighty five feet. Pyramid Peak, ten thousand and twenty feet.

23 Round Top distance one hundred and fifty one miles; bearing N.52° E. height ten thousand three hundred and eighty six feet.

24 Mt. Diablo; distance thirty six and two thirds miles; bearing North 78° E. height three thousand eight hundred forty eight and eight tenths feet by twice levelling. It sees Mt. Shasta fourteen thousand three hundred and sixty feet eleva-

tion, when the refraction is large.

25 University of California: The Library Building is distant eighteen miles; bearing N.85° E. Height four hundred and twenty two feet above Bay; Clock tower visible over the North Hall.

26 Mocho Mt. E. line Coast Range, overlooking San Joaquin Val. dist. 65 mi. S.78° E. Height 4091 feet.

27 Lick Observatory, Mt. Hamilton dist. 65.5 mi. S.69° E. Height of top of Northern Dome, 4261 ft.

28 San Jose; Court House dist. 56 mi. S.59½° E.

29 Loma Prieta or Black Mountain. Culminating peak of crest line of the Peninsula of San Francisco, dist. 69 mi. S. 53° E. Height 3798 feet.

30 San Bruno Mountain; 17⅗ miles. S.42° E. Height 1314 feet above Bay.

31 Sierra Morena; in crest line of Peninsula of San Francisco; dist. 38 miles; bearing S.39½° E. Ht. 2414 ft.

32 The Cliff House, & Sutro Heights These are on the Western slope of Point Lobos. The distance of Point Lobos is 10.8 miles; bearing S.35° E. Ht. three hundred eighty one ft.

33 The Golden Gate: The narrowest part, only one statute mile wide is not visible on account of the Point Diablo hills hiding it.

34 Montara Mountain. Two miles inside Coast line near Point Montara. Distance twenty six miles; bearing S. 29° E. height one thousand nine hundred and forty feet.

35 Pt. San Pedro South of Cliff House; the northern termination of the range of the Pen. of San Francisco. Distance twenty two and one half miles; bearing S.25° E. height 640 feet.

36 Montara Point and Light House. Most Southern coast visible from Tamalpais; distance 26.5 miles bearing S.26⅝° E. Height 55 feet.

37 The Gulf of the Farallones. Point San Pedro, the groups of the Farallones, & Point Reyes are the seaward limits of this Gulf. The depth of water over this plateau ranges from six fathoms at the bar of San Francisco to about fifty fathoms at outer limit of the Gulf.

38 San Francisco Bar. This bar within the six fathom limit, sweeps around from abreast Lake Merced, at the South to Point Boneta at the North. The Western limit is six miles outside the Heads.

39 Fog & Lightship off San Francisco Bar. This vessel is No. 70, & lies 3¼ miles outside the bar in 17¾ fathoms at low water, & nearly on the range of Fort Point & Alcatraz Island Lights. Distance 13¾ miles; bearing S.10⅘° W., & height of Light 52 feet above the sea.

40 The South East Farallon & Light House. Distance 28 miles; bearing S.39° W. Height of focal plane of the light, 358 feet above the sea.

41 The Middle Farallon. A small, low, black rock, 2.5 miles N.W. by W. from the S.E. Farallon.

42 The North West Farallones. This group is hidden from the Eastern Peak of Tamalpais. From the Western Peak they are distant 29⅛ miles; bearing S. 53° W.; highest peak 155 feet above the sea.

George Davidson

From the foregoing Original & valuable paper of this eminent geographer, appears the fact; so far as I know, heretofore unrecorded in history; that from the Peak of Tamalpais may be seen with a sweep of the eye, the trinity of points which marked the completion of Christianity's encirclement of the globe.

In 1579 Sir Francis Drake's Chaplain held the first Church services in English on the shore of Drake's Bay. A couple of centuries or so later, the Greek Church coming from the West, arrived at what is now known as Fort Ross, and in 1817 the Franciscans coming from the East met them with the Mission San Rafael Arcangel. These two terminals are about equally distant in longitude, one East & the other West from the place of Drake's landing

When a great railroad is completed, Golden Spikes are driven with Silver Malls and Cannon boom.

Christianity is less demonstrative but a small Chapel, placed where it commanded this inspiring view would become in time, of world wide fame, and I know of none other than that of the Holy Sepulchre which has more geographic reason for placement. Herewith the "Golden Hinde" gives One dollar to start a fund for its construction. Please be next. Make the contributions small but numerous Address the Purser of the Golden Hinde and acknowledgements will be made in these columns.

These columns from The Golden Hinde *list the points George Davidson was able to locate from the top of Mt. Tamalpais during his various stays there. (Courtesy of Mill Valley Library)*

Above: George Davidson (in skull cap) and crew on Mt. Tamalpais, possibly in the 1870s. The canvas-covered hut may be the first structure built on the Mountain.

Left: Ellinor Davidson, whose diary for 1859 tells us: "In January went into camp life with my husband on the top of Tamal Pais, carried across the bay in small sailboat & up the cattle trail on pony to the top of mountain where no woman had ever been & no habitation within miles. Snow on the ground & we lived in tents. At night could hear bears prowling around. Slept with pistol by my side as I was completely alone, my husband & brother being at work through the night at observatory 3 miles distant. . . . Moved to another station going on horseback & dropping into a quagmire where my horse sank up to his belly. Returned to San Francisco & in November 59 my first child was born."

The baby boy, shown at left with his mother, must have been the first child conceived on the Mountain; unfortunately he lived only a few months. (Courtesy of the Bancroft Library)

Brewer's delight in the view from Mt. Tamalpais has been matched by that of the many thousands who have succeeded in reaching the top. People seize their cameras to record the splendid panorama while others scan the scene with binoculars to identify San Francisco buildings, the ships in the bay, and mountains in the distance.

It is fascinating to compare today's views with the list of sites and objects which George Davidson identified with his telescope when he was up there doing his triangulation work in 1858. Take along a compass, because Davidson's directions are based on magnetic north, not true north. You may be surprised to find Point Reyes bearing south of west!

In addition to such familiar nearby sights as Mt. Diablo, Mt. St. Helena, the Farallon Islands and Mt. Montara, Davidson reported seeing the Sierra stretching 56 miles from Mt. Lola to Round Top, at a distance of over 150 miles. (Visibility was better in those pre-smog days.) Other points were Lick Observatory, 65 miles away; the capitol building in Sacramento, 75 miles; Mt. Monticello in the Coast Range, 37 miles; Vaca Mountain in the same range, 41 miles; and even the San Jose Court House. Some people have mistakenly reported seeing Mt. Shasta, but the cone-shaped, snow-covered peak visible just west of Mt. St. Helena is probably 6,000-foot Snow Mountain, beyond Clear Lake, or perhaps one of two peaks in the Mendocino National Forest, Black Butte (7,448 feet) or Sanhedrin (6,138 feet).

CHAPTER NOTES

There is no simple, adequate study of the Mountain's geology. Most helpful are sections of the *Geological Guide of the San Francisco Bay Counties,* Bulletin 154, Division of Mines, Department of Natural Resources, State of California, 1951. Though it contains no specific discussion of Mt. Tamalpais, the material on the history and structure of the coast range is applicable.

Again, no single publication relates specifically and comprehensively to the Indians who lived near the mountain, or even to the Coast Miwoks as a tribe. Two classics on Indians are A. L. Kroeber, *Handbook of the California Indians* (1953), and Stephen Powers, *Tribes of California* (1976). Recently two new sources have become available. Otto J. Sadovsky, professor of linguistics at California State University at Fullerton, claims in a recent article *(The Californians,* November-December 1984) that the Coast Miwoks (including the Marin, Bodega and Lake Miwoks) migrated by boat from the River Ob in Siberia. Catherine A. Callaghan, also a professor of linguistics at Ohio State, has published two Miwok dictionaries, for the Bodega and the Lake Miwoks. A third, for the Marin Miwoks who lived on the shore edges of Mt. Tamalpais, is in preliminary form but not yet published.

A useful summary account of Spanish explorations will be found in George Davidson, *The Discovery of San Francisco Bay* (1907), a reprint from *Transactions and Proceedings of the Geographical Society of the Pacific,* Vol. IV, Series II, (May 1907).

John Galvin's beautiful book *The First Spanish Entry into San Francisco Bay, 1775* contains some of the maps mentioned in this chapter, as well as the superb description of Marin Miwoks from the diary of Padre Vicente Santamaria. See also Neal Harlow, *The Maps of San Francisco Bay from the Spanish Discovery in 1769 to the American Occupation.* The Hoffman map is available at the California State Library in Sacramento.

Wilkes' visit to Fort Ross is recounted by William Heath Davis in his *Seventy-five Years in California,* originally published in 1867. Davis talked to Wilkes when he was here.

The Goycoechea story comes from an article by the distinguished historian of early California, Henry R. Wagner, in the quarterly of the California Historical Society, December 1931.

The report of the suffragettes' yellow banners appears in a small volume, *California Women: A Guide to Their Politics, 1885-1911,* p. 134. (no publisher or date).

12

South Soleta St Francisco   California

Ships of many nations stopped in San Francisco Bay to take on fresh water, meat, and vegetables, as well as to trade manufactured goods for cowhides and tallow. In 1842 the U.S. Sloop of War Cyane, *exploring Pacific waters, stopped in San Francisco Bay. Crewman William Meyers kept a remarkable journal of his travels, complete with water colors. His style, both in writing and painting, was extremely lively; the journal is a mine of factual information, and is one of the treasures of the Bancroft Library.*

Meyers, hearing Spanish place names, spelled them as best he could: "St. Francisco" referred to the entire bay; Sausalito became "South Soleta," and Sonoma he called "St. Omar." The picture above shows his ship at anchor at "South Soleta St. Francisco." The mountain behind the harbor looks remarkably like Tamalpais, although considerable artistic license must have been used. Below are excerpts from the journal. (See also Chapter Four.)

December 13 1842: At 8 came to an anchor in South Soleta, 3½ fathoms water muddy bottom.

December 14: Plenty of deer about, looking at the ship with wonder. This is a magnificent bay indeed, but they have queer names for things. A large island here is called mint island because there is no such thing as mint near it. The town is called Good Herb, and not a good herb grows within 10 miles of it. . . .

December 18, Sunday: Mustered all hands, divine service as usual, a severe lecture read to the men. Went on shore with a rifle, saw liberty men on shore lying about in spots damnably drunk.

Dec 23 Friday: Commodore Thos. Catesby Jones and suite returned from their visit to Colonel Vallejo at St. Omar, about 6 days.

Dec 27 Tuesday: General Vallejo and suite arrived at the watering place. Saluted him with 13 guns, he is the brave officer who fired with 30 soldiers upon a single man asleep. . . General going to stay on board all night.

Dec 29 Thursday: Pilot Capt of the Port Capt Richardson came on board, got under way at 12, came to anchor 1 mile where we started from.

Dec 30 Friday: . . . Fired a gun for the Pilot at 8 bells got under way. (Courtesy of the Bancroft Library)

CHAPTER TWO

Commercial Activities on the Mountain

Until the coming of the European and Yankee immigrants, not much use was made of the Mountain's natural resources. Little was done to disturb nature: the Indians harvested acorns and herbs, and hunted animals and fished, but their numbers were small and their techniques primitive. What they took was for subsistence only; their work produced nothing for sale. Economic use of nature's resources began with the San Rafael Mission, whose large herds of Mexican longhorn cattle ranged freely over large areas. At the annual round-ups, the animals were slaughtered for their hides and tallow, which were then exported via the Yankee sailing ships, bringing the Mission its only cash income.

The Spanish government discouraged this trade, but when Mexico took over California in 1821, she weakened commercial restraints, and encouraged the development of this industry. Bryant, Sturgis & Co. of Boston was the first to send ships to California for hides and tallow, used in New England for the manufacture of shoes, soap, and candles. Their three vessels plied the coast between 1831-1833, taking away hides estimated variously to number from ten thousand to forty thousand.

Two Years Before the Mast, Richard Henry Dana's classic description of his voyage from Boston to California in 1834-1836 aboard the brig *Pilgrim,* records that Yankee traders were rounding Cape Horn with cargoes of goods to trade with the Californios. Dana tells how the hides were collected and delivered to the ships in San Francisco Bay in 1835:

> Large boats, or launches, manned by Indians, and capable of carrying five to six hundred hides apiece, are attached to the Missions, and are sent down to the vessels with hides, to bring away goods in return.

This system was organized by William Richardson, an Englishman who first sailed into San Francisco Bay on August 2, 1822, as mate of the British whaler *Orion.* He returned in 1835 to establish a commercial town or pueblo, "Yerba Buena," authorized by the Spanish Governor. Near the cove whose beach was to become Montgomery Street, he set up the first habitation, a tent, later replaced by a wooden house that Dana saw when he was here. Three years later, Richardson became the grantee of Saucelito Rancho, and moved across the Bay in 1841.

When David Douglas, the famous early collector of West Coast plants, was in Northern California in 1831, he learned about cattle raising as well as the hide and tallow trade. Douglas's biographer, William Morwood, notes that beginning about 1830, the trade jumped geometrically because of rapidly growing demand for leather shoes in the United States and Europe. Three factors were at work:

(1) For the first time in history, shoes were comfortable to wear because a distinction had been made (as recently as 1818) between the fit of the right and the left feet; (2) shoe manufacture, traditionally the work of individual cobblers on a custom basis, was being standardized in factories that turned out ready-to-wear shoes at lower prices; (3) industrial populations, which had once made do with sandals, carpet slippers and wooden clogs, were taking to leather shoes as symbols of urban sophistication.

As Dana had reported, the missions brought the Mexican longhorn cattle to California, but the big private land owners were also soon engaged in the trade. When the missions were secularized in 1833-1834, some of their stock was slaughtered but much was sold to the owners of the ranchos, giving impetus to private cattle raising. Besides getting free land, free feed, free water, and cheap livestock, the ranchers also now had cheap Indian laborers who had been released from the missions. So they were ready to profit from the rising demand for hides. They became cattle barons, with tens of thousands of animals roaming the vast grasslands around the bay.

How these developments affected Marin County has never been studied in detail, but certainly cattle-raising was big business. A special issue of the *Marin Journal* (October 1877) reports, "In the valleys and in the rolling hills, thousands upon thousands of cattle found rich pasturage, and grew fat on the wild oats with which they were covered." Some of these cattle undoubtedly had belonged to Mission San Rafael, whose herds, according to Bliss Brown, had numbered three thousand head in 1834. And Munro-Fraser says, "In those early times the principal trade of San Rafael was shipping cattle. Longhorned Mexican steers roamed over the adjacent hills in thousands and were the only meat procurable in the country."

Five land grant ranchos spread out on the slopes of Mt. Tamalpais: Richardson's Saucelito Rancho, the Briones Rancho las Baulinos (Bolinas), Rancho San Quentin, which included a large area west and north of San Rafael in addition to Point San Quentin itself, John Reed's Rancho Corte Madera del Presidio,

and Rancho San Geronimo, where Woodacre is today. Cattle were run on the Mountain wherever there is now grassland: the Bolinas area, including Bolinas Ridge, Throckmorton Ridge where the Dipsea Trail crosses, the Bon Tempe area, Potrero Meadows, Bald Hill, the Phoenix Lake area, and the slopes down into San Geronimo Valley. Many areas now overgrown with trees or chaparral were probably grassland in those days.

Hides and tallow were loaded at Sausalito, where sailing ships often stopped to take on fresh water, or were brought in small boats from landings close to the ranchos to ships anchored in San Francisco Bay. The trade gradually came to an end during the goldrush years as the ranches began to convert to dairy farming. A growing population in San Francisco demanded fresh milk, butter, and beef for the table. Clark & Moylan built a slaughterhouse in San Rafael in 1850 and shipped beef carcasses to San Francisco.

Hunting and Trapping

Trapping, which played such a considerable role in the early days of the Sierra and the Central Valley, never was of any great importance in the Mt. Tamalpais area. Hudson's Bay Company trappers operated in the Delta in 1828-1843, but that was as close as they came. The Russians and later the Yankees took tens of thousands of sea otter pelts from the waters of San Francisco Bay, bringing the otters to the point of extinction.

Hunting on land also began early as a commercial enterprise on Mt. Tamalpais, as Joseph Mailliard, owner of Rancho San Geronimo, reported:

In the earlier days hundreds of deer were shot in this county and sold in the San Francisco markets. Near the head of Big Carson Creek, at the crossing of the Pine Ridge trail, was located a deer hunters' camp of such importance as to have been named on some of the early maps of that region. It has been stated by old settlers that as many as seven hundred deer have been shipped out of this camp in a single season.

William Kent, in his *Reminiscences of Outdoor Life,* remarks that "the growing population close at hand had created a surprising market for game, and market hunting rose to be an important profession.

This delicate pencil drawing from a sketch book made by Edwin Moody shows the Reed Rancho in 1856. The adobe house (slightly left of center), built in 1836, stood near today's La Goma and Locke Lane in Mill Valley. Widow Reed (Hilaria Sanchez Reed, 1813-1868) was the proprietor of the house and the immense Rancho Corte Madera del Presidio, having inherited it from her husband John Reed (also spelled Read) on his death in 1842.

In its early years the Rancho was used for grazing the wild Mexican cattle, which were slaughtered for their hides. But John Reed began importing purebred cattle very early, and thus may be thought of as the father of the dairy industry in California. His descendants leased their lands to Portuguese immigrants, many from the Azores, who eventually operated almost all the dairies on the Reed and Richardson Ranchos.

Widow Reed's adobe was a stopping-off place for travelers. The sailboat pictured here brought visitors from San Francisco, who stayed at the Widow's house and then rode north on horses, usually supplied by the Widow. (See the narratives of Ellinor Davidson, p. 10, and Lt. Craven, p. 34.) (Courtesy of the Bancroft Library)

There were thousands of crested California Valley quail and throughout the fall and winter innumerable ducks and geese," besides quantities of Columbia black-tailed deer.

Jack Mason, West Marin historian, claims that in the 1840s grizzly bears were being shot on Mt. Tamalpais to be used for steaks in San Francisco. There is considerable doubt that grizzlies, though numerous at one time, were still common on the Mountain as late as the 1840s. Hunting for sport continued, of course, for many years until the area was made a game preserve.

Logging

Yankee whalers and other trading vessels that visited San Francisco Bay in the 1820s and 1830s went to Sausalito not only for water but also for firewood, which the whaling crews needed in quantities for their trypots. The first commercial logging was in Larkspur in 1816, when cordwood was cut for the Spanish troops, thus supplying the name "Corte Madera del Presidio," the place where wood was cut for the Presidio. Then in 1834, John Thomas Reed, who had come to Sausalito as the first settler, received a grant from the Mexican government to Rancho Corte Madera del Presidio, including the entire Tiburon peninsula and much of present-day Mill Valley, Corte Madera, and Larkspur. Two years later, in 1836, William Richardson was granted Rancho Saucelito. The big attraction was timber.

Much of the Marin shore on the northwest side of San Francisco Bay was originally heavily forested, some of it in redwood, as shown on the Canizares maps of the Ayala expedition in 1775. When Richardson and Reed became owners of these lands, commercial logging began. In 1836 Reed built a sawmill on Cascade Creek in Mill Valley, the original frame of which still stands in Old Mill Park, a California State Landmark. Reed built his mill to supply lumber for his own ranch buildings, but later supplied redwood lumber to the Presidio. With millstones he acquired from the Russians at Fort Ross, he could also grind wheat and maize.

The old hand-whipsawing method was soon superseded by steam-driven circular saws when, in 1849, Robert Parker and his partners, Botts and McCormack, started up a new mill on the site of old Saucelito. The logs came from near the head of Richardson's Bay and were rafted around to the mill. Some part of the lumber used in Yerba Buena and for the new city of San Francisco came from here. The early 1850s were the big years. Captain Leonard Story ran a large bark and Charles Lauff and William Hood took over a raft of 88,000 feet, the largest ever floated across the bay. Before the end of Richardson's Bay became filled in with silt, flat-bottomed schooners and barges could said right up to where Tamalpais High School now stands.

Early logging took place on the lower slopes of the Mountain, primarily in the gulches where the redwoods grew and where the logs and lumber could readily be moved to tidewater. As William Kent says, first the redwoods were cut for finished lumber and pilings, then other woods for cordwood to heat San Francisco buildings and to supply the brick kilns scattered here and there in Marin County. To make the bricks the land was skimmed of its clay after the trees had been cut. Had Kent been writing a different sort of book, he might have observed that the big Marin landowners were beginning the exploitation of the county's resources which his own conservation movement was later to halt.

All the choice redwoods had been taken out of Mill Valley by 1852, when the steam mill was moved to Bolinas. But the Corte Madera area was being actively logged. John (Juan) B.R. Cooper, having received a Mexican land grant in 1840 to Rancho Punta de Quentin, stretching from Point San Quentin into the Ross Valley, made an agreement in 1847 with Captain Joseph L. Folsom of the San Francisco Presidio for a government sawmill to furnish lumber for the rapidly expanding American army base at the Presidio. And in 1849 the Baltimore and Frederick Trading and Mining Co. shipped a sawmill around the Horn and hauled it by oxen to a West Baltimore site.

Thus began a continuous chain of activity: in 1857 James Ross acquired the San Quentin Rancho to complete the cutting of the timber. He established a trading post on Corte Madera Creek known as Ross Landing, now Kentfield. In his fleet of shallow-draft schooners, Ross shipped logs, cordwood, and bricks down the creek to San Francisco. After Ross died in 1862, Isaac Shaver built his own wharf there to ship out lumber he was processing in a variety of

A lumber schooner at Ross Landing (now Kentfield) on Corte Madera Creek in 1874, photographed by Eadward Muybridge. The lumber probably came from the Isaac Shaver mill. (Courtesy of the Bancroft Library)

The Pioneer Paper Mill, shown here in a painting by Thomas Hill (1829-1908), supplied paper for three San Francisco newspapers: the Alta, *the* Call, *and the* Evening Bulletin. *Built in 1855, this mill was replaced in the 1880s by a larger one, which operated until 1915. (Courtesy of the Fine Arts Museums of San Francisco; Gift of Mr. H.K.S. Williams)*

mills, one of them on Cataract Creek, near the present site of Alpine Dam. Shaver's Lagunitas Mill, built in 1865, commenced shipping lumber that same year. Shaver and his partner Mitchner, "enterprising and energetic men," as the *Marin Journal* called them, constructed a road from the mill to Ross Landing, going over what is still known as the Old Shaver Grade. They turned out about sixteen thousand feet of lumber daily and sent it out to Ross Landing and on by barge to San Francisco. The mill was moved into San Rafael in 1873.

On the other side of the Mountain, Woodville (sometimes known as Dogtown) became a major logging and lumber center beginning with its first mill in 1851. Logs and lumber were hauled from the mills to the head of Bolinas Bay by ox-carts with solid wheels cut from redwood logs, lightered to Bolinas and taken by schooner to San Francisco. One source reports that in 1862 the mill was turning out 12,000 feet of lumber, 10,000 laths and two or three thousand pickets every 24 hours, the mill running night and day.

Joseph Mailliard supplied a picturesque footnote in recalling logging in the 1870s:

> In summer, huge wagons drawn by twelve or fourteen oxen hauled great loads of cordwood over the roads then existing. The depth of dust by this heavy traffic grinding up the dry earth was almost unbelievable. This dust bed was a delight to the bands of quail that dotted the roads, dusting themselves to their hearts' content.

Logs were used as pilings for wharves and for the foundations of buildings constructed on filled land. Before the extensive logging in this area, Bolinas Lagoon was much deeper, permitting vessels of ten-foot draft to come in at any tide. Skidding logs down the hillsides gouged out ruts, and then the rains washed the silt down into the lagoon.

Logging continued in the Bolinas area throughout the 19th century, much of it to supply cordwood for San Francisco houses and for the steam locomotives on the railroad which came through in 1875. By 1880, if Munro-Fraser is correct, fifteen million board feet of lumber had been cut near Bolinas. There were "as many as ten schooners making each two trips a week during the busy season." Much cordwood also came from the big Shafter-Howard properties and was shipped by railroad to Ross

Landing. Some was burned at San Quentin prison, but most of it went across the bay to San Francisco. Finally, Jack Mason points out, "Introduction of oil (1902), gas and electricity ended cordwood's supremacy."

Charles Augustus Lauff, one of Marin's earliest non-Spanish settlers, was born in France, came as a child to New York, shipped out before the mast at age 17, was shipwrecked in the Straits of Magellan, spent three days on a floating timber, was rescued by a whaler enroute to Alaska waters, and finally landed in San Francisco in 1839. He worked first in lumbering and then in ranching. During his logging days he worked at Rancho Corte Madera as a whipsawyer. Two years later, after a stint in the Mexican War, he worked at Ross Landing for James Murphy, and early in the 1850s he came to Bolinas to get out timber for San Francisco wharves, having a sub-contract under Hoff and Hatch. Yet Lauff appears as an early conservationist when he bemoans the indiscriminate cutting of redwood on the Corte Madera uplands: "A shame its big timber was ever cut. It was the grandest one could rest eyes upon."

Another major logging location was on the north slope of San Geronimo Ridge, where Isaac Shaver put up a portable sawmill in 1874 on the White Ranch, one mile south of San Geronimo station, and a year later another mill on the road between White's Hill and San Geronimo. These mills supplied redwood ties and heavy studding for the 1,300-foot-long White's Hill tunnel for the North Pacific Coast Railroad, then being built from Sausalito to Tomales. When the railroad was completed it carried lumber from the mill to San Francisco via Ross Landing. Later the line was extended beyond the Russian River to Cazadero, opening up a big new territory for logging, with a center at Duncan's Mills.

Hikers exploring the Mountain away from established trails often run across overgrown old sled trails used by the loggers to send logs downhill to a mill or to transportation. An excellent description of one of these sled operations has been recorded by Mrs. Rothwell, whose father, Robert Stedman, had a lumber business in what is now Lagunitas in the 1860s and 1870s. Stedman, originally from Lenox, Massachusetts, had made a fortune in the gold rush. One of his major lumber products was fence posts, in the era when the big ranches were being subdivided for dairy farms. Mrs. Rothwell's account:

> When the cordwood was being cut on the Taylor property in the vicinity of the Hogsback area, it created quite a transportation problem. Mr. William P. Taylor, the superintendent of the Taylor Pioneer Paper Mill, asked my father's assistance to remedy, if possible, this condition. . . . A sled road, running perfectly straight down the steep incline was constructed. . . At the upper end my father designed a rather unique contrivance. He had the carpenter at the Taylor Paper Mill build an exceptionally heavy and durable wood-sled. The two heavy runners were capped with tires made of four inch wide bands of steel. The loading platform on which the empty sled was to be placed operated with a system of balancing. The top surface of this platform was kept oiled with a generous supply of axlegrease. When the load was finally piled from the wood-wagon onto the sled, it was lashed securely with a heavy rope in readiness for its final wild plunge down the steep incline. The teamster, with a stout pole, would tilt upward the rear end of the platform and the loaded sled would shoot off into space, rapidly gaining speed as it went down the steep incline until it finally landed in a pile of loose dirt at the stock pile below., The teamster would then unhitch his horses and descend by another circular roadway to the bottom of the sled road where he would unload the sled and pull it back up the hill on the same circular roadway.

Mr. Stedman was certainly not the sole inventor of the sled for bringing logs downhill; there were many other sled trails. One of these, the Old Sled Trail, came down the ridge above Alpine Lake to Liberty's Ranch. Old-timers say that the trail was used to bring dairy products down by sled from the ranch in the valley across the ridge. It serves nowadays as a trail for hikers going in to Little Carson Falls.

The Pioneer Paper Mill, referred to by Mrs. Rothwell, was an extraordinary enterprise, producing paper for three San Francisco newspapers, the *Call,* the *Evening Bulletin,* and the *Alta,* as well as wrapping paper, paper bags and soft tissue. The mill, on what is now Paper Mill Creek, dates from 1855; its machinery was shipped around the Horn. Raw material consisted of rags and scrap paper collected in San Francisco and sorted by Chinese, who lived in a camp downstream from the mill. In its earliest days the mill shipped paper by ox-cart on a road that Taylor had built up Bolinas Ridge and along the Ridge for six miles to the lumber roads down to Bolinas Bay, whence the paper went by schooner to San Francisco. This route sufficed until 1874, when the railroad came through the valley. A sharp rise in the price of newsprint made the mill so profitable that in the 1880s Taylor built a new and much larger mill. This one lasted until 1915, when it burned. Remains of its foundation can still be seen.

The mill originally ran by water power, furnished by a dam on the creek. When the mill was converted to steam in 1884, it required quantities of cordwood, supplied by independent woodcutters whose cabins sprang up everywhere. Elsewhere on the Mountain wherever trees were being cut, such cabins were built, most of them rude and temporary, located of necessity near a stream or spring. But a few, such as Tucker's Camp in Bill Williams Gulch, achieved some permanence. Swede George, a woodcutter, is reported to have had a cabin in the gulch which bears his name, but its site is not known. No doubt there were many others.

The area drained by upper Lagunitas Creek (where Alpine Lake is located) was logged around 1868, according to Marin Municipal Water District records, and the lower drainage area, where Kent Lake is, during the years 1888-1903. That just about ended first-growth logging on and near Tamalpais. A second round of cutting occurred in the area to be flooded for Alpine Lake, around 1918. Considerably later, a second cutting took place along lower Lagunitas Creek. When the Water District acquired this area in 1946, it continued a logging lease from the Lagunitas Development Co. to A.H. Ruoff of San Rafael. Ruoff's mill, on the bank of the creek, about half a mile south of where Big Carson comes in, continued to operate until 1951, when it was dismantled. The site was flooded after Kent Lake dam was completed in 1953. Between 1946 and 1951 the mill had produced 21,079,896 board feet of timber. One can still walk down from Bolinas Ridge on logging roads which date from these years, but there is no sign of the mill itself except when the lake is very low.

The last logging in the area was on the Righetti Ranch on the west side of Bolinas Ridge, an operation that led to legislation requiring a state-approved

Above: The Bolinas waterfront in 1873. Logs, finished lumber, and cordwood were brought by barge from the head of the lagoon to this port and shipped to San Francisco. By 1880 15 million board feet had been cut in the vicinity. Left: Crates of eggs are barged to Bolinas in the 1880s, towed by McKennan's launch. (Both photographs courtesy of Thomas Barfield)

harvest plan to assure good harvesting procedures and plans for regeneration. More recently, in 1979, a flap developed over a proposal by a board member of the Marin Municipal Water District to sell logging rights to the Kent Lake watershed — all second or third growth timber — to help compensate for the drop in revenue following the drought in 1973-1974. The proposal was defeated following a major outcry by environmentalists.

Munro-Fraser was critical of the lumbering operations long before the current concern for environmental protection, but he was ahead of his time. In the early 1860s and for a long time afterwards, Marin County, he writes,

> . .suffered irreparable injuries. . . Magnificent forests were swept away that never can be restored. Fine redwood groves stretched between San Rafael and San Anselmo. Even the stumps are gone. Great madrone trees grew on the ridges. . . Not a tree of them remains. . . The devastation wrought through Ross Valley and along the foothills and canyons down to Corte Madera was nothing short of sacrilege.

Except for Muir Woods, all first-growth timber on Mt. Tamalpais has been taken out. But the Mountain can hardly be said to have been permanently defaced; the big old redwood stumps one finds in many areas are not eyesores, and many are surrounded by "family circles" of younger trees.

Dairy Farming

When William Brewer was going up and down California in 1862-1864, he found Marin County the "finest grazing district I have yet seen," his journal records.

> But the whole county is covered with Spanish grants and held in large ranchos, so settlers cannot come in and settle up in small farms. The county is owned by not over thirty men. . . As a consequence, there is but one schoolhouse, one post office, etc., in the whole county, although so near San Francisco.

He cites county surveyor's records showing that out of a total of 330,000 acres in the county, all but 1,500 acres of public land was divided up into twenty-three land grants, of which seventeen were over eight thousand acres each, and one was 56,000 acres.

But even as Brewer was complaining of the backwardness of the county, forces were at work to diminish the monopoly of the large landowners and to change the character of Marin land use. The population explosion in San Francisco after the gold rush radically increased demand for dairy products. As new settlers brought in more productive eastern and European livestock, the supply of dairy products shot upward. "Prices of $300 to $500 for a good milk cow were common," one report says, and the high prices stimulated the importation of more stock. Herds were driven overland across the Missouri River and all the way to California.

In the 1860s most of the big Marin land grants were broken up, the land fenced and devoted largely to dairy ranching. By 1868 half the Marin acreage had been enclosed. Marin was a good place for dairy ranching, because of its proximity to the San Francisco market and its grassy, rolling hills. By 1889, the Marin assessor reported 25,390 cows, the largest number for any county in the state, according to an article in the *Overland Monthly* (1941). The article quotes a Marin dairyman:

> Marin County, by its situation on the coast, and climate, hilly conformation, resembling Switzerland, and abundance of good water all the year, seems specially adapted for butter dairies, and has been selected by many Swiss and Italian dairymen who understand its advantages.

For the county as a whole, production of butter grew very rapidly from 200,000 lbs. in 1862 to a peak of 4,387,500 lbs. in 1872. Cheese output reached a peak of 456,000 lbs. in 1864-1865. Later, as transportation improved, dairy farms shifted from butter and cheese to fresh milk and cream. Cooperative creameries were organized, and the state began to require pasteurization; by the 1880s milk production had become big business.

A few of the ranches on and around Mt. Tamalpais had other specialties. On the east side of Bolinas Lagoon, for example, Isaac Morgan raised apples on his Belvidere Ranch for thirty years beginning in 1853. Hugh McKennan, in the same area, sold ducks; at one time he had 2,000 ducks and shipped 1,000 eggs a day to San Francisco.

Top: The Boyle house, Cypress Knolls, built in 1871, was the center of a thriving dairy farm; it still stands on Manor Terrace in Mill Valley. Below: The White Gate Ranch overlooks Willow Camp (Stinson Beach), empty except for a small store in about 1880. (Courtesy of the Mill Valley Library)

Top: Liberty Ranch operated as a dairy until 1876, then became a combination ranch and resort, run by Vincent Liberty and his widow. The site was covered by Alpine Lake in 1917, as the lower picture shows. (Courtesy of Nancy Skinner)

But in the main the ranches on the slopes and valleys of Mt. Tamalpais were dairy farms, many of them on the Sausalito Rancho, which Samuel Throckmorton had acquired from William Richardson in 1856. By 1859 the rancho had been divided into small ranches ranging in size from 500 to 1,500 acres, leased by tenants, most of whom were Portuguese. By 1888 the rancho consisted of 24 dairy farms. The tenants leased not only the land and buildings but sometimes even the cows themselves. A newcomer from Portugal or the Azores could buy (or earn through his labor) a share of the dairy operation from the chief tenant, and thus had an interest in high production. This early example of profit sharing provided a lifeline for immigrants who needed help to settle in a new country. By 1880 all of Throckmorton's tenants were Portuguese; the same was true of the Reed dairies on the Tiburon peninsula. Many Mill Valley residents recall when dairy cows roamed freely on the hills above the town.

Many dairy ranchers also raised hogs, feeding them the oceans of skim milk left over from butter production. These too were shipped to San Francisco by boat from Bolinas, often causing much excitement on the old *Owl,* the most famous of the boats on the route. The hogs often got loose and ran about the decks with much squealing, and sometimes were lost overboard.

In 1902, William Kent purchased some two thousand acres of land which included Steep Ravine and ran down to Willow Camp (Stinson Beach), extending north and west from the property of the North Coast Water Company in Frank Valley and including the Lone Tree tract. Most of this land was being used as dairy ranches; the price was $25 an acre.

On the west slope of the Mountain, the large Diaz and Brazil ranches continued to operate until taken over by Mt. Tamalpais State Park in the 1960's. The White Gate Ranch was taken over by the Golden Gate National Recreation Area in 1974. This last ranch is probably the best known because its buildings were visible until recently from Panoramic Highway just above Stinson Beach, and because the Dipsea Trail ran through it. It was a landmark until the GGNRA tore down the buildings. In its heyday in the 1920's, its 3,200 acres were leased by the Silva family from William Kent. The family owned about 300 cattle, milked 150 cows, and had about 200 pigs.

Cream was taken twice weekly by four-horse cart to Bolinas Lagoon, where it was loaded on schooners for San Francisco.

The north side of the Mountain also supported dairy ranches until they were bought by the Marin Municipal Water District to clear the way for Alpine Lake. One of these, Liberty Ranch, has given its name to Liberty Gulch at the head of Alpine Lake. In 1857 Loomis Curtis set up a dairy on the property. Though his wife continued the work after his death in 1875, she had to sell out at auction the following year, disposing of 64 milk cows, a few horses, hogs and equipment.

Shortly after the auction, the Vincent Liberty family moved in, leasing 1,100 acres from the Howard-Shafters. Liberty ran some cattle, and in 1881 put up a new house which included some rooms for paying guests who wanted to spend time on the Mountain. The ranch was on the stage road running from Ross Valley to Bolinas, following down Lagunitas Creek before going over Bolinas Ridge. Travelers could stop off at Liberty's.

But Liberty was plagued with bad luck; on September 10, 1885, a fire destroyed house and outbuildings. Though he rebuilt the house immediately, the ranch never fully recovered, and a few years later (1891), Liberty moved to Contra Costa County. His wife continued to run the place both as ranch and resort until 1894, when she sold out to a Mr. Barfoldi. When the Marin Water District acquired the property in order to flood it for Alpine Lake, the buildings were torn down. Souvenir hunters have found a few artifacts, all that is left of Liberty Ranch.

Another dairy ranch, owned by the Porteous family, stretched from the Phoenix Lake area, up Fish Grade and over to Deer Park. The ranch house was just above the lake, where a Water District superintendent now lives; some of the orchard trees still stand.

After her husband's death, Janet S. Porteous leased a portion of the property to the Marshall Ranch, which sold dairy products under the name of Hyppolite Dairy. The original lease was for 400 acres, from the lake-site up Fish Grade, and over to the ridge (then called Nebraska Ridge) separating this property from the 500-acre Deer Park section of the Porteous property. The ranch house was in what we now know as Hidden Meadow — one of the most delightful little valleys on the Mountain. The site of the house can still be seen. The Deer Park portion was leased to the Lezzini family in Fairfax, but when Mr. Lezzini died the Marshall people took over the lease and operated both portions. When Mrs. Porteous died in 1904, the heirs sold the entire property to the Marin County Water Co., which the next year built Phoenix dam. The Water Company terminated the Marshall lease and ran its own cattle on the property until the new Marin Municipal Water District took possession in November, 1916.

The buildings at Bon Tempe Ranch, another well-known dairy, had to be abandoned about the same time because of plans for Alpine Lake. The ranch straddled the area now occupied by Bon Tempe Dam, which was built much later, in 1949. A small knoll on the ranch was bulldozed down to supply fill for the dam. Some say that the little red barn at the Lake Lagunitas parking lot belonged to the ranch. But ranch activities did not cease when the buildings were demolished. Until 1930, William Barr of San Rafael leased some 1,200 acres for grazing sheep at ten cents a head.

This reversion to grazing occurred not only at Bon Tempe, but elsewhere in lands acquired by the Water District, including 945 acres near the Meadow Club, 351 acres along Bolinas Ridge, 500 acres of the Porteous Tract, 102 acres of the Worn Spring Tract (Bald Hill), and a number of smaller tracts including Cataract Gulch, around Lake Lagunitas, Potrero Meadows, Liberty Gulch and even fifteen acres on top of Pine Mountain. For the most part these tracts were used for grazing sheep. Thus land use came full circle, from the free running of longhorn cattle on the Mexican land grants, to grazing dairy cows and sheep on fenced properties. The last of these grazing leases was not phased out until 1969.

Cross-country hikers still find the remains of fences only partially torn down, sometimes fence posts but more commonly barbed wire. In one gully on the ocean side of Bolinas Ridge is a big roll of rusting barbed wire. Many find it sad that so much fine oat grass is not being used, and that present-day painters can no longer put cattle in their Tamalpais landscapes, as Thad Welch frequently did. But the days of grazing and of dairy farms on Mt. Tamalpais are over.

The Mailliard Ranch

One of the original land grants on the north side of the Mountain remained intact for a long time — the Rancho San Geronimo, granted to Rafael Cacho in 1844. Cacho sold it in 1846. Shortly thereafter it was bought by Joseph Warren Revere, a nephew of Paul Revere, who was one of the Bear Flag troops in Sonoma in 1846. Revere sold the property to Rodman and Francis Price, who paid him $7,500 apiece. They mortgaged half the property to the Ward family and lost it in foreclosure.

Meanwhile, Adolph Mailliard, related to the Bonaparte family, was growing up in France in the company of Bonaparte princes. He came to New York and bought the ten-thousand acre Rancho San Geronimo sight unseen on June 1, 1867, for $50,000, from his wife's family, the Wards. Arriving in California, Mailliard bought 113 acres of Forbes's San Rafael subdivision, later called Fairhills. He lived in San Rafael for three years while his house in San Geronimo was being built.

Unlikely as it seems, Mailliard brought with him on the long voyage by sea, across the Isthmus of Panama and up the Pacific Coast by steamer a number of Jersey cows, whose tolerance for the inconveniences of travel must have been exceptional. Cows of this breed produce the richest milk, which makes the finest butter. For years Mailliard sold his butter for premium prices to Goldberg Bowen, the fancy grocers in San Francisco.

Mailliard also brought out his horses, some of California's first blooded stock.

Many famous people visited the showplace Mailliard Ranch, among them Alexander Graham Bell, who installed a telephone from the house to the barn, some 200 yards away. This may not have been the first telephone in the county, since one was put in by Samuel Hubbard in 1877 for the Marin Water Company, just one year after Bell's invention had been demonstrated at Philadelphia's Centennial Exposition. The wire, about six miles long, ran from the dam at Lake Lagunitas to the company's office in San Rafael. As reported in the *Marin Journal,* "The gentle tones of Superintendent Nye are distinctly heard at the dam in the tone of ordinary conversation, and George Kendall's response came back as distinctly as if spoken in the room."

Top: The Adolph Mailliard Ranch (today's Woodacre) was a showplace where blooded livestock grazed and Marin's second telephone was tested. The ranch house (below) became the Woodacre Lodge in 1914; it burned in 1958. (Courtesy of Betty Gardner)

Another distinguished visitor to the Mailliard Ranch was the sister of Mrs. Annie Ward Mailliard, Julia Ward Howe, author of the words to "Battle Hymn of the Republic."

Mailliard's daughter Louise and his son Joseph lived at the ranch — the house was completed in 1873 — until it was sold in 1912. The buyer, Lagunitas Development Company, planned to develop it, but World War I intervened. The house was used for some years as a summer hotel, and then as the home of the Woodacre Improvement Club; it burnt in 1958.

Mining

About the only thing known for certain about mining on Mt. Tamalpais is that none was ever commercially profitable. The locations of a few diggings are known, but they never amounted to much. Hikers on the Mountain are familiar with the Old Mine Trail which goes up and down from Pantoll, and with the Old Mine Road that parallels the trail out to the Deer Park intersection. Just below the trail, possibly 200 yards west of Pantoll, the remains of one of these luckless mines may be identified if one looks closely and uses his imagination. A State Park plaque indicates its location. The visible depression could easily be mistaken for a stream bed. The mine was discovered by Jim Whitehead, a State Park ranger, in 1952.

Subsequently, the Pantoll Ranger Station acquired a copy of a hand-written "Notice," dated May 28, 1863, and filed in San Rafael by Louis Denos and others, stating that the several undersigners "have claimed and located for mining purposes fourteen claims of two hundred (200) feet each of the quartz-ledge or vein" — the location being then described. Presumably, Louis Denos and his associates hoped to find gold, but Salem Rice, a geologist who has inspected the few tailings still visible, says he cannot be sure. Denos and his friends were no doubt suffering from a belated attack of gold fever.

Even Adolph Mailliard succumbed to gold fever, according to his grandson, who recalls that his grandfather borrowed money from the Bonaparte family in France in order to drive a shaft into a hill on his property.

Another old mine is located on Bolinas Ridge right alongside the Coastal Trail in an open field. Again, a small depression is visible, and tailings that look like the neighboring serpentine suggest that it was copper the miners were after. The entrance to the shaft has been bulldozed shut, but its location is clear. A much deeper digging, more difficult to find, is located on the north slope of the Mountain, below the Northside Trail, near the west branch of Lagunitas Creek, and between the Lagunitas Fire Trail and the East Peak Fire Trail. It is not known when this mine was worked or what it produced.

Copper deposits have been worked from time to time by various companies in Copper Gulch, on the west slope of Bolinas Ridge in the area known as Dogtown. The Union Copper Mining Company dug a tunnel several hundred feet long into the ridge in 1863, but found no significant ore body. Then in 1900 the Bolinas Mining Company shipped out some ore, but it was not until 1918 that the Chetco Mining Company was able to report production of 22,500 pounds of copper. There is no information for subsequent years, suggesting that the vein was not profitable. The Golden Gate National Recreation Area, now the owner of the property, has closed the shaft entrance and made the site accessible and safe for visitors. Some remains of the old equipment may still be seen.

CHAPTER NOTES

J.P. Munro-Fraser, *History of Marin County* (1880): This large volume is a necessary compendium for anyone interested in early Marin history. A useful supplement, available only in typescript, is Bliss Brown, *Marin County History* (1936). Other manuscript sources are James Hepburn Wilkins, *Early History of Marin County* (1915) and Bertha Stedman Rothwell, *Pioneering in Marin* (1959), available in the Marin County Library.

The best source on dairy ranching in West Marin is Anna Coxe Toogood's *Historic Resources Study, A Civil History of Golden Gate National Recreation Area and Point Reyes National Seashore, California,* 2 vols., June 1980. The figures quoted in the text are from this study. The study was issued, but unfortunately never printed, by the Historic Preservation Branch of the National Park Service.

A splendid oral history on Portuguese dairy farming, by Mary Bernard Silva, is included in *Both Sides of the Track* (1986), James Heig and Shirley Mitchell, editors. *Pictorial History of Tiburon* (1984), James Heig, editor, has a section on dairy farming.

Arthur Quinn's *Broken Shore: The Marin Peninsula, A Perspective on History* has interesting material on the sea otter trade and on ranching. It is unfortunately peppered with inaccuracies.

A special issue of the *Marin Journal,* October 1887, has useful background material, as does the *Marin County Almanac* (1976).

A story about White Gate Ranch can be found in the *Bolinas Historical Quarterly* (October 1984).

Jack Mason's several books about Marin County are excellent sources, especially *Early Marin* and *The Making of Marin*.

Extensive collections of oral histories in both the Marin County Library and the Mill Valley Public Library provide much valuable detail.

Records of the Marin Municipal Water District were useful in regard to grazing leases.

MOUNT TAMALPAIS

This engraving, from Harper's Weekly (1875), shows Mt. Tamalpais from Greenbrae.

30

Hunting at St Francisco

This hunting scene is from the 1842 journal of William Meyers, described on page 12. The mountain in the background is clearly Mt. Tamalpais, which places this scene somewhere to the south, above Sausalito. The watercolors were probably made after Meyers returned to the ship, however, so the landscape can hardly be thought of as precise.

A hunting party from the Cyane *had gone ashore on December 14, and had brought back two deer, some geese, ducks and curlew. Captain William Richardson provided horses for the hunters. Meyers looked forward to a similar foray:*

Tuesday Dec 20: Cold and drizzly, employ'd cleaning rifles. . . . getting my mocassons ready for a hunt tomorrow.

Wednesday Dec 21: Went ashore with Whiting, Middleton and Barraud, with our boy to carry whiskey and grub. Whiting and I took horse, rode about 8 miles over the mountains. Saw bear prints and panther. Plenty of deer but very shy. Returning horses got bogged in the swamp. . . . my horse drove both his feet into my breast. Couldn't faze me. Got under trysting tree, eat all the grub, and drank all the whiskey. Whiting pretty shiny, returned on board at sundown. (Courtesy of the Bancroft Library)

CHAPTER THREE

Hunting on the Mountain

Following in the footsteps of the earliest arrivals — cattlemen, loggers and would-be miners — came many others, to hunt, fish, hike, enjoy the views, or study the mountain's plant life. Because trails were few and poor, they came on horseback at first, but later mostly on foot. The earliest recreation on the Mountain was hunting, an activity that continued in the Carson area until the last hunters' camps were eliminated by the Water District's rangers in the 1970s. On the Mountain proper, it was stopped in 1917, when the game refuge was established.

A dramatic account of early hunts, perhaps somewhat embellished, is found in the reminiscences of Charles August Lauff, who sailed into San Francisco Bay aboard a whaling vessel on October 13, 1839, and stayed to become active in a variety of local industries. In the 1840s he was loading hides and tallow at the ranchos and bringing them down to trading ships anchored off Sausalito. A few excerpts from his stories about hunting with William Richardson, owner of the Sausalito Rancho, make it clear that in those years the lower slopes of Mt. Tamalpais were a hunter's paradise:

The elk were thick as bees on the flat in front of Mill Valley and we slaughtered twelve in one morning. . . . The wild cattle were as plentiful as the elk and deer. . . . The country around Mill Valley and Muir Woods was covered with immense trees and was the home of large black and brown bears. Captain Bull (Captain of the hide boat on the bay), Don Richardson, myself and three Indian cowboys went out one Sunday hunting. . . . We had four fine Russian dogs, and a few minutes after we got in the thicket we started up seven bears and three cubs. . . . (After a battle which he describes in detail) we killed the three beautiful specimens.(On another occasion) Captain Healy and myself, Mr. Richardson and six Indians started out over the trail to hunt grizzlies in Steep Ravine, back of Mill Valley. Mr. Richardson wanted some antelope, elk and bear to roast for Christmas dinner. As we. . . . turned along a trail to the Big Lagoon (now Muir Beach), we encountered a number of deer, elk and antelope. Captain Richardson being a good shot spurred his horse and shot a beautiful specimen of the antelope family. He told us to blaze away when we got at close quarters and I killed an elk and Captain Healy a large deer. The Indians hauled the animals to a tree under which they hung them after dressing them.

It was about 8 o'clock in the morning when we reached the bear grounds. We held a sort of hunter's caucus and Mr. Richardson planned the hunt. Two of the Indian hunters with eight dogs were to beat the brush in the center of the canyon, while the rest of the party were given stations at differ-

ent points of vantage. Mr. Richardson went a few yards through the brush at the center of the canyon, and very shortly we heard the report of his rifle and he returned dragging a large California lion at the end of his riata which was twisted around the horn of his saddle. It was a beautiful specimen.

In a few minutes we started again to our stations and we were horrified by the breaking of branches and the rush of animals through the thick underbrush. Mr. Richardson shouted for us to look out for bear and not shoot until we got a sure bead. In a few minutes we thought bedlam broke loose. Bears, deer, lions, wild cats and coyotes darted out in all directions. The barking and baying of the dogs created a noise that was hard to describe. Captain Healy got the bearfever and started down the hillside on his horse at breakneck speed. He was scared to death and never stopped until his horse stopped in a clearing a mile away.

Mr. Richardson and myself singled out a big brown grizzly and the first shot put him on his haunches; he turned around ready to charge us. I fired and put a bullet in his body. This only enraged the beast and he made a dash for one of the Indian hunters, who fired and broke his back leg. He plowed up the earth with his front paws and when the dogs came up he fought like a demon. It took seven shots to put him out of harm's way. Mr. Richardson estimated there were over a hundred bear and lion in the ravine.

The Indians skinned the bear and after taking about fifty pounds of the choicest cuts for our Christmas dinner, we returned to Sausalito. It was the most exciting bear hunt I ever experienced.

We don't know just how long this great variety of large animals persisted, but after 1850 the combination of hunting and logging brought a rapid decline in their numbers. In 1923 Joseph Mailliard of San Geronimo Valley wrote about the vanished elk and bear in "Earlier Days in Marin County:

In 1868 it was no uncommon thing to find bleached horns shed by elk, scattered through the brush on Tamalpais and on the adjacent ridges. . . . In those early days numbers of bears still existed on the Bolinas Ridge.

These, he thinks, were probably the Northwestern Black Bears, not grizzlies. The last bear he himself saw, in 1880, was near the head of Cataract Gulch. At about the same time the "last bear" was caught

in a trap in Muir Woods. Wildcats and mountain lions largely disappeared too.

But by the end of the 1880s such game had been almost completely killed off except for deer, which multiplied as the big predators were thinned out. Sportsmen continued to hunt deer and quail until 1917, when the legislature created the Mt. Tamalpais Game Refuge. Since then the deer have grown again in numbers, their natural predators having been largely eliminated. As the deer multiplied some people have thought that the wildcats and mountain lions might make a comeback, but this does not seem to have occurred; only rare sightings are reported. Muir Woods archives note "mountain lions occasional" in 1932; as recently as 1977, State Park rangers saw two on the Mountain. But don't expect to see one on your next hike, even if you are walking in the wild Carson area.

Margaret Dowd, in her oral history, recalls that young hunters "thought the Mountain was theirs." Her husband, Charles Dowd, son of the founder of the livery stable in Mill Valley, used to ride up on horseback with his friends to their own camp at Bootjack, while their gear was shipped by the Mountain Railway to West Point. No doubt such arrangements were common.

There were, besides, many highly organized hunters' camps which controlled large areas of the Mountain. These camps were male retreats, often quite remote, to which the members rode on horseback. One of the earliest was the Tamalpais Sportsman's Club, which leased a sizable area from the local ranchers sometime in the 1880s. Its headquarters was in Sequoia Canyon (which became Muir Woods National Monument in 1908), and later it extended all the way to Stinson Beach, as the 1898 trail map shows. Ben Johnson, the gamekeeper, lived in a log cabin near where the present Ben Johnson Trail comes down into the valley. When William Kent acquired the canyon in 1905, Johnson remained as his caretaker, but it is not known whether Kent continued the club's lease. It seems likely that when the National Monument was created in 1908 the club ceased to function, though it is still shown on the 1910 trail map.

Meanwhile members of another club, the Lagunitas Rod and Gun Club, could roam over an enormous area of 12,000 acres leased from the Berry Rancho, owned by the Howard-Shafters. Their range

Hunting the Grizzly Bear.

Another watercolor from William Meyers' journal for 1842 (see pages 12 & 30) shows a grizzly bear hunt which must have been based on stories told to Meyers by the hunters, since his journal contains no account of a bear hunt in which he himself participated. No doubt such stories were widely circulated, especially when a ship anchored at Sausalito and young crewmen went ashore, eager for adventure and information about the unknown land of California. The picture above matches up rather well with the narrative of Charles August Lauff, quoted at the beginning of this chapter, of a hunt which took place a few years after Meyers' sojourn. (Courtesy of the Bancroft Library)

This watercolor, on two facing pages of a small sketchbook, was made by Edwin Moody in 1855. It identifies "Saucelito Rancho" (far left) "Tamal Pais Rancho" (top center), "Corte Madera Rancho" (right), and "D.H. Carpenter Rancho" (bottom, just below sailboat). (Will Brooks Collection, Courtesy of the Bancroft Library)

The Journal of Lt. Tunis Augustus Macdonough Craven, U.S.N. Sausalito, 1847

Sausalito. Bay of San Francisco arrived here June 22. *My first deer.* On Friday July 7th [Lt. William T.] Smith & myself left the ship for a hunt, determined to bring back some kind of four footed game. We took a boat, and landed at the head of the bay, some four miles from the ship, at a place familiarly known as the "Widow Read's." This "widow" lives in a large house, which at the time of our arrival presented the appearance of a tavern, for there was a throng of idlers around, there were horses ready caparisoned, persons constantly coming and going, lazy Californians, and vagabonds of all other nations were busy doing nothing.

Let me introduce you to the "widow." She is a Californian of about 35 years of age, and *was* a "widow." Her former husband was a son of Erin, a man of some respectability, and by marriage with this fair dame — she was once pretty — became the possessor of an immense tract of land, which under his management soon became a thriving estate; for his cattle & horses increased rapidly, and all available land was speedily brought under the plough, a mill was erected, and his lumber brought into the market. Prosperity crowned his industrious efforts, he commenced the building of a fine house, and died, leaving a widow with four *very pretty children.* The disconsolate widow for some time found comfort in the *friendship* of a gay Californian, said to be a rogue, and well known as "Four-fingered Jack." Pleasantly she passed away some three years of widowhood in the enjoyment of Jack's society, and at last married him.... The widow's cavalier is Sr Bernardino Garcia, a gay, reck-

less, profligate, worthless handsome fellow; there you have him & the busy tongue of scandal says, "she is no better than she should be." But of this I will not speak for I have partaken of her — hospitalities.

On one of my hunts, I found myself in the vicinity of "widow Read's" establishment; everything there is Widow Read's for the most important matters, viz the property is all held in *her name.* Well, being nearer to her house than to the ship, I resolved to sleep at the Widow's. So I went to the house, and made known that I was hungry and wished to be accommodated for the night. These people of California are proverbially hospitable; the widow made many apologies that her house was full (& so it was to overflowing) and that I must put up with such as she could give, but she intended to have a room and bed for the especial use of such *distinguished* guests. A plentiful supper was soon placed before me, tea, hot cakes and stewed beef, to which I paid my respects most cheerfully; supper over, and the small hours of morning at hand, a bed was made for me on the settee in the "Sala" — I turned in, but fleas were in myriads. No sooner were the lights put out, than they *swarmed,* and sleep was out of the question. I tossed about and patiently waited for dawn, which no sooner arrived, than I sallied out, with my gun. I returned at about 10. The widow had just "made it day" — she was up, and preparing my breakfast to which I sate down and did justice. I then made known to the widow, that I was going back to the ship. "I sent my boy for horses, he will soon be back," said she, and sure enough, she fitted us out as well as she could, and we returned quite pleased with the kind hospitality of Widow Read. Everything was done for us, and we made as much at home as if we were in a Hotel, but no pay was expected, no not even a gift to a pretty little girl was permitted....

Let me now return to my hunt of July 7. Arrived at "the Widow's" we were soon furnished with horses, and in company with a youngster, half Californian, half Yankee, started on our expedition. Our guide was Dan Smith, the son of a runaway American seaman, who had married a native woman. Dan is a queer Arab, a regular Flibertigibbit, a rogue of the first water, but Dan is a smart boy, and his roguery is the result of a miserably neglected education. Careless & lazy, he is fit for nothing but riding on his horse, and in the saddle he is perfectly at home. Our road lay over mountains & through valleys, the scenery in some places really beautiful & always grand. I was much amused with the habits and manners of my guide, a boy of 14 speaking Spanish at one moment & very good English at another. It was worth the ride to see this wild youth; as free and easy in his manners as if he were our equal, he familiarly called us Craven and Smith, as soon as he found out our names....

After a ride of about two leagues we espied a small hovel in the bottom of a deep valley. "There is my father's Rancho," said the boy. We soon arrived there & what a spectacle presented itself. "Bill Smith" had on the 4th of July gone to the Widow Read's on a spree. There he had been taken very ill, & his wife left home to take care of him, leaving three small children (the eldest *scarce eight years old*) to take care of themselves. The children had managed to milk a cow, and were living on *milk and corn stalks,* thus they had lived *nearly a week in the wilderness,* the woods around being infested with bears, panthers & coati [coyote] (a species of wolf). My heart was saddened by such neglect on the part of the parents, and we divided our fare with the hungry children, who were overjoyed at the return of Dan....

Early day found me rambling over the hills in search of game, and as the sun was rising, I was on the summit of a high hill, and the landscape was so beautifully grand, that I for a moment forgot the chase.

The glorious sun was just showing itself above the mountains which bounded the Eastern horizon; to the Westward of me was a high and wild range, whose tops were here and there tipped with sunlight, which rested on them like gilding; a deep and thickly wooded valley lay below me, and the mountain sides were covered with the stately and beautiful "red wood." The grand bay of San Francisco was on my left, and the picture was completely beautiful. The deep shadows, the perfect outlines, the gilded mountains, the fertile valley, the rich forests, the herds of wild cattle, the silvery Bay; and I wished I were a Claude; but do you see those two deer there, on that ridge within a few hundred yards? So away I went and soon found myself within 60 yards of the stately animals. I marked the largest for my victim, fired, it leaped into the air and disappeared, I ran up the hill and found that the deer had been standing on the brink of a precipice down which it had probably rolled, and was concealed among the bushes below. I commenced a careful descent; it was just the place where one might meet a bear, so warily I searched the place and while watching the thickets and hunting the bushes for my game, [Lt.] Smith came up from the opposite side and drove a deer over the hill, he came within my range I fired and brought him down. There he is. Now in my eagerness to secure my "first deer," bears & panthers are forgotten, I rushed down the hill side crossed through the thicket & brook & climbed the opposite side of the ravine. The wounded deer had concealed itself in the brush, and I wandered about for some time, without finding it, but at last came upon him, put my foot on his head, drew my hunting knife, and cut his throat. I reloaded my gun & began now to consider upon the means of getting out of this place with my deer, for go without it I *would not.* That thicket below me is a very suspicious looking place; and even were it free of bears, I cannot get through to the valley below *with my game.* Let me look up the hill. It is so steep that I can scarce secure a foothold, but *up* I must go. So I tied my handkerchief to his heels, and commenced dragging or rather lifting him up the hill. After a toilsome and most fatiguing labor of about half an hour I reached the hill top, in triumph, and sate down to rest myself. [Lt.] Smith was nowhere in sight, so I determined to hang my game in a tree, go back to the house (about a mile) and bring my horse, but just now heard voices over in that thicket. There is Dan, and directly after out came Smith with his *third* deer. They were both mounted so we all three went in together & got our breakfast, packed our game, and returned to the ship, sure of being well received.

covered the whole north side of the Mountain and included most of the Lagunitas Creek watershed from just below Lake Lagunitas almost to Shafter Bridge on the Sir Francis Drake Highway. This club was probably started sometime in the late 1890s. The original clubhouse was located on Lagunitas Creek about a mile upstream from the present site of Alpine Dam, where the Rocky Ridge Trail came down to the creek. Later, in 1909, the club was re-organized, and in 1911 took over the old Liberty (or Pezzaglia) Ranch, farther upstream at the bottom of Liberty Gulch, on the north side of the creek. The club was used for hunting and fishing, as its name implies. Members patroled the area to keep off trespassers, and to watch out for fires.

Sometime about 1910 the club published a "Members' Map" of its Game Preserve with detailed instructions on how to reach the clubhouse. For San Franciscans: via ferry to Sausalito, train to Fairfax, and then by stage. For those coming by "teams," driving time from San Rafael is given as one hour and twenty minutes, but as only fifty minutes returning, perhaps because it is downhill. Automobiles, which could be rented from Auto Livery at the Union Depot in San Rafael, required forty minutes either way.

Several mementos have survived, including an announcement of the first annual barbecue in 1909. A few years later, in 1915, club president Samuel "Slim" Hubbard invited members to a feast. The fancy printed menu included roast venison with Spanish sauce. Hubbard wrote a poem in praise of the club in 1912; the first two stanzas follow:

THE LAGUNITAS CLUB

When I'm weary of the City,
* With its pavements, dust and noise;*
When I'm longing for the mountains,
* And a deer-hunt with the boys;*
When business cares oppress me,
* And I'm yearning to be free,*
Then the Lagunitas Club, my boys
* Is just the place for me.*

When it's early in the morning,
* And the stars shine overhead,*
And 'tis hard to leave the blankets
* On the fragrant fir boughs spread;*

When the horses are all saddled,
* And the Keeper brings the hounds;*
While our little Vale is ringing
* With joyous hunting sounds;*
Then we trail across the ridges,
* As the fog begins to rise,*
And the dawn steals up in splendor
* Behind old Tamalpais.*

This work, whatever its poetic merits, shows us that hunters, like everyone else, were under the spell of the Mountain. (Mr. Hubbard seems also to have been under the spell of Rudyard Kipling). The satisfaction of bringing down a deer or hauling in a string of fish was equalled by the joy of the surroundings.

At the time the property was acquired by the Marin Municipal Water District in 1917, preliminary to building Alpine Dam, the club had a frame building with ten or fifteen rooms, a stable for ten horses, a place to store hay and enough room for several wagons. There were also dog kennels, a stockade, and a water tank. The club, along with other structures scattered along Lagunitas Creek, was torn down in 1917, and the area was subsequently flooded by Alpine Lake.

Just at this time the state legislature, responding to the newly aroused conservation movement, created the Mt. Tamalpais Game Reserve, outlawing hunting on the main part of the Mountain, but not affecting the large watersheds of the Big and Little Carson Creeks overlooked by Pine Mountain and Geronimo Ridge. The Water District began to acquire these lands, looking ahead to the building of Peters Dam to create Kent Lake, finally accomplished in 1953.

In 1946, the District, using condemnation proceedings, acquired (for $165,000) some six thousand acres from the Lagunitas Development Company, one third of which was owned by Stanford University. The District took over a hunting lease held by the Big Trees (hunting) Club, covering 5,658 acres on both sides of Little Carson Creek and an additional 783 acres across the Fairfax-Bolinas Road from the Meadow Club, subleased to the Redwood Gun Club. This latter portion was on land draining into the Cascades above Fairfax. The Big Trees lease was held by John D. McKee and George Stevens.

Big Trees Club was on Little Carson Creek, below Little Carson Falls in a magnificent grove of redwoods; the name appears on a hiking map that

HUNTING FERAL PIGS

A new kind of hunting began on the Mountain in 1984 and continues today — hunting not for sport or even primarily for food, but for protection of natural resources. Herds of wild pigs have staked out large portions of the Mountain for their own. They are voracious, omnivorous, amazingly fecund, and extremely destructive. They root up huge patches of earth, devouring bulbs, acorns, small animals, virtually anything organic and bite size. They can ravage a meadow in one night. Their insatiable appetites have caused major changes in the ecology of the Mountain, silting streams in which salmon spawn, destroying snakes and rodents on which hawks feed, exterminating plant species.

Unlike wild pigs in other areas of California, these pigs have no European wild boar blood; they are descended from domestic pigs which either escaped or were released from a pigpen. In the wild, they grow longer tusks, perhaps as a result of hormonal change, and become far more muscular and faster on their feet. They grow to immense size, 300, 400, even 500 pounds, and are ferocious when cornered. With grizzly bears and mountain lions long gone from the Mountain, the pigs have no natural enemies except men, and so far men have proved unequal to the task of controlling them.

Plant lovers were the first to be alarmed by the pigs' depredations. Meadows at Potrero and Laurel Dell were so badly rooted up and trampled that grasses and the rare calypso orchid were disappearing, giving way to Scotch broom and thistle. The rooting caused so much silting

One of the troublesome pigs glares from a cage after capture.
*(*Independent Journal *photo by Bob Hax)*

in creeks that the Water District started a program of trapping and hunting which netted 70 pigs. Rangers for the Golden Gate National Recreation Area have accounted for a good many more. The *Chronicle* reported in March 1987 that 150 pigs had been served up at St. Anthony's dining room in San Francisco in the preceding year.

But a sow produces two litters a year, with up to ten piglets per litter. No one knows how many pigs are now ranging the Mountain. The herds seem to have retreated to Bolinas Ridge, but they move fast and are extremely elusive. Park managers are afraid they will invade Point Reyes National Seashore, and to prevent this are installing a seven-mile pig fence, running from Audubon Canyon Ranch along Bolinas Ridge northward to Olema, and back down to Bolinas Lagoon. A second loop is proposed further south, to enclose Muir Woods and adjacent areas. The cost: $13,000 per mile. It takes a very good fence to hold 400 pounds of streamlined muscle determined to escape.

Judd Howell, natural resources specialist for the GGNRA, believes that the fences are "the ultimate solution," the *Chronicle* reported. The pigs will be driven down the fenced enclosures toward hunters' guns. The cost of this exercise, high as it may be, is small compared to the amount of damage the pigs have caused. The "ultimate solution" may seem like an extreme measure, but there is no alternative if the ecology of the Mountain is to be preserved.

pre-dates 1918. Under the terms of the Water District lease, the club was restricted to twelve active members and two guests, sixteen horses and six dogs in camp at one time. Similar restrictions applied to the Redwood Gun Club. Members were required to provide fire protection and to man fire patrols.

The Water District was clearly concerned about fire hazards, but does not seem to have worried that the horses might cause pollution. The Big Trees Camp itself depended for drinking water on a spring, rather than on the creek, which might be polluted by cattle grazing further upstream. But the horses must have been a source of pollution for Kent Lake after its construction in 1953. Ostensibly for these reasons the lease was cancelled in 1971 "in the best interest and welfare" of the MMWD. The real reason was revealed in an article in the Sunday *Examiner and Chronicle,* which sharply criticized the Water District because the clubs were keeping out everyone but their own members. Also, the rental amounts were small: Big Trees paid $625 per year (eleven cents per acre), and the Redwood Club $350 per year (45 cents per acre). The newspaper article supplied the names of many of the clubs' members. These read like a Who's Who for Belvedere, Atherton, Kent Woodlands, San Rafael and elsewhere, though a spokesman for one of the groups declared, "We're all just working men." The Big Trees Camp was torn down by MMWD in 1972, but the site is easy to locate.

Established earlier, and surviving longer, was Mailliard's Camp, probably established by Joseph Mailliard, himself an ardent hunter. He referred to this camp in his article "Earlier Days in Marin County." It too was torn down by the Water District in the 1970s; the site, below the Saddle on the upper reaches of Big Carson Creek, is visible today.

Still another hunters' camp appears on the Northwestern Pacific map of 1925, but nothing else is known about it. "Hunters' Camp" was at the top of Bolinas Ridge, next to the trail, about a mile and a half north of Ridgecrest.

The Kent family had its own cabin, built some time before 1898, on Lagunitas Creek, possibly where Van Wyck Creek empties into Alpine Lake. Around 1909, George H. Jackson, vice-president of the Rod and Gun Club, took over the site, tore down the cabin and built a small house and stable. In 1914

he built a house, barn, bridge, keeper's house and corral. The site, not far from Liberty Ranch, was flooded when Alpine Lake was filled. Though people have searched diligently when the lake has been drained, no trace of the structures has been found.

Hunting, for those who enjoy it, is undoubtedly great sport, but hunting and hiking in the same areas became increasingly incompatible, and hikers objected. Besides the danger from a vagrant shot, hikers resented being excluded from hunting preserves which took up very large areas of Tamalpais. They were confronted by signs put up by the Tamalpais Sportsmen's Club: "Hunting, Fishing and the Building of Fires Strictly Forbidden on these Grounds. Trespassers will be Prosecuted." Such prohibitions sparked the campaign by the Tamalpais Conservation Club and their hiking allies for the designation of the Mountain as a game refuge. The Sportsmen's Club retaliated by posting patrols to prevent the TCC from holding its second annual convention at Rock Spring in 1913; the hikers met at Rattlesnake Camp instead. The conflict intensified the campaign for a game refuge, which was finally established in 1917. The refuge included all of what we usually think of as Mt. Tamalpais, and also took in the Lagunitas Creek watershed below Alpine Dam, as far as Little Carson Creek, where Pine Mountain Tunnel was being built.

But the sportsmen did not give up; they made several attempts to get the legislature to relax restrictions. In 1951 a proposal was made, but defeated, to reduce the size of the game refuge and to permit controlled hunting to reduce the deer population. Again, in 1964, the Associated Sportsmen of California sought to weaken restrictions imposed in the state's game refuges, including Tamalpais. Nothing came of these proposals, even though they had the support of the Fish and Game Commission. Their defeat was attributable to the Tamalpais Conservation Club and other hiking clubs, who by this time had the strong support of the Marin Conservation League. Though the Tamalpais Game Refuge was not diminished, neither has it ever been extended beyond its original boundaries. Hunting has been halted elsewhere by the Water District and more recently by the GGNRA.

Though hunters and hikers did not enjoy sharing the mountain, it is only just to note that the hunters were, in their own way, conservationists. Not only on Mt. Tamalpais, but statewide, hunters and their organizations try to prevent depletion of the animals they hunt.

Hunting is no longer the manly sport it was in Teddy Roosevelt's day. Even TR was revolted by the commercial slaughter of wild animals; his biographer says, "For all his zest for hunting, Roosevelt possessed both the naturalist's compulsion to conserve and the democrat's desire to share." Marin's own conservationist, William Kent, like his father, was fond of shooting and indeed was a noted marksman. Yet without his contributions Mt. Tamalpais could not have become the sanctuary it is.

CHAPTER NOTES

Information on Recreational hunting comes almost entirely from fugitive sources, not easily located. A section of Charles Lauff's autobiographical notes is available in the Mill Valley Public Library, as reprinted in the San Rafael *Independent Journal,* June 12, 1971.

A Naval Campaign in the Californias, 1846-1849: The Journal of Lieutenant Tunis Augustus Macdonough Craven, U.S.N., United States Sloop of War, Dale, edited by John Haskell Kemble, was published by the Book Club of California, Ward Ritchie Press, 1973. It contains the complete account of Craven's excursion on the Mountain and his visit to the Reed household.

Joseph Mailliard: "Earlier Days in Marin County" makes good reading, but has only limited references to hunting. It appears in *Trails,* the official publication of the California Alpine Club, for 1923, Vol. II, No. 2.

California Out-of-Doors, official publication of the Tamalpais Conservation Club (available in the Mill Valley Library), has an article on "Mt. Tamalpais Game Refuge," in the Fall issue, 1964.

Harold French, an early and enthusiastic hiker, published an article in *Overland Monthly* for 1913 (Vol. 61, p. 424) entitled "Mt. Tamalpais' Game Refuge."

Above: The rare native clematis (Clematis lasiantha) is covered with white blooms. (Courtesy David Fairley) Left: Another rare sight is the flower head of the squaw grass (Xerophyllum tenax), which is said to bloom only after a fire. (Courtesy of Hermann Zutraun)

CHAPTER FOUR

The Changing Flora of the Mountain

Much of the charm of Mt. Tamalpais is due to the beauty and diversity of its plant life. Every hiker, whether rank amateur or professional botanist, finds something memorable. Perhaps it's the lovely little orchid, *Calypso bulbosa,* or a fantastically contorted Madrone, or the largest tree of some particular species, or a specimen of one of the eight species found only on Mt. Tamalpais. The regular hiker will look for the first bloom of each species and mark the succession of blooms as the season progresses. Some will notice the characteristic groupings of plants in different localities. Others will observe the successional changes as grassland gives way to chaparral, or shrub to fir trees. And some will be angry at the proliferation of broom and other exotics. But all will agree with Alice Eastwood, who called Tamalpais a garden spot.

There are said to be some seven or eight hundred species of plants on the Mountain. These include some of the Sierra species, some for which the Mountain is the southern boundary, some for which it is the northern boundary, and a few which are known only on Mt. Tamalpais. John Thomas Howell, in his *Marin Flora,* lists eight of these latter, including a lupine (the Tamalpais Lupine, *Lupinus Douglasii* var. *fallax*), and a gooseberry (Victor's Gooseberry, *Ribes Menziesii* var. *Victoris*).

The variety of plant life on the Mountain is extraordinary; with the possible exception of Point Reyes, the diversity is greater than anywhere else in Marin.

Sir Francis Drake was the first to report on plants he found in Marin, but their identification is as uncertain as the location of his landing. Later explorers often had naturalists in the party, so there is a record of the plants they identified. Among them were Archibald Menzies, with Vancouver in 1790-1795; Dr. Georg von Langsdorff with Count Nikolai Resanov in 1806; Adelbert von Chamisso with Otto von Kotzbue's first visit in 1816; Johann Friedrich Eschscholtz with Kotzbue on his second expedition in 1824; David Douglas in 1831, from the Royal Horticultural Society of London; and Karl Theodor Hartweg, in 1846 and 1847, also from the Royal Horticultural Society.

Menzies is remembered in the name for Madrone *(Arbutus Menziesii),* and he discovered the California laurel *(Umbellularia californica).* Chamisso was the first of these botanists to visit Marin, but he did so in October when little was in bloom. Eschscholtz came to Mission San Rafael and walked from there to Bodega. He found two of our common shrubs, Blue Blossom *(Ceanothus thyrsiflorus)* and Coffee Berry *(Rhamnus californica).* Our California state flower, the Golden Poppy, *(Eschscholzia californica)* is named for him. Douglas is well known for a number of plants named for him, such as the lupine and the Douglas fir. Hartweg made the first collections definitely known to come from Marin, including Fritillaria *(Fritillaria lanceolata* var. *gracilis)* which he found in Corte Madera.

Only after the United States took over California was the first extensive collection of Marin plants made by John M. Bigelow, botanist with the Pacific Railroad Survey. In April of 1854, he made a collecting trip through redwood country north of Mt. Tamalpais, in the Carson area. Among other early spring flowers which he found were Fetid Adder's Tongue *(Scoliopus bigelovii),* which is named for him, and Modesty *(Whipplea modesta).*

After the establishment of the California Academy of Sciences in 1853, many botanists roamed the Marin hills, collecting specimens. Most notable was Alice Eastwood, Curator of Botany at the Academy for fifty-seven years, from 1892 to 1949, when she resigned at age 90. She is of special interest here, because Tamalpais was her favorite haunt. Among botanists, she is best known for her work on manzanitas *(Arctostophylos),* of which she identified and named five different species on Mt. Tamalpais. Miss Eastwood was eager to share her knowledge with other hikers. She wrote for the publications of hikers' clubs a series of articles which she later collected and published in a slim volume, *A Collection of Popular Articles on the Flora of Mount Tamalpais,* now unfortunately long out of print.

Though Alice Eastwood roamed all over the state in the course of collecting plants for the Academy's herbarium, her lifelong love was Mt. Tamalpais. Her first visit to the Mountain was in 1891, soon after her arrival in San Francisco. For many years thereafter she hiked on it regularly. Carol Green Wilson, her friend and biographer, writes that Miss Eastwood "kept in condition. . . because while she was at home she climbed Tamalpais Sunday after Sunday."

Miss Eastwood was a prodigious hiker. One of her friends has described her: "I remember a famous plant-hunter — a hatless, short-skirted, broad-shouldered woman of wonderful strength — who used to trudge easily twenty miles a day. .carrying her heavy plant presses on her back." She herself claimed that she had often walked more than thirty miles in a day. On one occasion, fortunately accompanied this time by John Franklin Forbes, she was crossing Cataract Creek in a storm when she slipped on wet moss, fell in and was carried downstream to a pool. The accident was greatly exaggerated in a San Francisco *Examiner* story which reported that she had fallen off a 200-foot cliff.

Those who like old trail maps of the Mountain will find an Eastwood Trail, running up to West Peak from the Rock Spring Trail not far from West Point. Originally it connected near the top with the Arturo Trail, which ran down the northern slope to Rifle Camp and Potrero Meadows. But when the radar station was built in 1952, its chain link fence interrupted this route. In 1985 the Mt. Tamalpais History Project won permission from the Golden Gate National Recreation Area to reconnect these two trails.

Miss Eastwood was also commemorated by the establishment of Camp Alice Eastwood, a daytime camp administered by Mount Tamalpais State Park, and located on the site of the Mountain Railroad's Muir Inn. Camp Alice Eastood was dedicated on May 1, 1949, by the Tamalpais Conservation Club, of which Miss Eastwood had been a founding member and president. She celebrated her 90th birthday on that date.

Since Alice Eastwood's time, botanists have become increasingly interested in ecology, an understanding of which adds to one's enjoyment of the trees and wildflowers. John Thomas Howell, who followed Alice Eastwood as head of the Botany Department at the California Academy of Sciences, and who now is Curator Emeritus, distinguishes a number of "life zones" or "plant associations" in his authoritative book, *Marin Flora.* Four of these are clearly represented on Mt. Tamalpais: the Redwood Forest, the Tanbark Oak—Madrono Forest, the Chaparral and the Mountain Meadow. For each zone, Howell lists the plants commonly found there.

While Howell's plant groups are a recognizable feature of the Mountain today, they are constantly subject to a variety of forces which change not so much their composition as their extent and their distribution. Big changes have occurred in the hundred or more years for which we have a record, and changes are still going on. Most striking, as old photographs and paintings show, the upper slopes of the Mountain, now densely covered with chaparral and scattered trees, once were largely bald.

Above: Alice Eastwood devoted her life to the study of plants on Mt. Tamalpais, as part of her distinguished career at the California Academy of Sciences in Golden Gate Park. (Courtesy of the Archives, California Academy of Sciences) Left: John Howell, author of Marin Flora, *discovered a number of new species of plants in the county. Here he gives a lecture to plant enthusiasts on Mt. Tamalpais. (Courtesy of John Howell)*

When Robert Louis Stevenson first saw Mt. Tamalpais in 1879, he wrote, "Yet a little while and perhaps all the hills of sea-board California may be as bald as Tamalpais." He had just had a harrowing experience with a forest fire near Monterey, and assumed that Mt. Tamalpais had once been covered with redwoods, and that its baldness was the result of fire. He was, of course, incorrect; there is no evidence that the distribution of redwoods has changed markedly in centuries.

But he is probably correct that before the white man came fire had kept the foliage down so that from a distance the Mountain appeared quite bare. There seems to be no other explanation, despite the fact that lightning storms are infrequent. Since the Anglos supplanted the Indians most of the major forest fires have been man-made. This is true of the fires of 1881, 1889, 1890, 1904, 1913, 1916, 1923, 1929, and 1945, all of which resulted from human carelessness, from sparks from wood-burning locomotives, and in one instance from the sun shining on broken glass.

Earlier methods of containing fires created the present network of access roads and fire breaks that can still be seen running down the Mountain. Modern fire-fighting methods have made these obsolete, although rangers now patrol the roads. The firebreaks have been narrowed by encroaching chaparral until they remain only as trails, poor ones at that because they are so steep.

Since the last big fire in 1945 the county's fire fighters have succeeded in preventing any serious conflagrations, thanks to accurate spotting and the use of airborne tankers which drop thousands of gallons of fire retardant. So effective, indeed, has fire prevention become that the fire authorities now have a new worry. Chaparral, usually vigorous and healthy until about 25 years old, then deteriorates, becoming dry and very flammable. Some varieties are very resinous, especially Chamise. Large areas of the Mountain are covered with dead or dying chaparral, and this accumulation creates a serious fire hazard. The Marin Fire Department in 1983 began a program of controlled burning, using a napalm-like chemical dropped by helicopter in selected small areas, first in the Carson area, and later on the south side of the Mountain. Some years must pass before the project's success can be judged. Meanwhile skeptics protest against the ugly black scars left by the burns, and are concerned lest the extreme heat produced by the chemical fire may interfere with the recovery of plant life. Others point out that burning will destroy young fir trees that have popped up through the chaparral. Left to themselves, the firs would eventually cover large areas of the Mountain, as they have already done in many canyons, thanks to years of fire prevention.

Studies show that after a natural fire, though some species are killed, many plants appear or reappear as soon as the rains come. Two species of manzanita *(Archtostaphylos glandulosa* and *A. Cushingiana)* provide an interesting example of how evolutionary forces have worked to protect them from lasting fire damage. New growth, often at an accelerated rate, develops from the stumplike root crowns, some of which are so ancient that botanists speculate these plants may be as old as the giant redwoods. The seeds of some other plants germinate as a result of the heat. And the spectacular blossoms of Squaw Grass *(Xerophyllum tenax)* rarely appear on Mt. Tamalpais except after a fire. Thus a naturally burned area is soon as beautiful as ever.

We cannot overlook the very great damage a major fire might cause. Many in Marin remember the 1929 fire, which swept down the south side of the Mountain to Mill Valley, where it destroyed 117 houses. Now that houses have crept even further up the hillsides all along the crescent from Mill Valley to Fairfax, the danger is greatly increased.

Fires are by no means the only factors causing changes in the flora, although they are the most dramatic. Other factors include logging, grazing, the introduction of exotics and the process which causes ponds to become swamps, swamps to become meadows, and meadows to become covered with brush and eventually trees. Logging has reduced the stands of the old redwoods; new ones have grown up mostly from the roots of old trees, but also from seeds in areas kept moist by summer fogs, as along the top of Bolinas Ridge. In general it seems that logging has left but few scars. The end of grazing has contributed to the reduction of grassland areas, and thus to a growing coverage of chaparral and trees. Broom is overgrowing grassland and elsewhere is crowding out native shrubs. The pond in Potrero Meadow has become a swamp; the High Marsh is drying up, and lagoons appearing on old maps are no more.

Alice Eastwood tramped the Mountain for decades, gathering specimens for her original research in botany. (Courtesy of the Archives, California Academy of Science)

The shrinkage and disappearance of ponds and swamps has been accompanied by what some old-timers claim has been a decline in the flow of streams and the disappearance of springs. Water district data do not show any long-range reduction in rainfall. It may be that runoff has been reduced by the great quantity of new trees and chaparral, which soak up water and then lose it into the atmosphere through transpiration. The natural erosion and silting of water courses has been accelerated since the coming of the white man. Every act of man, whether undertaken to exploit some resource on the Mountain or to conserve natural features and protect them from fire, has its consequence on the ecology and the rate of change.

At the same time, other factors are at work to keep things as they are — the character of the soil, the extent of exposure to sun or rain. Serpentine areas are probably much the same as they were a hundred years ago; at various times fires destroyed the Sargent Cypresses so typical of the area, but they have grown up again much as they were before.

The many serpentine areas on the Mountain are of great interest botanically, because their plant life is so radically different from areas underlain by other types of rock. Since serpentine soils contain very little potassium, calcium and sodium, they cannot support many common plants. And some unusual plants are found only on serpentine. No firs, for example, but the typical Sargent Cypresses. Even the cypresses very rarely grow to more than a foot in diameter. Yet in one spot where the serpentine vein runs through a stream there are two enormous Sargent Cypresses. Members of the Tamalpais History Project have been responsible for their being cited as "Twin Champions" in the United States, in the *National Register of Big Trees,* published periodically by the American Forestry Association.

The inquiring hiker, even when he has become familiar with the accepted explanations of ecological change, finds questions he cannot answer. For example, why is half of Pilot Knob grassy while the other half is forested? Is it the exposure, or soil, or something else? In many places one finds a perfectly straight line between grass and chaparral. Why? Maybe the line marks a vanished fence which restricted cattle to the grassy side. But in that case why hasn't chapparal moved in? Why did most of the pines planted on Oat Hill die? Too much sun, too

little water, wrong soil? After the redwoods were logged off the eastern slope of Bolinas Ridge above Redwood Creek, why did tanbark oaks take over so completely? Why not other trees? Will other trees eventually displace them? Why are Calypso Orchids found only under fir trees? Or are they? Is it the soil, or do their roots have some affinity to the firs' roots?

Large areas of Mt. Tamalpais are covered with grass, and many of them probably have always been so. Grass likes an alkaline soil, and this does not change over the years. But the type of grass does change. Before the Spaniards and Mexicans came, the predominant grasses were perennials, including the bunch grasses. But within a relatively few years after their arrival these grasses were almost completely displaced by several species of oat grass *(Arena spp.)* and later by several species of Bromus *(Bromus spp.)* not to be confused with Broom, *(genus Cytisus).* The new grasses are annuals which die down after the rains, making the hills brown. It is generally thought that seeds of the invading grasses were brought over from Spain in the the packing and hay and in the debris from livestock. Then, of course, birds accomplished the wide distribution. The change was dramatic.

While "the extent and composition of pristine coastal prairie are not well recorded," as Professor Heady says, there is one interesting source of information about the original grasses: the adobe bricks of the Spanish Missions. Scientists, crumbling these bricks, have found seeds of the plants which lived in the Mission days. Bunch grass is most commonly found.

Recently, since grazing has stopped on the Mountain, some of the perennial grasses are making a comeback. A stand of native perennial grass can be found, for example, on the right hand side of the highway, half a mile or so below Pantoll as one heads west.

The end of grazing, along with the end of fires, has had the additional effect of allowing shrubs to creep into grassland at the edges, so that the grasslands are becoming smaller. The most active invader is Coyote Brush *(Baccharis pilularis).* From an ecological point of view there may be something to be said for again allowing cattle to graze on the Mountain, for example on Bolinas Ridge. It is sad to see the grassland shrinking. Young firs and canyon oaks crop up on grassy slopes, though deer help keep

The fire of 1929 was the most devastating on record, sweeping over most of the southern slopes of the Mountain and destroying many houses in Mill Valley. Many residents today recall the catastrophe. "It was tragic," says one witness, "like watching the death and cremation of someone dear to me." (Courtesy of the Mill Valley Library)

Firefighters work frantically to contain the 1929 fire, then run for safety. (Courtesy of Nancy Skinner)

them down. Bracken fern is taking over in some areas where soil is shallow and the grass is thin. Since deer don't eat bracken, they don't help prevent this encroachment.

Field flowers are not so abundant as they once were. Mrs. Thomas Kent says in her oral history that she had noticed a decline in wildflowers in her sixty years in Marin. She recalls that the hills above Stinson Beach used to be "sheets of gold and sheets of blue, acres and acres, and it was that way all down the coast." Lupine and poppies have become less luxuriant since then. Can it be that the fields are missing the fertilizer supplied by the cattle? Wildflowers have suffered the effects of highway construction and real estate development, as well as of the increasing stream of casual visitors who, perhaps unintentionally but inevitably, destroy the wild plants.

Some people, sad to say, pull up flowers by the roots. Practically all the wild rhododendrons *(Rhododendron macrophyllum)* have disappeared from the Mountain, and most of the Leopard (or Tiger) Lilies *(Lilium pardolinum)*. Some of the vandals are householders who want to replant specimens in their gardens. But this practice may destroy the species entirely. One botanist, Peter H. Raven, writes that "many species of Calochortus, Dudleya, Fritillaria and Lilium are threatened directly by those who take them from the wild to gardens, in which they may persist for only a short time. Native plants should be introduced into cultivation only by means of seeds and cuttings, and the rare plants of California should be stringently protected in the wilds."

Of course not all native plants are desirable, including bracken fern, and many would be happy if poison oak could be eliminated even though it is not a serious menace to those who stay on trails, and it is beautiful in the fall when it turns a bright red. Its ill effects were deplored as long ago as 1826 by Captain Beechey:

The most remarkable shrub in this country is the yedra, a poisonous plant affecting only particular constitutions of the human body, by producing tumours and violent inflammation upon any part with which it comes in contact; and indeed even the exhalation from it, borne upon the wind, is said to have an effect upon some people.

And Stevenson remarks in Silverado Squatters:

In all woods and by every wayside there prospers an abominable shrub or weed, called poison-oak, whose very neighborhood is venomous to some, and whose touch is avoided by the most impervious.

The invasion by exotics is another factor changing the Mountain's flora. Some of these, like forget-me-nots and scarlet pimpernels, are easy to tolerate and even to welcome unless one is a purist who abhors all exotics. But many people think that exotics are quite undesirable and should, if possible, be eliminated. These include broom, thistles, pampas grass, gorse, and among trees, acacias and eucalyptus.

Broom, though its bright yellow blossoms are beautiful, is considered the worst villain. Janet Mountjoy, writing in *Fremontia,* says, "Broom is a growing threat to native plants here in Marin and many other areas of California. It chokes the trails here on Mt. Tamalpais. It obscures the views. It crowds out native species on the grassy hillsides. It is a fire hazard — and, as it ages and becomes lank and woody, it is ugly." Broom is classified as a "pest weed" by the California State Department of Food and Agriculture.

There are in fact three species of broom (genus *Cytisus*), all of which were introduced from Europe for ornamental purposes. Elizabeth McClintock, writing in *Fremontia,* says that the French, or Montpelier broom, is the most widespread and damaging. A native of Europe's Mediterranean region and the Azores, it was the first species to arrive here, being offered for sale in 1858 by William C. Walker in his Golden Gate Nursery in San Francisco. Scotch broom *(C. scoparius),* also of European origin, the only one of the brooms found in the British Isles, appeared in the same nursery in the 1860's. Spanish broom *(C. junceum),* relatively rare, and mostly from the Canaries, dates here from 1871.

The brooms are now so widespread on the Mountain, they reproduce so rapidly from seed and are so difficult to eradicate, that little progress has been made in eliminating them. The State Park has done a major job on Angel Island by spraying, but not much so far on Mt. Tamalpais. The Water District, concerned over harm to its water supply, has avoided sprays, but in 1985 dug the broom up by the roots on the edges of Phoenix Lake, and has a continuing program elsewhere, using the Marin County Youth Corps. Over the years, many private organizations and many individuals have done what they could to stem the advance of this tenacious invader. The Marin Native Plant Society was prominent in a shortlived ad hoc "Broom Control Committee" consisting of various conservation groups. The Tamalpais Conservation Club has also been active.

Despite these worthy efforts, most people agree that the job is simply too big for volunteers or for state or county agencies with their severely limited budgets. A thorough job would require an effort on the scale of work done by the Civilian Conservation Corps in the 1930's. Unfortunately, this seems out of the question nowadays.

Besides broom, the exotic which has stirred the most controversy is the eucalyptus. These trees were originally imported from Australia in many different species. A number were planted near the Tourist Club, above Muir Woods, and along an avenue approaching the parking area for Lake Lagunitas. These latter were planted by William T. Coleman as part of his plan to develop the area. Coleman built Lake Lagunitas to supply water for his real estate development in San Rafael, and for a hotel he planned to build below the dam. About half of these eucalyptus have recently been cut down by the Water District.

The Plan for Mt. Tamalpais State Park, drafted by the staff in 1979, called unequivocally for the removal of all eucalyptus trees in the Park. But the Park and Recreation Commission disagreed, ruling that no more than ten percent a year should be removed, and then only if they are replaced with compatible native plants. By 1986 this program was well under way.

Plantings of other trees, many of them native to the Mountain, were carried out on a much larger scale by the Water District from 1929 to 1935. The object was reforestation. A survey by Carl O. Bachem of Mill Valley recommended planting Bishop and Monterey pines, redwoods and Port Orford cedars, with a preliminary planting of tanbark oak acorns, since tanbark oaks are a precondition to the success of conifers. By 1935, some 24,000 trees had been set out.

The program was discontiued in 1935 because mortality was very high among all species except pines, and because it was feared that even these would be killed by fires. In some areas, for example Oat Hill, practically none of the plantings survived, perhaps because the soil was not suitable. Elsewhere many pines did survive and have grown to substantial size. Most conspicuous are those near the Double Bow Knot, at West Point, near the East Peak parking lot, and between Lake Lagunitas and Bon Tempe.

Many are familiar with the Coulter pines along the east side of Lake Lagunitas, planted by Jim Roof and others. Elsewhere a stand of Monterey pines, planted to produce Christmas trees, was abandoned and became an eyesore; park staff have made it into a very attractive walk-in campground.

The only pines one sees on Mt. Tamalpais proper are those that have been planted. But the exploring hiker will find a number of stands of Bishop pines elsewhere, in that vast and gorgeous country north of Alpine Lake, where Big and Little Carson Creeks drain into Kent Lake. Here a number of groves have sprung up since the devastating fire swept over the whole area in 1945. Harold Gilliam calls them "expatriate Bishop pines" in his beautiful Sierra Club book, *Island in Time.* Fred Sandrock, a student of Bishop pines, calls them "invaders from Pt. Reyes." Bishop pines are believed native only to the granite formations of Point Reyes and to other similar areas west of the San Andreas fault. Were seeds from Point Reyes brought over by birds, or did the westerlies carry them over?

The whole subject of plant succession and plant distribution seems to this writer to be still in its infancy. There is so much no one seems to know.

CHAPTER NOTES

Much the most useful book on the Mountain's plants is John Thomas Howell's *Marin Flora*. Besides his detailed classification of wildflowers, trees, shrubs and ferns, Howell has a long introduction covering the physical environment as it affects plant life, the geographic distribution of plants in the county, a very useful analysis of "life zones and plant associations," the effect of fire and much more. The book includes beautiful photographs by Charles T. Townsend.

Very helpful to the layman, if one can locate a copy, is Alice Eastwood's *Collection of Popular Articles on the Flora of Mount Tamalpais*. Carol Green Wilson's biography, *Alice Eastwood's Wonderland: The Adventures of a Botanist,* is a worthy tribute to a great lady. Another book, also issued by the California Academy of Sciences in honor of Alice Eastwood, is Susanna Bryant Dakin's *The Perennial Adventure, A Tribute to Alice Eastwood, 1859-1953*.

Information on the Water District's tree planting program is from District records and from a manuscript by James Roof, *History of Reforestation on the MMWD Lands,* a copy of which is in the Mill Valley Library.

The effect of differences in soils is dealt with in an article in *California Living* for June 1, 1980, "A West Marin Trip" by Nancy Wise. She quotes the naturalist Clerin Zumwalt, formerly with the Water District. Zumwalt is largely responsible for a fine report put out by the MMWD, *Environmental Planning Study,* with excellent photographs.

A very scholarly compendium is the grandly titled *Terrestrial Vegetation in California,* edited by Michael J. Barbour and Jack Major. (This book presumably omits mention of Spanish moss, mistletoe and air plants, which might be termed extra-terrestrial vegetation.) Included are articles on California Scrub and on the historic transition from native perennial grasses to imported annuals, mostly oat grasses. Most useful is the article by Professor Heady.

Alice Eastwood is the authority for the estimate of 700 or 800 species of plants on the Mountain, of which about 100 are trees or shrubs. These species belong to some 350 genera, representing some 80 orders.

Overleaf: This small section of an enormous map printed by H.H. Bancroft & Co. in 1873 shows "Tamalpais Mt." with a small patch of "Public Land" on its eastern flank, at the time the only land not in private ownership in the entire county. Samuel Throckmorton, with 16,482 acres (below the portion shown here), and Shafter & Howard, with 10,110 acres, are the largest landowners on the Mountain. Many old Marin families can trace their names on this map; a magnifying glass helps.

The narrow-gauge North Pacific Coast Railroad, established just one year earlier, enters at lower right from Sausalito, skirts the east side of Strawberry, goes up to Ross Landing (Kentfield) and on through the San Geronimo Valley, with a spur leading to San Rafael. The rival route was the very short San Quentin & San Rafael Railroad, which connected with a ferry to San Francisco. Mill Valley, Corte Madera, Larkspur, San Anselmo and Fairfax did not yet exist.

The San Rafael-Bolinas Trail is clearly marked. "Bolinas Bay" is a navigable means of getting farm produce and lumber to the little port of Bolinas Landing for shipment to San Francisco. Across the channel is "Isaac Andrews Sand Beach", later called Willow Camp, and finally Stinson Beach. Steep Ravine ends at Rocky Point, with a "Horse Coral" near its mouth. The Mount Diablo Base Line runs due west from Mt. Diablo. Just below it, in Coyote Valley, are two buildings labeled "Hoppys." Could a cowboy named Cassidy have lived there? (Courtesy of the Bancroft Library)

H.H. Bancroft & Co.   1873

The Alonzo Coffin and Thomas Kelly families, pioneer residents of Mill Valley, enjoy the view from the summit of Mt. Tamalpais in 1893. (Courtesy of Nancy Skinner)

CHAPTER FIVE

Hiking in the Nineteenth Century

"On a fair spring morning in the month of May, 1850, a single horse with two riders might have been seen threading its way up the steep mountain trail leading from Bolinas to San Rafael," relates Helen Bingham in her 1906 classic, *In Tamal Land.* The riders were Senorita Maria J. Briones, daughter of Gregorio Briones, and Francisco Sebrean, on their way to be married at Mission San Rafael, and their precipitous path was the Bolinas-San Rafael Trail.

Shown on an 1860 map of Marin County, their route was the earliest trail for which there is such definite information. From San Rafael it followed Lagunitas Creek as far as the site of Alpine Dam, climbed steeply to the top of Bolinas Ridge and then descended to the shore of Bolinas Lagoon. How long the trail had been in existence before 1850 we don't know; chances are it was used by Indians long before that.

No such romantic canter is recorded for another beaten track which may be even older: the Lone Tree Trail, still very much in existence as the Dipsea Trail and labored over by the hundreds of runners in the Dipsea Race each year. Today the path starts in Mill Valley, climbs 420 feet via 671 redwood steps to the top of Windy Gap, drops down steeply to Muir Woods, rises northwest up the southern slope of the Mountain, passes the "lone tree" (a redwood, not a pine as many people say, and now no longer alone), descends into Steep Ravine, then mounts to overlook the Pacific and ends at Stinson Beach.

According to Jack Mason, San Jose Jesus Briones, Maria's brother, "said he remembered driving cattle past Captain Easkoot's house above Stinson Beach, across the high land and from there following the trail to Sausalito." For at least a portion of the way he must have coaxed his herd along the Lone Tree Trail.

Neither of these early trails went to the top of the Mountain, but another one did, on the north side, going up Rocky Ridge to West Peak (until 1952 the highest point on the Mountain at 2604 feet). Whether one started from San Rafael or Ross Landing, there were two possible ways to get onto Rocky Ridge: follow Lagunitas Creek to where the trail comes down, or climb up Fish Gulch and cross the level Bon Tempe area and up to Rocky Ridge. The way up the ridge is quite straight and relatively open. When wild cattle roamed the mountain they must have grazed here.

William H. Brewer's expedition from San Rafael to Sausalito, noted earlier as the first thoroughly documented record of a climb to the top, clearly took him up Rocky Ridge, though he does not provide us with any details.

A few years later, in 1869, Albert S. Evans, editor of the San Francisco *Daily Alta,* rode up on horseback. He went by ferry — quite likely the *Petaluma* — from San Francisco to Point San Quentin, and though he does not explain what route he followed it seems certain to have been Rocky Ridge. He and his party were after bears but had to settle for quail. He had nothing to say in his account of the climb about his feelings at the summit, pleasurable or not; later he wrote, "There is no finer mountain for its height on all the continent of America, than Tamalpais. . . " But after his climb his enthusiasm waned:

> As I have already remarked, Tamalpais is one of the finest of the lesser mountains of California, an attractive mountain to look at from Russian or Telegraph Hill. It is there all the time. You may see it any day; and you may have it for all of me. The experience of that trip disgusted me with it for all time, and I go there no more. *Adios,* Tamalpais.

From the early 1870s we have records of only two ascents, both on horseback. One, probably in 1873, is recounted by Munro-Fraser in his 1880 *History of Marin County.* He and his party rode up the Fish Gulch Road, which was being used to construct Lake Lagunitas Dam, and then up a horse trail that may have followed Rocky Ridge, though his reference to a ravine raises a question about the route. The trail, he says, "is steep and leads through chaparral, with some hard climbing for the horses." He continues:

> The ascent is. . . .through a ravine leading to the summit ridge, which is indicated by the numerous trails of horned cattle, migrating to and from either side of the mountain, for change of herbage and water. The scenery is wild and romantic, showing abrupt declivities and deep ravines; a wilderness of redwood, cedar (he probably means cypress), chaparral, in which are frequently found the blanched antlers of the elk, an animal now extinct, or hardly ever met with in these glades. The mountain summit is gained from thence by a succession of outcroppings between barren stretches, with here and there a stunted cedar, or patches of low brambles.

The summit they reached he calls the "central summit" and gives it an elevation of 2,594 feet. He notes that it has been selected for the Flagstaff Station of the U.S. Coast Survey, but the station was actually built on West Peak.

On May 1, 1874, according to the *Marin Journal,* a group of students from the San Rafael Academy rode horseback up the Mountain. They went up the Fish Gulch Road to "Mr. Coleman's dam at the Lagunitas." (William T. Coleman, leader of the San Francisco Vigilantes in 1856, needed the water from the lake to supply his extensive real estate developments in San Rafael.) From the dam, they "took the trail for the summit, riding up the mountain in single file, led by a brave boy mounted on a beautiful steed." Another boy commented, however, that the trail was "broad and good. . .even ladies could go up safely." They reached the signal station of West Peak and then hiked to the East Peak, "a pretty rough walk I can tell you." Then they returned to the lake and went rowing.

These few reported climbs in the early 1870s were undoubtedly only the tip of the iceberg; there were certainly many more, and after 1875 the pace increased. For one thing, the population of San Francisco was growing at an exponential rate — from 34,776 in 1852 to 233,959 in 1880. Marin County itself had 11,324 people in 1880.

During these years access to the Mountain was becoming easier as the ferries and the railroad began operation. The first ferry service was supplied by the little *Princess,* which in 1855 began making stops at Point San Quentin on its way up to Petaluma, at that time a thriving waterfront town. Then, on May 10, 1868, the Saucelito Land and Ferry Co. started ferry service from Sausalito to San Francisco, at first using the *Princess,* but soon putting on the larger *Petaluma.* The fare was 25 cents. But even with the ferry service, a trip to Tamalpais was not to be undertaken lightly.

With the opening in 1874 of the North Pacific Coast Railway from Sausalito to Fairfax and beyond, access became much easier. San Franciscans looking for a Sunday in the country could board a ferry in the city, transfer to the train in Sausalito, and get off at any one of several stations along the route, from Ross to Fairfax. When a railway spur to Mill Valley was inaugurated in 1889, the way was opened for the major invasions of subsequent years.

These transportation improvements were fostered by real estate and lumber interests. The North Pacific Coast Railroad was built mainly to

Top: A party of well-dressed travelers is ready to depart for the summit on donkeys in 1893, when the Alonzo Coffin house on the hill was just finished. Below: Twenty men and two women, all probably railroad workers, pose at the summit around 1900. (Courtesy of the Mill Valley Library)

Above: Wheeler Martin (right) stands in the doorway of his store, his aproned clerk beside him, at the corner of Throckmorton and Bernard in Mill Valley. In the early 1890's hikers could buy provisions here for the arduous climb to the top. Opposite, above: Miller Avenue ends at Lytton Square with the Wheeler Martin store (center) and the depot (right, behind trees); the Coffin house on the hill is barely begun in 1892. Below: The hotel and restaurant at 38 Miller Avenue, offering ice cream, lunch parlors and the Examiner, *draws a fine brace of customers.*
(All three photos courtesy of the Mill Valley Library)

Blithedale Road leads through pastures in 1896. Below: Miller Avenue is a muddy track along the railroad in 1903. "Maples," the Jacob Gardner house at left, is still imposing today. (Courtesy of the Mill Valley Library)

bring down redwood lumber. The Saucelito Land and Ferry Co. was started to promote the town of Sausalito. And the railroad spur to Mill Valley was timed to promote the auction of Mill Valley land in 1890. The enormous benefit to hikers was incidental.

The rapid increase in hiking on the Mountain is recorded in visitor registers maintained on the East Peak of the Mountain by the Tamalpais Club from 1880 to 1887. Volume I of the registers, for the years 1880—1884, contains the signatures of 850 men, women and children who had hiked to the top, in most cases from starting points on the railroad. If so many made it in those years the number during the late 1870s must also have been substantial.

Moreover, several of those who made the climb in the 1880s noted in the register that they had been up before, some of them many times. One F. D. Russ said he had visited East Peak seventy times between 1874 and 1884. A number of others made almost equally amazing claims. Of special interest is the statement of Fred D. Marsh, who wrote in 1885 that he had first ascended about ten years before, and that he had "possession of a part of the old book from the other (West) Peak. There is some very old dates in it." We shall owe a great debt to any descendant of Marsh or of his climbing partners who can locate that book.

These East Peak registers were simply kept in a crevice in the rocks, along with a pen and a bottle of ink. The books are now in the Mill Valley Library. One entry complains that someone else has spilled the ink. Although most of the entries are at least legible, the books are not in good condition, for reasons which soon become obvious. An entry in the first volume reads, "Found the book badly soaked by the thoughtless exposure of the parties who used it last." The second volume (early 1884 to July 1887) is in better condition except for two gunshot holes through its 435 pages. The reaction of later visitors is well expressed by this entry: "Confusion on the fellow who spilled the ink and double toil and trouble on the miscreant who defaced the book, presumably by firing bullets into it."

Very little is known about the Tamalpais Club, and nothing about its origin, except that its members were mostly German. The club secretary, Edward Ziesche, was an immigrant from Prussia who arrived in a wagon train in the 1860s and owned a tobacco

store in San Francisco. He is remembered in the name for Ziesche Creek, close to Rock Spring. Other members included August Bergman, president, Frederick W. Bach, Edward Reichert, Theodore Angelis, F. D. Russ, and Julius Paulsen. Many early hikers brought their love of hiking with them from Germany, Austria, and Switzerland.

Though the first trail map did not appear until 1898 ("Tourist's Map of Mt. Tamalpais and Vicinity," compiled by A. H. Sanborn and P. C. Knapp), a number of routes are reported in the registers: from Tamalpais Station (later Kentfield), Sunnyside Station (Ross), Cushing's Sanitarium in Blithedale Canyon, from Sausalito, San Rafael, Fairfax, Bolinas. Some climbed up the north side, but the majority came up from the south. Almost all came on foot; only a few rode horses. In 1884 the Eldridge Grade was built as a carriage road up the north side to West Peak, making the top accessible to those unable or unwilling to climb.

Probably the best known people among the climbers in the 1880s were Joaquin Miller, the poet, and Eugene Schmitz, who later became mayor of San Francisco. Miller scribbled down a short verse, unfortunately in pencil and thus not wholly legible. Many well-known San Franciscans are listed: T. Evans, city editor of the *Evening Bulletin,* Frederick W. Macondray, M. Hall McAllister, Charles Sutro, C. Van Wyck, and Hugo Eloesser, uncle of Dr. Leo Eloesser. A number were trail builders — Frank J. Murphy, for example.

Visitors came from all over the United States, and from Germany, Austria, England, Scotland, Ireland, Denmark, Quebec and Nova Scotia as well. At least a third were women, and many were children. One party of 34, of which half were women, reported the number of times each had climbed to the top; nine had been up five or more times. In October, 1886, seventeen first-grade boys from Washington Grammar School were led to the top by their teacher, Prof. C. H. Ham.

The registers are adorned with drawings, poems and spicy comments, some of which must be seen to be appreciated. Of those who express their enthusiasm in verse, several use German script; one quotes Goethe. Other comments are in Spanish, Italian, Latin and Greek. As one might guess, literary quality is far from uniform. For the most part, the remarks are ecstatic: "Glorious views of the snow-capped Sierras and the sea." "I have been travelling all over the world but never found a more glorious spot than this." "This trip is a case of hard labor well repaid. . . Will we ever be able to get nearer to heaven than it has been allowed today?"

One climber reported that she was glad she got up, and that she'll be gladder still when she's down. Another wrote, "The views are magnificent. The skies are clear. The air still. The sun warm. But one has paid for it all by the horrible climb."

Far and away the biggest complaint was lack of water. "O for a drink." "Our kingdom for a beer" (with a drawing of a stein showing one of the party drowning in it). "We arrived safely but dry as a Cork Leg." Old-timers advised that one could quench one's thirst at a near-by spring, probably Redwood Spring, only a short distance down from the saddle between East and Middle Peaks.

Many entries dealt with food. Some climbers hadn't brought any. A Dane yearned for "1 lb. limburger cheese and 1 pint of beer." A party which had walked up was counting on lunch being brought up by buggy, but the buggy never arrived. Two men reported that they were the first in their party to arrive "because we were sensible and eat 4 chickens under Bingo Rock." One party, afflicted with curious syntax, shot a deer at their campground near Lake Lagunitas, skinned it on the spot, cooked it, and "devoured the venison most ravishingly. We started when the last remains of our delicious repast had vanished and traveled upward."

One entry for February 1887 reported finding snow a foot deep on the way up. In September 1881 there were reports of fire: "Foothills and southeast side of mountain on fire — burning for three days. Passed along fire line coming up." This was before there was any organized fire fighting service. "Too much smoke to see. I only saw *je ne sais quoi,* which means in English, 'Goddam the smoke.'"

Some climbers left brief reports of their experiences on the way up. A party from San Francisco City College camped for the night on the way: "Favored guests of Mr. Kent. Fruit and things. Toiled up several small mountains just for practice, nothing more. Learned to wade through sage brush as if blue grass." The next morning, "Climax: we stand upon the heights, 7:30 a.m." (The reference is to Albert Kent, father of William Kent.)

J.R. Fiedler with two others: "Started from the 5:30 p.m. boat, stayed overnight at Mrs. Peter Smith's Flea Palace, Tamalpais Station (Kentfield). That which was left of us after the fleas had had their supper started for the mountain at 6:30 a.m. and crossed Col. Kent's *mudfield* in spite of all his wire fences, fierce bull-dogs, loaded shotguns, etc."

A party of boys and girls camped on the very peak of the mountain in May 1885, and proclaimed themselves : "First party to camp on the highest point." They very well may have been.

Some of the climbing times seem remarkable, though old hands claim they were not at all impossible. Two climbers reported that it had taken them an hour and a half. One of these, who had left from Sausalito, added sourly, "and I heartily sympathise with every unfortunate who undertakes the same trip." The other, who came up from Tamalpais Station, had killed a 3'8" rattler with 14 rattles. The time of these climbers was more than matched by Dad Burnett, who left Tamalpais Station at 6:21 a.m. and arrived at the summit at 7:33 — "the best time on record," he said, and several corroborated his story.

One climber, Paul Trommulitz, was a San Francisco contractor who built the Eldridge Grade road, using Chinese labor. He came up first on September 7, 1884, "ahead of the trail (the road then under construction) for the purpose of taking survey in fog and winds." He later reported coming up five times, very likely using his own road, which wound upward from near Phoenix Lake to West Peak.

The man who conceived the road and raised the money to build it was John O. Eldridge, San Francisco merchant and owner of the San Rafael Gas Works. There was no problem about acquiring land for the right of way. The deed reads, "In consideration of the sum of one dollar, a forty-foot right of way was secured from Susanna M. Throckmorton, D. W. Doughthitt, William Craig, J. H. Meredith, Nathaniel Holland, William T. Wallace, Clarence Greathouse, Gordon Blanding and J.H. Turney." There is no record of objections by conservationists. But the deed required that the right of way be dedicated "forever to public use." This provision has been complied with, and the road is still in use today, both as an access road for the Water District and as a trail for hikers, horseback riders and bike riders. One boy who signed the register in February 1885 announced, "We'll ride down the new road

Top: The A.A. Lundquists, with sons Carl and Ivar, found a rocking chair indispensable while camping at Throckmorton & Eugene, Mill Valley, in 1893. Below: The Upham family brought plenty of furniture and clothes to their camp in Blithedale Canyon on July 4, 189?. (Courtesy of the Mill Valley Library)

Left: The Summit House, on the Bolinas-San Rafael stage road, began welcoming travelers in 1890. This early picture shows a stylish party in a fringed surrey with a matched team, during the period when Larsen ran the inn. (Courtesy of the Jack Mason Collection, Dewey Livingston, curator) Top: Another fringed but less elegant rig is ready to depart from Bolinas. (Courtesy of the Marin County Historical Society) Below: Tally Ho parties left the Hotel Rafael for the eleven-mile trip to the summit along the Eldridge Grade Road. This wagon, built for McPhail Livery Stable in San Rafael and now on display at the Ford Museum in Dearborn, Michigan, had a quiver for guns, an ice box, and a long tally ho trumpet. (Courtesy of Jack McPhail)

on our bicycles as soon as weather is settled." Bike riding on the Mountain is not new.

The wagon road was officially opened on December 14, 1884. Three two-horse carriages conveyed dignitaries from San Rafael to the summit. Eldridge died two months later, just as his road was "rapidly growing in public favor and the daily travel to its great elevation increases." As the *Marin County Journal* (October 1887) reported, it "has replaced the ragged horse-trail which preceded it and which made the ascent as difficult as the mythological ascent of Mt. Parnassus by those who courted the muses. . . . Formerly the climb and return was such a hard day's work, with such unpleasant concomitants as scratched hands and torn clothes, that few attempted it."

In 1896 access to the Mountain became even easier when the Mill Valley and Mt. Tamalpais Scenic Railroad was opened. This elegant, exciting and above all effortless way to reach the East Peak is described later in Chapter 10. Some people now rode up and hiked down, though most passengers, including great numbers of out-of-town visitors to San Francisco, were non-hikers.

Still, many people scorned the train and continued to climb on foot and on horseback. Beginning in 1890 groups from San Rafael made climbs annually on Washington's birthday to greet the sunrise from the summit. A boy of 14 tells of his first such trip in the *Independent Journal* (February 22, 1904). The party left San Rafael on foot about 6:30 in the evening and climbed up through Kent Canyon (not today's Kent Canyon, but the canyon west of Kentfield). They continued up "a rugged steep path marked by boulders" (now called the Indian Fire Trail). The last 400 feet, "steep as a ladder," led up to the observation station built by the *Examiner* in 1901, where they arrived at 3:30 a.m. It was so cold on top that the group withdrew to the Tavern run by the railway, only to find it locked up tight. They spent the rest of the night huddled in a stone stairway, and watched the sun rise over "the glistening white Sierra."

The first trail map, issued in 1898, showed many of the trails we know today: Lone Tree (today's Dipsea), Cataract, Kent, Throckmorton, Bootjack, West Point (now Rock Spring). The Rock Spring area, named on the map, probably dates from 1882. Unnamed, but shown as trails are several on the south side, coming up from Mill Valley, Baltimore Canyon, and Kentfield, and those along Corte Madera and Blithedale Ridges. Today's hiker would miss such familiar landmarks as Laurel Dell, Barth's Retreat, Potrero Camp, Rifle Camp, Bootjack Camp, Mountain Home, Northside Trail, Fern Creek Trail, Steep Ravine Trail and Ben Johnson Trail, none of which yet existed.

A few of the trails shown are now obsolete, for example, one from Rock Spring to West Peak, connecting there with the Eldridge Grade, and a steep trail down into Muir Woods, the counterpart of the Zigzag Trail up from Mill Valley. Most striking are a number of trails into the Carson Creek watersheds and up to Pine Mountain. Apparently that whole area, including Little Carson Falls, was a more familiar attraction in those days than it is today.

Only the well-informed hiker knew where to find springs for drinking water. Thirsty travelers could stop at two hostelries: Liberty Ranch and the Summit House, both along the stage road from Ross Valley to Bolinas, not very handy for most hikers on the Mountain. After the trains began running three taverns or inns were opened by the railroad: East Peak Tavern (1896), West Point Inn (1904) and Muir Inn (1908). But for the most part these catered to passengers, not hikers.

Summit House stood on top of Bolinas Ridge where the stage road reached its highest point and where, today, it intersects with Ridgecrest Blvd. It was also called Halfway House. Its site is well-known, though little remains: a couple of fruit trees, an enormous ivy climbing a big redwood, the old well, and a quarter-mile down the Bolinas side of the ridge, a spring with some of the pumping equipment scattered about. The buildings burned down, but it is not known precisely when or how.

For some years after it was built in 1890 the Summit House was run by a man named Larsen and was popularly called Larsen's. But a real estate advertisement from 1891 suggests that Larsen was not enchanted with the place:

Summit House — Bolinas Ridge, 8 miles from Ross Station, overlooking Pacific Ocean, 20 acres of land, fine well of water, several good springs, substantial improvements, tract magnificently wooded with tanbark and redwoods. House doing a good business; a grand place for a summer residence. For sale at a great bargain.

Top: The Bostwick and Stuart families, camping in 1890, win the prize for neatness and elegance. Below: A more relaxed group includes John Spottiswood, Sausalito poet Daniel O'Connell, and Roger Magee, age 11. (Courtesy of the Mill Valley Library)

Around the turn of the century Larsen sold out to Constantine Desella (or de Cello). William Kent was familiar with what he called the "lodge and cafe" when it was run by Constantine, whom he refers to as "the Greek." Charles Keeler stopped there after walking along the road from Ross:

Mine host Constantine, surnamed the Old Pirate, who had concocted stews on the ferry boat for many a year, was there with his good wife to receive us, and as soon as wet boots and clothes were steaming by the open fire we sat down to a festive board and devoured plates of inimitable chowder a la Constantine, savory chicken and many other Greek dishes he proudly set before us. Swapping yarns the while with our host and entertaining his festive goat while the master's back was turned. We slept in one of his cabins before a roaring fire, lulled to sleep by the raindrops trickling in through his leaky ceiling. A twenty mile tramp to Olima (sic) on the morrow was one succession of splendid views of forests and mountains, with the ocean far below.

Keeler does not say when he made this walk but it was before 1903, the publication date of his book.

Still a third proprietor, named Wright, took over the roadhouse from Constantine, but eventually it failed, was closed and ultimately burned down in 1945 in a "general conflagration." Sometime after the fire the property was acquired by Mrs. Thomas Kent, who owned it until the Golden Gate National Recreation Area took it over. She and her family and friends used to picnic there, where they had a fine view of Bolinas Lagoon and the ocean. Now the trees and brush have grown so tall that the view is completely hidden. Mrs. Kent recalls that Larsen, the earlier proprietor, then lived nearby on the west side of Ridgecrest where a few of his orchard trees are still visible.

Several more establishments are noted on the 1898 trail map. About Mason's Camp, on Lagunitas Creek below the site of Alpine Dam, nothing is known except that it offered some sort of accommodations to the hiker. Its location has recently been discovered. At Stinson Beach were Willow Camp and the Dipsea Inn, terminus of the Dipsea Race in its early years.

Besides the Tamalpais Club, founded before 1880, two other well-known hiking clubs were organized. The Cross-Country Club, which dates from January 14, 1890, grew out of the Sightseers Club, founded in 1887. According to a 1923 report, the Cross-Country was an auxiliary, "for fast-hiking men, decreeing somewhat ungallantly perhaps that women of the Sightseers should not accompany them, because too slow of foot. The Sightseers thereupon perished, while the Cross-Country Club men have been sprinting ever since." A very few women were nonetheless admitted to associate membership, among them Alice Eastwood, who evidently could keep up the pace. Hikes in the old days were often called "tramps," and Cross Country Boys hailed each other as "fellow tramps."

Miss Eastwood and a few boon companions who formed a sub-group of the Cross-Country Club were referred to as the "Hill Tribe" by Benjamin Brooks, writing in 1905. This is how Brooks described them:

A plain, rough-shod set of people, who prowled these hills year after year — never fished, never hunted (though trout and deer were to be had), never "picnicked" with the usual defacement of surroundings, but always prowled on, over the endless trails, light of pack and light of heart, covering the ashes of their fires, and hiding their camp-kettles in mysterious places, leaving no sign behind them. Their sole object seemed to be the hills, and for wide views from them, and the silent places.

Beginning in 1909, according to one report, the Tribe inaugurated an annual Thanksgiving Day dinner at Rock Spring, near a huge madrone nearly 15 feet in diameter. They were not far from an even larger California live oak, now split in two, but still most imposing.

One of this group, John Franklin Forbes, is now remembered by a stone bench erected in 1981 by his son, John Douglas Forbes, on a small knoll above Rock Spring, where club members used to enjoy the view of the Golden Gate.

The Sierra Club, as is well known, was formed by John Muir and others to protect and expand Yosemite National Park. Articles of incorporation, signed June 4, 1892, include the following statement of purposes:

To explore, enjoy and render accessible the mountain regions of the Pacific Coast; to publish authentic information concerning them; and to enlist the support and cooperation of the people and the

Top: The Locator, a telescope, helped visitors spot landmarks; this woman's hat looks like a large bird which has found its aerie. (Courtesy of Nancy Skinner) Below left: Magnificent hats and elegant gowns could arrive at the peak unruffled, thanks to the railroad. Right: This couple look as if they have exerted themselves a bit on the way up. (Courtesy of the Mill Valley Library)

Our Sierra Mountain Boot

as perfected from suggestions of a member of the Sierra Club, is certainly the best boot in America.   The stock is the best calf; the color is a beautiful shade of tan; the sole is double, and has a good extension which runs from heel to heel, giving good protection to the upper.   This extension in shank enables the climber to step on sharp rocks in center of the foot without danger of hurting the boot or slipping.

For this season we will carry an assortment in stock, but advise those contemplating an outing to call as soon as possible, and if it is necessary we will make them to measure at same cost.

The prices range from $5 to $7.50.   It takes four weeks to get these boots made to order.

WALK-OVER SHOE CO.

924 & 926 Market St., San Francisco—111 S. Spring St., Los Angeles

F. F. WRIGHT & SON, Proprietors

In the summer of 1903 the Sierra Club organized a walk on Mt. Tamalpais; these pictures are from the Sierra Club Bulletin *for June, 1904. Although hiking costumes like these were certain to preserve decorum, the Sierra Club men and women apparently enjoyed an easy informality on their outings. A gentlemen normally did not remove his jacket or tie in public; his hat was an essential part of his costume, and had to be tipped or removed according to strict rules of etiquette. The ladies wear cool blouses, but their long full skirts must have been very cumbersome on the trails. Their splendid hats must have been easier to wear than to carry. Hiking shoes for ladies had only recently been perfected, as the advertisement from the* Bulletin *shows.*
(Courtesy of the Sierra Club Library)

government in preserving the forests and other natural features of the Sierra Nevada Mountains.

Mt. Tamalpais and other Bay Area localities soon became hiking objectives, and a Sierra Club Local Walks Committee was started in 1906. J.H. Cutter was the first chairman. Cutter was also a member of the Cross Country Club and was first president of the Tamalpais Conservation Club. He was the son-in-law of General Mariano Vallejo.

Two other early clubs which sponsored hikes on the Mountain were the Columbia Park Boy's Club (1894) and the Sempervirens Club (1900). The former is still very much alive, but has not had hikes on Mt. Tamalpais for forty or fifty years. The California Camera Club, dating from 1890, made the Mountain one of its special interests. The club office was at 819 Market Street, San Francisco; for years members maintained a display of photographs in a cabin near the beginning of the Pipeline Trail.

The Dipsea Race

The Olympic Club, a well-known San Francisco athletic club, was the inspiration behind the Dipsea Race, the oldest cross-country race on the West Coast and the second oldest in the United States. The race was first run in 1904 and has been run every year since, except during World War II when major parts of the Mountain were closed by the military. According to Mark Reese's *The Dipsea Race,* several members of the Olympic Club, lunching one day at the Dipsea Inn at Willow Camp (renamed Stinson Beach in 1920) decided to organize a hiking group to be called the "Dipsea Indians." The name is cross-country salute to the Huckleberry Indians of the New York Athletic Club, but the origin of "Dipsea" itself is unknown; William Kent built the inn, but his daughter-in-law, Anne Kent, did not know where he got the name.

The first activity of the Dipsea Indians, a race between two members over the Lone Tree Trail, aroused so much interest that the group decided to make the race an annual event, beginning the next year. Since then sponsorship has changed several times. The Dipsea Indians, all members of the Olympic Club, turned sponsorship over to the Club itself in 1924, which then handled the race from 1925 through 1931. After two years when no race was held, it was resurrected by the Sunrise Breakfast Club which ran it through 1938. Then the Mill Val-

ley Chamber of Commerce, working with a real estate promotion firm, Marvelous Marin Inc., took it over until the war intervened. In 1946 the race was reinstituted by the Stinson Beach Progressive Club. In 1954 the South of Market Boys' Club took it over. Then in 1963 the Mill Valley Jaycees became sponsors, but were later disbanded. Today the race is handled by certain dedicated individuals.

The first official race in 1905 was won by G. Hassard in 1 hour, 12 minutes and 45 seconds. But Hassard had a ten-minute handicap; scratch winner was C. Connelly in 1 hour, 4 minutes and 22 seconds. Ninety contestants finished. Over the years, the winning time has been cut down to the present record of 44 minutes, 49 seconds, established in 1974 by 21-year-old Ron Elijah, of the Mad River Track Club. The course at that time was 6.8 miles. There were 1,063 finishers that year, so Elijah, who started from scratch, had to run through these and many more starters to win the race. That same year, Debbie Rudolph, age 13, established the women's record of 56 minutes, 10 seconds. In 1981 the course was lengthened to 7.1 miles. Record holders as of 1984, at the new distance, are Rod Berry in 1983 (47:33) and Pat English in 1984 (56:38).

The number of participants has increased spectacularly from the 90 finishers in 1905. So many want to race now that the entrants are limited to 1,500.

Dipsea runners include men and women of all ages, even some past retirement age, and many children. Awards go to the winner (handicap), to the one with the fastest scratch time, to the first woman (handicap), to the fastest woman, to the fastest person over 40, to the leading 5-man team, and to the fastest father-and-son, mother-and-daughter, and husband-and-wife combinations. Though women were not allowed to enter the regular Dipsea until 1971, it is interesting that more than 60 years ago a special women's race was run, the "Dipsea Trail Hike for Girls," sponsored by the *San Francisco Bulletin*, on April 21, 1918.

Among long-distance runners, the Dipsea Race is considered about the toughest. The initial hundreds of redwood steps up from Mill Valley are followed by steep grades, heavily wooded and very rough. Wrenched ankles and even broken bones are not uncommon. And yet well over a thousand com-

Olympic Club members gather at the Dipsea Inn at Stinson Beach, circa 1905, perhaps to discuss their ideas for the Dipsea Race. In the front row are (from left) Edward Anstett, Dave Cowlen, William Greer Harrison, president of the Olympic Club, Phil Winerman, Doc Rogers, and H.V. Ramsell. (Courtesy of the Mill Valley Library)

Above: Entrants in the 1912 Dipsea Race gather in Lytton Square, Mill Valley, for the start of the grueling run. The winner was Donald Dunn of Berkeley High School, who has a dark diagonal stripe on his singlet, in the right half of the picture. Mason Hartwell, third-place winner under handicap rules, set a course record of 47:56 which stood until 1937. (Courtesy of Charles Ford)

Below: The fourth annual Dipsea Girls' Hike in 1921 drew an astonishing number of competitors, wearing costumes that would have been unthinkable ten years earlier. World War I, the 19th Amendment, and bobbed hair had liberated women to a remarkable degree. But the event was discontinued the following year, according to Dipsea historian Mark Reese, because of clergymen's worries about the morality of the hiking costumes, and physicians' concern about excessive stress on women's bodies. Women were not permitted to enter the regular Dipsea until 1971. (Courtesy of Charles Ford)

Top left: Emma Reimann, No. 211, placed first in the 1921 Women's Dipsea, with a time of 1:16:15, faster than many men can manage even today. (Courtesy of the Mill Valley Library) Top right: Gail Scott, of Colorado, breaks the ribbon in the 1986 Dipsea. (Courtesy of Gene Cohn) Below left: Two stalwart runners climb the Cascade Steps in the 1963 race. (Courtesy of the Mill Valley Library) Below right: "King of the Dipsea," Sal Vasquez of Alameda, has won the race four times; at age 47 he is one of the leading marathon runners in the U.S. (Courtesy of Gene Cohn)

pete each year. A good many run the Double Dipsea, Mill Valley to Stinson Beach and back.

Best known among the many who have run the course over the years is Jack Kirk, the "Dipsea Demon," who has run every Dipsea beginning with the 1930 race, a total of 51 Dipseas through 1986. He made the best time in 1931 and 1940, and won in 1951 and 1967.

Today, thanks no doubt to the Dipsea, one sees almost as many runners as hikers on the Mountain's trails. One group, the "Tamalpa Runners," run the trails every Saturday morning. These are not joggers, but serious runners, many of them in training for the Dipsea Race.

CHAPTER NOTES

Helen Bingham's *In Tamal Land* (1906) and Mark Reese's *The Dipsea Race* (1979) are the only books with direct bearing on this period. For the most part, sources are scattered.

The visitor registers kept on the East Peak, 1880-1887, are at the Mill Valley Library, and are available on microfilm.

Two articles by Fred Sandrock on the history of Mt. Tamalpais trail maps, "The Trails Make the Maps," appeared in the *Mill Valley Historical Review,* published by the Mill Valley Historical Society, December 1980 and Spring 1984. The first one deals with the early maps.

For two fascinating accounts of hiking on the Mountain in the early days, see Harold French, "A Vacation on the Installment Plan: Wild Places on Tamalpais," in *Overland Monthly,* October 1904, and James Hepburn Wilkins, *Early History of Marin County* (1915, but recounting events from earlier decades), typescript in Marin County Library.

Jack Mason's *The Making of Marin* has a useful chapter on Mt. Tamalpais. Mason's *Early Marin* and *Last Stage from Bolinas* are also very informative..

George H. Harlan is the leading expert on the history of the Bay's ferries. See *San Francisco Bay Ferry Boats* (1967).

Fred A. Stindt's *The Northwestern Pacific Railroad* (3rd edition, 1978) is the best source on Marin railroads.

See also Harre W. Demoro, *Electric Railway Pioneer: Commuting on the Northwestern Pacific, 1903-1941* (1983).

78

Courtesy of the Mill Valley Library

CHAPTER SIX

The Heyday of Hiking

The number of hikers on the mountain, by 1900 already very considerable and growing rapidly, swelled to a maximum during the years from 1910 to 1941, when thousands of weekend wanderers swarmed across the Bay to visit their favorite spots. This period saw the founding of the Tamalpais Conservation Club (1912), the Tourist Club (1912), the California Alpine Club (1914), the Contra Costa Hills Club (1920), and the Berkeley Hiking Club (1922). All are still active. And between 1896 and 1930 the Mt. Tamalpais & Muir Woods Railroad carried thousands of sightseers each year from Mill Valley up to the East Peak and down into Muir Woods.

Every weekend a veritable multitude arrived from San Francisco and the East Bay, some to spend the weekend camping out, even more just for Sunday. The weekenders typically took an early afternoon ferry on Saturday (which in those days was a workday until noon), and the Sunday contingent came over on an early ferry Sunday morning. The Northwestern Pacific Railroad met them at Sausalito and carried them to Mill Valley, to which a spur had been opened in 1890, or to Kentfield, Ross, San Anselmo, Fairfax, or Lagunitas to begin their hike. Sunday evening they all returned by the same means, but often by a different route. So great was the interest that during the 1920s the San Francisco *Ex-* *aminer* included in its daily weather report a prediction of weather on Mt. Tamalpais.

It is difficult to convey the sense of pleasurable release, the excitement, of the throngs aboard the ferries and trains. Photographs help, and there are many personal accounts in oral histories, but there are no recordings of the singing aboard the ferries, and no way to recapture the high anticipation, the strong community spirit that people felt on their way to the wilderness after five and a half days of labor.

Ferry service was phenomenal. Ferries operated day and night, sixty trips daily in each direction in 1925. The ferry *Ukiah,* rebuilt and renamed the *Eureka* by the railroad in 1923 (and now on exhibit at the Hyde Street Pier in San Francisco), was the largest ferry in the world, carrying up to 4000 passengers. Traffic was often so heavy on Sundays that the train which met the early boats had to run in two sections.

One published account, which may exaggerate the numbers, nevertheless probably conveys a correct impression. Samuel Dickson, in *Tales of San Francisco,* describes the Ferry Building in San Francisco on a Sunday morning:

There would be a seething mass of humanity, noisy, exuberant humanity. There were boys in

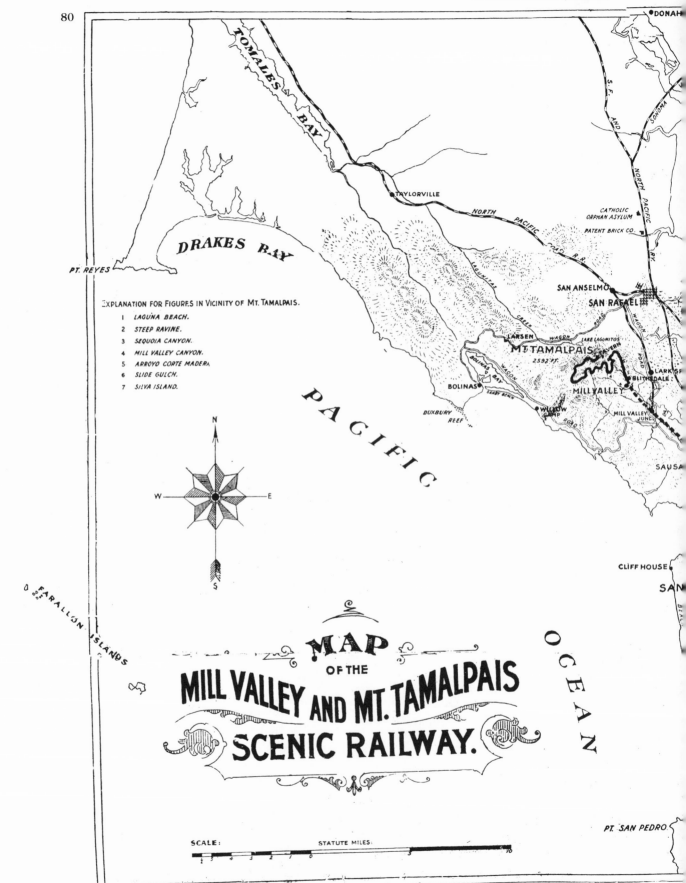

MT. ST. HELENA
56 MILES DISTANT FROM MT. TAMALPAIS

DONAH

TOMALES BAY

DRAKES BAY

PT. REYES

TAYLORVILLE

NORTH PACIFIC COAST R.R.

CATHOLIC ORPHAN ASYLUM

PATENT BRICK CO.

S.F. AND NORTH PACIFIC RY.

SONOMA

SAN ANSELMO

SAN RAFAEL

LAGUNITAS CREEK

Lake Lagunitos

LARSEN

WAGON ROAD

WAGON ROAD

MT TAMALPAIS
2592 FT.

TAVERN

LARKSP
BLITHEDALE

MILL VALLEY

BOLINAS BAY

BOLINAS

SANDY BEACH

WILLOW CAMP

MILL VALLEY JUNC.

DUXBURY REEF

SAUSA

EXPLANATION FOR FIGURES IN VICINITY OF MT. TAMALPAIS.

1   LAGUNA BEACH.
2   STEEP RAVINE.
3   SEQUOIA CANYON.
4   MILL VALLEY CANYON.
5   ARROYO CORTE MADERA.
6   SLIDE GULCH.
7   SILVA ISLAND.

PACIFIC

N
W   E
S

FARALLON ISLANDS

OCEAN

CLIFF HOUSE

SAN

PT. SAN PEDRO

MAP
OF THE
MILL VALLEY AND MT. TAMALPAIS
SCENIC RAILWAY.

SCALE:

STATUTE MILES:

5 4 3 2 1   0   10

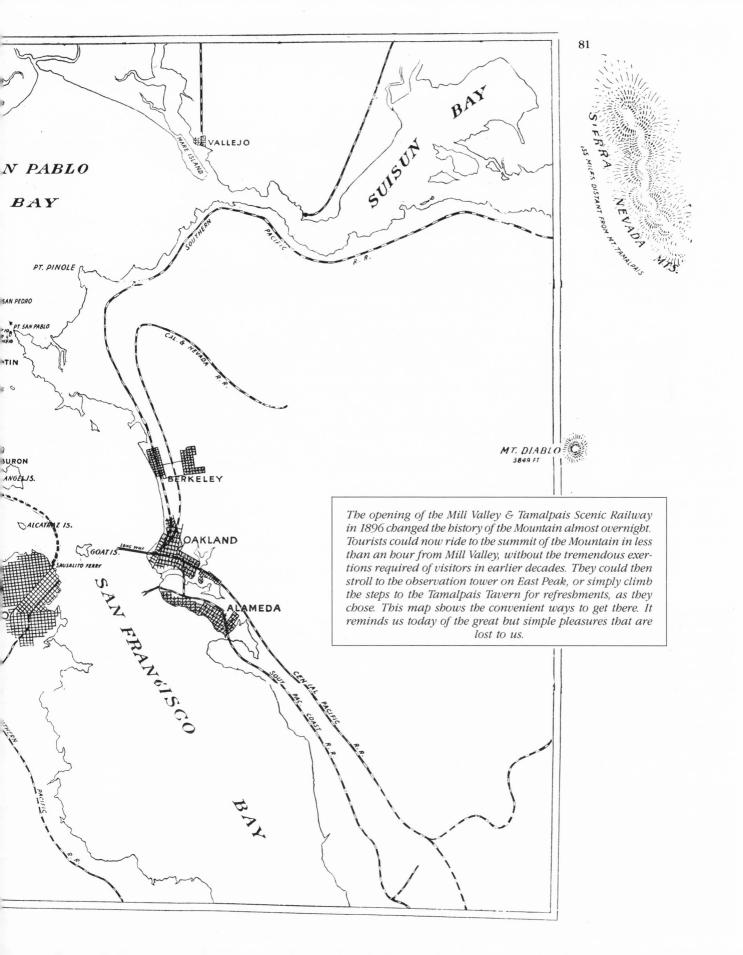

SUISUN BAY

VALLEJO

MARE ISLAND

SIERRA NEVADA MTS.

155 MILES DISTANT FROM MT. TAMALPAIS

N PABLO BAY

PT. PINOLE

SAN PEDRO

PT. SAN PABLO

SOUTHERN PACIFIC R. R.

CAL. & NEVADA R. R.

MT. DIABLO
3849 FT

TIN

BURON

ANGEL IS.

BERKELEY

ALCATRAZ IS.

GOAT IS.

LONG WHF.

SAUSALITO FERRY

OAKLAND

SAN FRANCISCO

ALAMEDA

CENTRAL PACIFIC

SOUT PAC. COAST R. R.

R. R.

PACIFIC

BAY

R. R.

The opening of the Mill Valley & Tamalpais Scenic Railway in 1896 changed the history of the Mountain almost overnight. Tourists could now ride to the summit of the Mountain in less than an hour from Mill Valley, without the tremendous exertions required of visitors in earlier decades. They could then stroll to the observation tower on East Peak, or simply climb the steps to the Tamalpais Tavern for refreshments, as they chose. This map shows the convenient ways to get there. It reminds us today of the great but simple pleasures that are lost to us.

Above: The ferryboat Tamalpais *leaves the ferry building in San Francisco on the first leg of a trip that thousands of passengers took each weekend. Yerba Buena Island looks peacefully unaware of its future as an anchor and tunnel for the Bay Bridge. (Courtesy of Nancy Skinner)*
Left: The observation tower on East Peak was the ultimate destination for tourists who, on February 12, 1922, included two sailors, two respectable married couples, and a couple of boys in caps. (Courtesy of the Mill Valley Library)*

corduroys, girls in short hobble skirts and sweaters, old men with rucksacks hanging from straps over their shoulders, and old ladies in sweaters and skirts and high leather boots. We'd crowd noisily aboard the ferryboat, and I use the word "crowd" advisedly. It was nothing to see between thirty and forty thousand San Franciscans head for Muir Woods on Sunday. We'd reach Mill Valley, head for the little store across from the Mt. Tamalpais Railroad depot, and buy dill pickles and Saratoga chips and chocolate bars. And we'd start out, scornfully ignoring the few dozen staid, antiquated beings who planned to go up the mountain on the little one-lung train. We'd start walking, perhaps just my girl and I, or perhaps a party of a dozen.

One long-time hiker recalls seeing a steady stream of lights along the Dipsea Trail heading for Willow Camp the night before the Dipsea Race. The same hiker tells of the reverse migration back to San Francisco on Sunday evening:

I remember when hikers used to come off the mountain like locusts (and) head for a certain train out of Mill Valley. . . . (They) were made to sit in the rear cars so the refined people wouldn't get their clothes dirty from the dust the hikers brought with them. Each group had its own singing club; all the way to San Francisco by boat, music was heard coming from every place. One sometimes couldn't hear the engines that turned the paddles. A popular fare was 48 cents from San Francisco to Mill Valley.

When the ferries stopped running on February 28, 1941, there was a series of "last ride parties." As one observer wrote:

On February 23 an organized group of railroad employees ran an excursion that included a ride on the boat and trains to many of the old points of interest that were reached and developed by the railroad. On the evening of February 26 the Sierra Club sponsored a last ride trip. There was a large gathering of club members, also representatives from all the Bay Area hiking clubs. A program was prepared and presented by the Sierra Club while all those present were enjoying their last ride on the ferries. On the evening of February 28 a grand celebration was held on the boats and trains. The stopping of the boats and trains has taken something from hiking that never can be replaced. The ride on the boat, the freedom on the trains and the fact that members of the clubs and hiking par-

ties were always all together up to the time they started their hike.

The hordes that landed at Mill Valley had many destinations and traveled many trails, but the biggest contingent went up the Pipeline Trail, so named because it followed a water pipe which brought water to Belvedere Dam in Mill Valley from the east fork of Fern Creek. After climbing the steps from Mill Valley, hikers usually set out along what is now Edgewood Avenue, passing by Mountain Home Inn (opened in 1912). Across the trestle over the tracks of the Muir Woods branch of the Mountain Railroad, the trail split. The Upper Pipeline Trail swung around to Bootjack, more or less as the Matt Davis Trail does now. The other branch went lower down, and has been replaced by Panoramic Highway and the Troop 80 Trail. Some hikers stopped at Bootjack or at one of the Rattlesnake Camps, while others went on to Rock Spring, Laurel Dell, Barth's Retreat, Potrero Meadows, Rifle Camp, perhaps climbing up the Eastwood Trail to West Peak and then down the other side by Arturo Trail. So many used the Pipeline that, on weekends, there were several refreshment stands along the way where they could get sandwiches going up and beer or lemonade coming down.

The Northwestern Pacific Railroad, operator of both the ferries and the electric trains, provided free trail maps, embellished with photographs showing enthusiastic hikers. The text touted Marin County as "The Hiker's Paradise":

Towering above all is Mount Tamalpais, the goal of thousands of walking expeditions. The magnificent view from its summit . . . . is world famous . . . . Abounding as it is in natural beauty, this bright land is doubly interesting because of its colorful historic background.

There follows some remarkable "history" about the "warlike tribes of Indians," with a chieftain, Marin, "who for a time withstood the Spanish invaders." This was largely invention.

More accurate were the descriptions of the principal trails and the areas to which they led. And the map was a good one. It shows many changes from the earlier trail maps of 1898 and 1910. Because of the creation of Alpine Lake in 1918, several old trails and roads which had run along Lagunitas Creek had to be rerouted: the Fairfax-Bolinas Road was moved onto the north side of the lake; Kent Trail was moved higher up on the south side; and Lily Lake Trail, which had crossed the creek from Kent Trail, was cut off.

The ferry-train approach to the Mountain had one great advantage: hikers could start at Kentfield or Fairfax and end up at Mill Valley, or vice-versa. One such trip along Bolinas Ridge was recommended in 1936:

> Take the 7:45 a.m. Sausalito boat and train to Fairfax, thence by stage to Camp Taylor. From Camp Taylor ascend Wildcat Canyon and follow along the summit of ridge to lunch place at Hunter's Camp. (The Camp appears on the NWP map on the Bolinas Ridge Trail about two miles northwest of Ridgecrest.) Continue walk to Mill Valley via Rock Springs and West Point. A long walk offering many extensive views of sea, coast and foothills. Recommended for sturdy hikers. Miles 21. Elevation 2,100 feet. Fare, round trip, to Fairfax 60 cents.

The sixty-cent fare was "a special arrangement for the accommodation of hikers." The round-trip ferry ticket from San Francisco to Sausalito was thirty cents.

An alternate, more expensive way to make a round trip was to ride the *Owl,* a small cargo vessel only 60 feet long, with a combination of power and sail, plying between San Francisco and Bolinas. She began running in 1911, soon after being built in South Bend, Oregon, for her owner, Dr. Richard Gibson, and ran regularly until 1931 when the Depression and autos put her out of business. Though not licensed to carry passengers, she did so, as had her predecessors way back to 1850. The round-trip fare was around six dollars. One could leave San Francisco in the morning, from a pier adjacent to the Ferry Building, and be in Bolinas in about an hour. From Bolinas, one could take a launch, the *Alice F. McKennan,* across the lagoon to McKennan's landing. From there one climbed to the top of Bolinas Ridge on the old Bolinas-Fairfax Trail, and onward by several possible routes to Mill Valley. Or one could reverse this route. Such a trip might have been hilarious on Wednesday, which was hog loading day at Bolinas. Some of the porcine passengers are known to have been swept overboard in rough seas.

Many old-time hikers have shared their experiences in oral histories, collected at the Mill Valley and Marin County Libraries. One of these, Ralph Sterner, described his favorite trek with excusable exaggeration:

> I always went to Stinson. We'd go over Saturday and stay overnight. For a long time everybody in San Francisco had to work until one o'clock on Saturday. The first ferry we could make was the 1:45. Nobody ever waited for anyone else. If you fell dead, why you were dead and what of it? We'd run all the way from Mill Valley to Stinson Beach if we could, and then down and jump in the ocean.

He estimates that he made more than two thousand round trips from Mill Valley to the beach, and covered 31,000 miles, usually on the Dipsea Trail. Sterner says that a lot of people who walked to Stinson made the round trip in a day, "but as soon as I got wise I stayed there overnight."

> I stayed at Sea Downs, starting about 1921 or '22. The first few times I stayed at Mrs. Richardson's. That's up where Henry Lacase's house is. . . . She had a few tents in the orchard. Then I went down to the Sea Downs. Tom Kent built that. . . . When the State made that park there, they knocked down Sea Downs and all the little cottages. They had nice cabins, and a dining room. The best cabins were the ones south, on the dunes.

Sterner recalls that in Mill Valley on the way to the Dipsea Steps, he would stop at Hikers' Retreat to change into his hiking clothes.

> There were lockers and showers. You paid something ridiculous — $6.00 a year for the locker and 35 cents for the towel and shower! If you didn't have a locker there year-round, you didn't have a chance at all in the summer. That was a gold mine; it really was.

Hikers' Retreat was run by a British couple named Odlin. The lockers, Sterner says, are still there, in the basement at 153 Throckmorton. "About 1934, when Mrs. Odlin was getting along in years, she quit the hiking business and leased the location to Russ Sweeney, a bartender. Everybody who has owned the bar has been very nice to the fellows hiking."

One old-time hiker says her parents used to invite friends from San Francisco to come over at the full moon to climb to the summit by moonlight and

Hikers of the California Alpine Club, July 1923; compare with the Sierra Club hikers on p. 70. (Courtesy of the Mill Valley Library)

*The first hike of the Tamalpais Conservation Club at Rock Springs in 1913 marked the begin-
ning of an organization which for seven decades has led the fight to preserve the Mountain
for public use. Top: Members stand at attention for the raising of the flag. Below: The camera-
man looks north toward a club picnic. (Courtesy of Nancy Skinner)*

wait for the sunrise; with the moon full they needed no lanterns. Another recalls the remarkable feat of her father, who climbed the Mountain from Mill Valley in thirty minutes. He had bet his companions in the Sequoia Saloon on Miller Avenue that he could do it. The Tavern at the top phoned down, within the allotted time: "Fred Merriman is here." On May 18, 1915, the Mountain Railway sponsored a race from the Mill Valley depot to the Tavern at East Peak. It was won by Olivar Millard of the Olympic Club in 37 minutes.

Malcolm Steel recounts how, as a boy, he raced the train to the tavern. As the train started up with his mother aboard, he rushed off up the Mountain, telling his mother he'd see her several times along the way. His route crossed the Bow Knot, the remarkable series of loops which the train went around to gain altitude, five times as he went almost straight up; he waved at each crossing. "We were able to be on hand just as the train was entering the Summit Station at the East Peak and to give the passengers a sixth greeting." Running time for the train, including a couple of stops for water, was 75 minutes, so he wasn't so fast after all.

Many people recall riding to the summit on the burros supplied by a company run by a group of residents, including Max Schmidt, head of Schmidt Lithograph Co. in San Francisco, "who saw in Mill Valley and Mt. Tamalpais a melodious echo of the Tyrolean Alps." August Wehr, outfitted in Tyrolean garb, was imported from Austria to serve as guide. The burros had such names as Bismarck, Lorelei, Sauerkraut, Maude and Nasturtium. This business was given up in 1906 as hiking became more popular, but the well-known livery stable run by the Dowds provided donkeys as well as horses for years afterward.

During the 1920s groups would congregate each weekend at Rifle Camp, Barth's Retreat, Potrero Camp, and Stinson Beach. Barth's Retreat was built by Professor Emil Barth, who began hiking on the Mountain in 1886. One of the regulars at Rifle Camp says that it dates back at least to 1917. And the Dipsea Inn at Willow Camp (Stinson Beach) goes back at least to 1905, when the first Dipsea Race was run.

Ralph Sterner and his friends, who went so often to Stinson Beach, enjoyed the luxury of shelter. At Rifle Camp, Potrero, and Barth's Retreat, the regulars camped or simply slept in the open. These places were convivial gathering spots for meals; sleeping quarters were some distance away. Hammer's Camp (later taken over by Balthazar Lavang, an Italian-Swiss) was just north of the Retreat. Barth had his own camp on the south side. Others later shared the area, including Dorothy Burley, who wrote a book, *This is Your Life,* about the wildlife around Barth's. Other visitors included Halbe, an Austrian artist, and his wife, and Karpechek, a Slavic partner of Lavang, who planted many trees, including some at West Point and later at the Tourist Club.

Charles Carillon, a French-speaking German from Alsace-Lorraine, was a regular at Barth's and at Rifle. Now almost ninety, the sociable Mr. Carillon has been hiking on the Mountain for seventy years. His friend Vee Krysiak, also in his eighties, has hiked all his life, not only on Mt. Tamalpais but throughout the West. He is a life member of the Sierra Club, and in 1941 was president of the Contra Costa Hills Club.

Rifle Camp was known by regulars as the "Down and Outers' Club," as well as for its international membership. Besides Carillon and Krysiak, a Pole, there were George "The Greek" Catalan and Camillo Scaposi, an Italian. Such men account for the name of the International Trail, built by the Down And Outers in the 1950s when their usual path over West Peak, the Eastwood and Arturo Trails, was cut off by the building of the radar station. The new trail was named by Joe Zapella, an employee of the Water District and a great friend to hikers. A plaque in his memory stands near Barth's Retreat.

Potrero Camp was not much used for overnight camping. Among the regulars were Frank Perkins, now in his eighties and still hiking regularly; Sibley, an Englishman, and two carpenters, both socialists, who enjoyed long arguments with their companions, especially the conservative Sibley. Others were Milton Brownstone and John I. Miller, who was the oldest of the group and a tireless trail builder. The Miller Trail is named for him.

These groups had dwindled by the late 1950s, and all but a few of the regulars are now dead, but some of them were to be found at the familiar locations into the 1960s. Then the hippies flooded the Mountain and forced them out with their noise and thievery; pots and pans and other implements could no longer be left from week to week.

The Tamalpais Conservation Club built a Trailman's Cabin at Bootjack, shown here in the 1930s, with Matt Davis, champion trailbuilder, on the porch. (Courtesy of Nancy Skinner)

Though not a camp, the Hot Sulphur Springs, as they are designated on the N.W.P. map, were frequented by many hikers. These springs are on the beach at the foot of Steep Ravine, below Highway #1. By digging a hole in the sand at low tide one could make a forerunner of the notorious Marin hot tubs. A rock slide has made the springs difficult to find, but barefoot strollers will feel warm spots in the sand and gravel. These springs led an early writer, impressed by the sulfur fumes, to conclude that Mt. Tamalpais was once a volcano.

Still other camps, well-known to hikers but not so much congregating points for week-end regulars, were privately owned; they were built in the early days when the owners of the tracts did not care. Ziesche's, Hogan's, Cooper's and Matt Davis's were among these. Much the oldest was Ziesche's, on Ziesche Creek not far from Rock Spring. Edward Ziesche, a German immigrant, was a friend of Professor Barth and Alice Eastwood, who visited him often at this camp. Camp Hogan, just off the present Stocking Trail, near Kent Trail, was dominated by a big redwood known as Hogan's Tree, now fallen. Under the trunk is said to be a sign, "Camp Hogan." John J. Hogan was a member of the TCC and the California Alpine Club.

Hikers today who follow the remnants of the old Berry Trail through the redwood grove near Azalea Meadow, cross a somewhat rickety bridge with a sign on a nearby tree reading "Cooper's Bridge, 1928." Cooper had an extensive camp just below on the east fork of Swede George Creek. He built a bridge of fir which rotted out after a few years; the present redwood bridge was built by Frank Perkins, one of the few remaining old-timers. Cooper is said to have dammed the creek to make a swimming hole, still visible above the bridge, spring-fed and much smaller now.

Matt Davis, "the dean of trail workers," as the Tamalpais Conservation Club called him, is best remembered as the builder of the much-used Matt Davis Trail, but he worked also on many others. Matt in his youth had been an Eagle Scout. He built his cabin near the Mountain Theatre, one of his great enthusiasms. He began it in 1932, but was still adding new conveniences at the time of his death in 1938. It was probably the best equipped cabin on the Mountain, with running water, a shower, heating stove, built-in cabinets, and sliding windows, and

room for a dozen weekend visitors.

Not all those who flocked to the Mountain had the discipline of the regular hikers, or shared their concern for its protection. During and right after World War I, a surge of rowdyism and vandalism caused as much damage and produced as much outrage as the more recent influx of hippies. The perpetrators were denounced in the *San Francisco Daily Commercial News* (January 1919):

> They are "vandals" and desecrators; they break into houses; they rend the air with piercing shrieks; they cast broken bottles, old cans and paper about; they leave fires...and they gleefully commit innumerable nuisances.

There were repercussions in quiet Mill Valley, where the weekend throngs had begun to take on the appearance of an invasion. Several residents asked the town board of trustees for "protection from lawlessness and disorder on the part of frequenters of the trains." The town, in a joint effort with the Water District, the Forest Fire District, the State Fish and Game Commission, the County of Marin, the TCC, the California Alpine Club and the Sierra Club, posted notices on the trails:

> It is unlawful to cut, break, injure, destroy or remove, trees, shrubs, plants....to hunt, shoot or carry firearms....to use vulgar, obscene, profane or offensive language, gestures or epithets, or to indulge in indecent or disorderly conduct. Help to preserve this wildwood park and be a law-abiding and welcomed guest to Mill Valley and Mt. Tamalpais.

A score of members of the TCC and the California Alpine Club volunteered to serve as deputy law enforcement officers.

It would be interesting to know how seriously these hiker-deputies might have taken the complaint of an out-of-town visitor who had walked on the mountain, and whose letter to one of the daily newspapers was paraphrased in *California Out Of Doors,* in August 1918:

> (The visitor) was exceedingly disturbed....by the costumes which young women hikers wore, and by the hilarious conduct of certain young men and maidens.... He seemed even more troubled by the costumes than by the conduct. He advocated the employment of chaperones to patrol the trails

for the purpose of protecting young men from women who wear knickerbockers.

Clearly times and customs were changing.

Outrage over vandalism and hunting led in 1912 to the founding of the Tamalpais Conservation Club, which proclaims itself, with much justification, the "Guardian of the Mountain." At that time the entire Mountain, except for Muir Woods, was still privately owned. One day R.F. "Dad" O'Rourke and his friend S.M. Houghton came upon some hunters dressing the carcass of a young deer near Rock Spring. Bad enough that hunters had succeeded in reserving very large areas of the Mountain for themselves, but here they were desecrating what was traditionally hikers' territory. O'Rourke and Houghton were so incensed that they persuaded William Kent, who owned large properties on the Mountain, to call a meeting of hikers and conservationists in Kentfield on February 18, 1912. At this meeting, with 135 people attending, the Tamalpais Conservation Club was formed, with J.H. Cutter as its first president.

The club's first organized activity was a massive clean-up campaign in which hundreds participated. A San Francisco newspaper headlined "There'll be Something Doing on Old Tamalpais Tomorrow: The Sentinel of the Gate Will Be Combed from Base to Summit by Loving Hands." The story continued:

> All the trails have been parcelled out to leaders of cleaning parties — twenty of 'em. The leaders are to have their aides, and the aides their sacks, kerosene, matches — and lunch. They are going to gather up the scattered papers, trash, tin cans, bottles and varied debris thrown about by careless, thoughtless, untidy persons. . .and they are going to burn the waste paper and bury the cans and bottles. . . . Then with the consciousness of having performed a duty, they will meet at Rock Spring, eat lunches and talk.

In a smug aside, the writer of the news story asks whether one can imagine "several hundred prominent New Yorkers — or Philadelphians or Bostonese" — doing this: "Can you see 'em? I guess not." One may wonder whether today's San Franciscans could be mobilized for such a job.

But the TCC has been much more than a collector of litter. Under the direction of a long succession of devoted Trail Chairmen, it has constructed and maintained trails, built bridges and stone cooking stoves, and dug out springs, often putting together rock structures to protect them. A plaque at Lone Tree on the Dipsea Trail, dated 1917, identifies the TCC as the builder. Even more important were the Club's political activities, which led to the founding of the Tamalpais Fire District and the Tamalpais Game Refuge. The Club's greatest triumph, as we shall see later, was the successful campaign to establish Mt. Tamalpais State Park.

But the TCC was not acting alone. Several hiking clubs had similar concerns. The California Alpine Club (CAC), formed in 1914, though it was later active mainly in the Sierra, concentrated in its earlier years on Mt. Tamalpais. In the 1921 issue of *Trails,* the club's publication, a list of the weekly "Local Walks and Leaders" showed that out of the total of 52 local hikes, nearly half were on Mt. Tamalpais. In 1935 the CAC bought a house on Panoramic Highway, not far from Mountain Home Inn, and converted it to a lodge.

The CAC held annual hikes and picnics at the Tamalpais Center clubhouse, near the railroad station in Kentfield. Something of the flavor of the CAC get-togethers comes through from the following description of one of the annual camp craft shows, held at Rock Spring on June 3, 1923. As reported in *Trails*:

> The Contra Costa Hills, Sierra, Tamalpais Conservation and California Clubs all produced their star performers. Jesse K. Brown tells the story: "A fowl was swathed in clay and baked in the coals. Diamond and other hitches were thrown. Fir bough beds were laid, and blankets neatly rolled. Model camps were established, and flapjacks juggled. Beef was roasted on a revolving spit, and a bandanna display covered the green, like a coat of many colors. Interesting information concerning bird life was given by members of the Sierra Club. The relative merits of rain-proof hammocks and sleeping bags were brought into contrast by two exhibits within the gaily decorated booths. Excellent speed was made in the water boiling contest held under strict rules; but no one was ready to take advantage of a fine shower bath duly demonstrated. A self-feeding fire aroused much hope but many skeptical comments on the part of spectators who had been separated from their beds in the chilly nights of high altitude.

The Touristen Verein—Naturfreunde *built an imposing chalet clubhouse. (Courtesy of the Mill Valley Library)*

Mountain Home Inn on the Famed "Pipe Line Trail" to Mt. Tamalpais

Mountain Home Inn, built in 1912, is dear to the hearts and memories of generations of hikers. The interior (above) is shown in the 1950s; the exterior shot was taken before 1923. (Courtesy of the Mill Valley Library and Nancy Skinner)

The Alpine Club, like the TCC, was interested in conservation, as shown by this excerpt from its constitution:

To make excursions into the trailed and untrailed portions of California for the purpose of bringing the people of the cities into the open, and to the full enjoyment of the natural wonders of the state; to aid in every way possible, the preservation of the woods, streams, game and natural resources of the country.

The Tourist Club, also called Nature Friends, was started in 1912 with only a few members, but grew rapidly to include several hundred. This club's Swiss-chalet lodge on the slope of Fern Canyon has been a gathering place for hikers and nature lovers for decades. Any thirsty hiker can buy beer at the lodge and eat his lunch on the spacious veranda while enjoying a wide view of the Mountain.

The club was an offshoot of the *Touristen Verein — Die Naturfreunde,* founded in Vienna in 1882, with branches in many countries now. Founding members in Austria were trade unionists with the usual socialist orientation. The club's purpose was to provide wholesome outdoor recreation for workers, to foster an appreciation of nature, and to educate workers to become "progressive people." Here in San Francisco, the founders were William Heidelman, J. Dencker and Hans Haedler, all natives of Austria, who brought over both the German language and the labor-socialist philosophy. For many years German was heard more than English at the lodge and on the trails, and for the first decade, programs for the annual entertainment and ball — called a *Stellungsfest* — were printed in German.

Hikers on Mt. Tamalpais generally — not just members of the Tourist Club — have been disproportionately Germanic. It is still common to hear German on the trails or to see a green Tyrolean hiking hat. In the early days San Francisco had many immigrants from Germany and Austria. In the 1900 census, much the largest contingent of foreign born were of those nationalities; they constituted 10.8 per cent of the whole population of the city, more than twice the proportion from Ireland (4.7 per cent), the next largest group.

The labor-socialist-cooperative tradition is reflected in the Tourist Club's constitution and by-laws. Candidates for membership are required to work at least two weekends on the lodge or on the surrounding grounds as a condition of acceptance. An early rule, no longer enforced, required that all club members belong to a trade union. In years past controversies sometimes arose over ideological issues, for example Hitler's rise to power. But as early members were gradually replaced, ideology became less important.

The Contra Costa Hills Club, organized in 1920, focused mainly on the East Bay hills, but its members have done much of their walking on Mt. Tamalpais, and the club has helped maintain trails and supported conservation measures in Marin. The Club's founder and first president was Harold French, long a member of the Sierra Club and the TCC, who first climbed Mt. Tamalpais in 1892, when he was fourteen. French drew much of his inspiration from John Muir, whom he knew well. He used whatever time he could spare from his job as director of the San Francisco Mint to campaign for the creation of the East Bay Regional Parks, finally established in 1934. The club's conservation efforts extended to Marin, where it worked with the TCC in the fight to set up the Mt. Tamalpais State Park, and later to extend the park's boundaries.

The Berkeley Hiking Club, founded in 1922, has sponsored many hikes on Tamalpais, and many members also belong to the TCC and the CAC.

No review of these years would be complete without mention of two eating places patronized heavily by hikers. Mountain Home Inn, known to all who visit the Mountain, was opened in 1912 by a Swiss couple, Claus and Martha Meyer, who said the location reminded them of the Alps. It had a Bavarian decor and served hearty German dishes to the throngs of famished wanderers coming in from the trails.

Claus Meyer was killed when his Model-T Ford, which he was cranking, started up and ran over him. Though his widow continued to run the inn for some years, she finally sold it in 1930 to Max and Katie Todd, who added a beer garden and five guest bedrooms. Max Todd was a close friend of Jack London. The Todds served sandwiches, sausages, potato salad, meat loaf; the most popular drinks were lemonade and buttermilk. Louise Lambert, the Todds' daughter, recalls that her father had a favorite source in San Francisco for each staple — rye

Above: California Alpine Club dedicates a monument to members who fought in World War I, November 9, 1919, on the summit of West Peak. Each member brought one rock for the monument, which held pictures and ashes of war dead. The Air Force bulldozed monument, plaque, ashes and all in the 1950's. Left: Henry Zaugg signs the West Peak summit register, July 1927. (Both photographs courtesy of Nancy Skinner)

Equality of women and men — at least among hikers — has progressed rapidly by 1923, when the Reeves family (originally Rewecs, from Hungary) and friends posed on the trail. Boots, trousers, even caps are virtually identical. Elsa Reeves, age 13, holds a puppy. (Courtesy Elsa Reeves Wilson)

Top: The concept of the hot tub was already old hat in the 1930s, when this group of hikers dug a basin in the sand at the foot of Steep Ravine and let it fill with hot spring water. (Courtesy of Elsa Reeves) Below: The Pipeline Trail follows an actual pipeline near bridge over the railroad track in the 1920s. (Courtesy of Nancy Skinner)

bread, white bread, lemons, sausages — and traveled all over the city for provisions.

The Todds were followed by a Scottish couple, James and Millie Drummond (1944—1952), who dropped the German tradition. But in 1952 the German *Kuche* was brought back by Patrick and Marian Vincent, who ran the inn for twenty-four years. By the end of this time their customers were more likely to be motorists than hikers. Many celebrities dined there.

Early in 1976 the inn was purchased by a couple whose plans for it never materialized. It was closed for a couple of years, reopened as a French restaurant, and closed again in 1980. In 1985 this beloved landmark was rebuilt and opened as a country inn with restaurant, bar, and guest rooms.

Another favorite stop, Joe's Place, near Muir Woods, dates back at least to World War I. Joe Bickerstaff, dressed in an army uniform, sold sandwiches and soda pop to hikers, and ran a dance hall, popular with young people on weekends. Around 1936, when the Muir Woods Inn was built nearby, Joe's went out of business. The building became a residence.

The Muir Woods Inn, next to Joe's Place, was another old-time eating place. In 1970 it was moved into the Park, grew substantially in size, and is now the cafeteria and gift shop which swarms with visitors.

After 1930, hiking declined as a result of the Depression and of the growing use of automobiles, especially after the Golden Gate Bridge opened in 1937. The heyday of hiking ended when the Sausalito ferries stopped running; in the next few years much of the Mountain's hiking area was closed off by the military.

CHAPTER NOTES

Sources for this period are all fugitive; no books deal with it in any detail. Almost all the materials listed are available at the Mill Valley Library.

The TCC's *California Out of Doors* (1914 to date) is the best single source, though not always completely reliable. *Tamalpais Magazine* was published by TCC in 1913-14. *Trails* (1921-24), annual publication of the California Alpine Club, is a useful source.

Two typescripts are informative: *History of the Tamalpais Conservation Club, 1914-1926,* and *History of the California Alpine Club,* by Caroline J. Waldear.

A photocopy of the complete CAC Visitors' Register (1937-38) from West Peak is interesting.

For more detail on the Pipeline Trail see Fred Sandrock's article in the *Mill Valley Historical Review,* Spring 1985.

Oral histories are available at the Mill Valley Library and Marin County Library.

A seven-man crew wrestles with one of the thousands of boulders which the Civilian Conservation Corps used to improve the beauty and utility of the Mountain Theatre in the 1930s. (Courtesy of the National Archives)

CHAPTER SEVEN

The CCC on Mt. Tamalpais

When next you sit in the Mountain Theatre near the top of Mt. Tamalpais, take a few minutes to think of the men who quarried the stones for the seats and set them in place. Most of the work was done during the Great Depression by men on relief, enrollees in the Civilian Conservation Corps (CCC). All were unemployed. Their headquarters was a CCC camp located near Muir Woods. Another CCC group had a camp not far from the head of Alpine Lake; they worked on north side projects.

The CCC, created by President Franklin D. Roosevelt in April, 1933, was the first of the New Deal agencies, and Roosevelt's favorite. In his inaugural address, Roosevelt said, "I propose to create a Civilian Conservation Corps to be used in simple work, not interfering with normal employment, and confining itself to forestry, the prevention of soil erosion, flood control and similar projects."

He later wrote,

This enterprise will pay dividends to the present and future generations. It will make improvements in national and state domains which have been largely forgotten in the past few years of industrial development. . . . More important, however, than the material gains will be the moral and spiritual value of such work. The overwhelming majority of unemployed Americans, who are now walking the streets and receiving private or public relief, would infinitely prefer to work.

Two categories of men were employed on CCC projects: single young men on relief, and veterans (mostly veterans of World War I but also some from the war with Spain) who were employed without regard to age or marital status. Though each camp was headed by an Army officer (usually retired) and the Army was responsible for the enrollees' pay, clothing and food, the camps were civilian in character. There was no military drill, no manual of arms, no military discipline; a civilian project supervisor directed the work of each camp.

The inclusion of veterans in the program may well have been due to the fact that the bonus marchers had recently swamped Washington. The first "Expeditionary Force," during the Hoover administration in 1932, had been driven out by troops and their tents burned. After Roosevelt came in, the second group of bonus marchers was treated with consideration; Mrs. Roosevelt went out to visit. One vet said, "Hoover sent the Army; Roosevelt sent his wife." Most of the men in this second group were in the CCC two weeks later.

Under initial CCC regulations, enrollment was for six months, thus insuring rapid turnover, and pay consisted of a cash allowance of $30 a month, of which $22—$25 went to the man's family. A total of 1,468 camps were authorized, their activities to be determined by the Department of Agriculture for forestry work and by Interior for work in public parks. One significant change was made early in the CCC rules, both to increase efficiency and to counter labor opposition: skilled men, hired at prevailing wages, would supplement the work of the unskilled men from relief rolls. For example, skilled woodsmen were added to forestry projects.

By early July, 1933, there were already 250,000 enrollees, and at the CCC's peak in August, 1935, the number had risen to 505,782, working in 2,652 camps in every state. By the end of the CCC's eight years of operation 2,920,000 people had been put to work, at a total cost of $634 million.

Some critics characterized the CCC as "this crazy dream" and "a political gesture." But the program was very popular, and was neither threatened with budget cuts nor attacked on grounds of illegality (as were other New Deal programs). In mid-1933, Roosevelt, with justifiable pride, called the CCC "the greatest peacetime movement this country has ever seen." He wanted to make it a permanent part of the country's social legislation. But World War II created huge demands for manpower, and the CCC program was ended in 1943.

Mt. Tamalpais was an ideal site for CCC work, embracing three public jurisdictions: Mt. Tamalpais State Park, Muir Woods National Monument, and the Marin (County) Municipal Water District. Like most public agencies, each of these had more plans for improvements than funds to carry them out, and each was eager to sponsor CCC work. All the Mt. Tamalpais projects were under the general direction of the National Park Service, Department of the Interior.

Muir Woods Camp's first enrollees — young men from New York State — arrived in October 1933, and went to work at once on building fire breaks, cutting forty-foot swaths down from the top of the Mountain to Lake Lagunitas (these are now known as the East Peak and Lagunitas fire trails). They realigned the Ocean View Trail and were beginning work on the Ben Johnson and Bootjack trails. According to *California Out of Doors* (January 1934), all the projects were "under the direction of competent engineers, acting with a careful regard to scenic and natural features."

This first camp did not last long; all personnel were transferred in April 1934, bag and baggage, to Elk River, Idaho. The second, known as Mt. Tamalpais Camp, was on the site of today's Camp Alice Eastwood. It was an extensive enterprise with some fourteen buildings — barracks, mess hall, recreation room, hospital, offices, warehouse, blacksmith and repair shop. The new enrollees were primarily veterans between the ages of 35 and 64, including "experienced mechanics, rockmen, catskinners, woodsmen, etc." The Park Engineer observed, "The Camp's juniors or veterans have one feature in common; viz., willingness to put forth honest effort. The juniors are more anxious to learn; the veterans, to do a fair amount of enduring work with their more expert and specialized knowledge."

At first these men put up fences and stile gates along Muir Woods' south and west boundaries to keep cattle out; then they built redwood footbridges, a sod stage and rock aisles for the Mountain Theatre. They worked on many trails, cleared slides and brush, and built firebreaks. Their three major projects have had lasting value: work at the Mountain Theatre (not completed until the 1940's), stone riprapping (facing a stream bed with stones in an overlapping, shingle-like pattern to keep it from washing away) on Redwood Creek in Muir Woods, and building the fire lookout on East Peak.

The work was sufficiently impressive to evoke strong support from the Mill Valley Chamber of Commerce, meeting in January 1934:

> The citizens of Mill Valley and of Southern Marin County. . .are particularly impressed with the excellent character of these men, and their conduct and behavior. . .and salute their excellent accomplishments which have reduced the tremendous fire hazard, together with its potential loss of life and property, and which has been ever present in this community, three times in the last 20 years threatening its complete destruction.

The devastating fire of 1929, which destroyed many Mill Valley houses, was still vivid in people's minds.

When the CCC began its work on Mt. Tamalpais, a substantial trail network had long been established, with many trails dating back to the 1870's and 1880's. Until the CCC era, all these trails had been built by volunteers. Besides building miles of fire-breaks and truck roads, the CCC relocated or rebuilt several trails, including the TCC Trail and the old Pipeline Trail, renamed the Troop 80 Trail (Boy Scouts of Troop 80 no doubt did some work on it, but the major work was done by the CCC). During one six-month period the CCC workers devoted 5,062 man-days to trail construction.

The CCC built a great many footbridges and benches hewn out of redwood logs, put in redwood steps on steep slopes and stone culverts to prevent erosion, and built the outer edges of contouring trails with rocks and redwood ties. Many of the footbridges — those with hewn redwood stringers — are just as strong today as when they were built fifty years ago: look along Bootjack Trail below Bootjack Camp, Steep Ravine Trail, Cataract Gulch Trail, TCC Trail, Troop 80 Trail and Ben Johnson Trail. Troop 80 Trail also has a fine example of the massive hewn redwood benches so enjoyed by hikers.

Much work was done on the Steep Ravine Trail which runs close alongside Webb Creek. The camp superintendent summarized the work for October 1935 to March 1936:

> (The Steep Ravine Trail) is a splendid example of the 'primitive' type of construction with its dips and bends and rough hewn puncheon bridges. . .
> The actual construction is of a permanent nature; all means of support being very massive, placed as nearly as possible to conform and blend with the natural surroundings. The bridges are all located with ample clearance and above extreme high water even in the worst storm periods.

Those who loved the Mountain and were concerned for its natural beauty were full of praise for the CCC projects, which were handsome and harmonious with the landscape, and which avoided disturbance of plant life. Indeed, the signs and trail markers put up by the CCC had too much aesthetic appeal; they have all disappeared, as have their replacements, installed by the TCC and more recently by the state park, no doubt at the hands of souvenir hunters.

CCC workers also improved several popular camps along the trails. Once used by overnight campers, these areas are now limited to daytime picnic use, but many of the CCC-built features are still in place. At Bootjack Camp, for instance, the CCC built a convenience station, tables and benches, fireplaces, an incinerator, a sink, drinking fountains and water tanks.

Redwood Creek, flowing through Muir Woods National Monument, is the only creek on Mt. Tamalpais that received extensive protection. The object was to keep storm waters from washing away banks, trees, trails, and picnic grounds. The main job involved facing the stream with large rocks, especially on sharp turns. Work began in November 1933, but was not completed until 1938, because of interruptions each winter when heavy rains came. The rock came from a nearby quarry, where a derrick was built to handle it.

Several major stone structures were built in Muir Woods. Three check dams were built across the creek to prevent erosion and to stop channel cutting. The dams used big redwood logs across the stream, reinforced and supported at the ends by stone abutments. Each dam had a fish ladder, in the form of a pool on its face, to permit salmon to leap up as they go upstream to spawn.

A particularly outstanding bridge, built of reinforced concrete and stone, spans Fern Creek just above the junction with Redwood Creek. Its fine design and durability testify to the architectural and engineering skills that guided the work of the CCC men. Further down Redwood Creek are several other bridges, supported by enormous redwood logs forty or fifty feet long and weighing more than five tons each. These were expected to last a hundred years, as they no doubt will.

As a final contribution, one of the CCC enrollees carved a large cap for the entrance arch that still greets visitors: "Muir Woods National Monument, National Park Service, Department of the Interior."

Because the East Peak of Mt. Tamalpais is the highest point in Marin County and is located in the heavily forested area most subject to big fires, it has long been used for fire-spotting. The Marine Observatory, erected there in 1901 by the San Francisco *Examiner,* was used as a fire lookout beginning in 1921. Then, in 1935-36, the CCC moved that building out of the way and erected a much more substantial structure. The lookout site, commanding a 360-degree view, presented two major problems to engineers: insuring stability against winds that sweep the peak at speeds up to 115 miles per hour, and getting massive construction materials to the site. The first problem was solved by combin-

Top: CCC workers construct the observation tower which surmounts East Peak today. Below: The Mountain Theatre was based on classic Greek theatres, especially those in Sicily. (Courtesy of the National Archives)

ing stone and concrete with a structural steel skeleton for the building. Part of the second problem was that the last several hundred feet to the summit of East Peak is a roadless wilderness of jagged rocks. The solution was to construct a "highline" — an overhead cable powered by a gasoline engine — running a thousand feet up from the roadbed of the old Mountain Railway (closed in 1930). The cable was rugged enough to bring up stone blocks weighing as much as a ton.

The new lookout, named in honor of Edwin Burroughs Gardner, first chief warden of the Tamalpais Forest Fire District, is not only structurally sound but has all modern conveniences — electric lights, telephone and running water. To get water up there, CCC workers built a stone pumphouse nearby and laid all the pipes. When they had finished the lookout station and the fire breaks, they helped fight fires on the Mountain and elsewhere in the county.

The lookout is manned throughout the summer months of maximum fire danger. Resident fire spotters, working with other spotters on Mt. Barnabe, use the surveying technique of triangulation to pinpoint the location of a fire and phone the information to headquarters — an invaluable method of early detection. Since the lookout opened in May 1937 only one major fire (1945) has swept the Mountain; it was stopped before it reached inhabited locations.

A footnote to this subject: As a result of Prohibition-era raids by government officials on illicit stills in the Mt. Tamalpais vicinity, the CCC camp inherited a supply of redwood water tanks, six of which they installed along the roads for fire protection. Some of these are still in place, along with smaller ones used to supply water for picnic areas.

Without doubt, the most remarkable CCC project was the Mountain Theatre, sponsored by the newly created Tamalpais State Park. To be eligible for the work, the Mountain Play Association had to deed the land to the state. But even before the CCC started its work, the Association had set aside some money for improvements on the theatre. Some terracing work had begun as early as 1923. Then in 1925 a well-known landscape architect, Emerson Knight, drew up a development plan (for a fee of $200) which was subsequently followed by the CCC, with Knight supervising the work.

By 1931, the Association had already spent some $1,150 to build a terrace wall, install the first row of stone seats, and expand seating capacity by 1,000. But the Mountain Play lost money that year and in 1932 and 1933. The Theatre Board must have heaved a unanimous sigh of relief when the CCC took over early in 1934.

The theatre was still for the most part a natural, grass-covered amphitheatre, despite the work already done. There was very little separation between the spectators and the players, who had to perform precariously on the slanting hillside. There were no dressing rooms, no backstage, no comfort stations, no drinking fountain, no landscaping. Though Kent's toll road (later Ridgecrest Blvd.) was in use, most people, including the players, came by foot, either all the way up from Mill Valley or more than a mile up from West Point, a stop on the Mountain Railway. During the days of preparation the cast and crew lived at the West Point Inn and walked back and forth for rehearsals.

Despite these drawbacks the theatre provided a magnificent view of San Francisco Bay. Players were eager to perform there and spectators waxed lyrical. Mrs. D.E.F. Easton, in an article titled "The Mountain Play" in *Trails* (1922), praised the "backdrop of the natural stage, which no human hand could paint, no human mind conceive. It presents to the audience a panorama of the ship-dotted Bay... In the words of a writer in *Theatre Magazine*... 'There seems to be no limit to the scene. The whole world appears to be spread out behind the actors on this mountain side, placing the Mountain Play in a place of its own, in a God-made theatre.'"

What the CCC accomplished was to turn this natural area into a replica of a Greek theatre while preserving its sylvan character. Far and away the most impressive feature of the CCC work was the building of the stone seats for thousands of people, in forty rows, each three hundred feet long. Emerson Knight reported that the seats required some five thousand stones, each weighing six hundred to four thousand pounds, and "buried so deeply that only a fraction of their upright bulk is visible. Because so much of their bulk is hidden, they rest firmly in place."

Quarrying the stones and trucking them almost four miles to the theatre site were tedious jobs but

This picture suggests the scale of the work at the Mountain Theatre, and the size of the boulders, which had to be moved into place with the aid of the improvised machinery shown. (Courtesy of the National Archives)

required no unprecedented skill. The difficult part was finding a way to move the stones from the top of the slope to the point of emplacement. The procedure has been explained by Donald Hobart, who was employed at the time by the state to inspect CCC projects. Two tripods were erected perhaps fifty feet apart near the top of the slope and connected by a wire cable. Each rock was slung under the cable and then let down to its position by a winchman who ran a donkey engine located at the top. It took very skilled maneuvering to get the stone located just right.

To make a level stage, a massive rock retaining wall was built with "huge boulders so interlocked that it should last indefinitely," according to Knight. This wall is now pretty well hidden, but several other stone structures of continuing utility and beauty are seen by everyone who visits the theatre: the rock wall and ramp that serves as entrance and exit, comfort stations, and drinking fountains. A large landscaping project completed the job. Arthur H. Blake wrote, in *California Out of Doors* (January 1936):

> In the Mountain Theatre planting of backstage screens and wings with chinquapin and other shrubs is now underway. Very careful preparation has been made to insure survival and some very fine clumps are being brought in. From many years of experience in trying to get a satisfactory backdrop of greenery ready for the annual Mountain Play, I can say no work being done there is of any more importance. Artificial touches or scenic effects are absolutely out of place. Concealed entrances and exits through these blocks of shrubbery will be utilized by future directors to dramatic advantage.

And Emerson Knight, understandably enthusiastic about the project's outcome, wrote:

> The completed theatre tended soon to take on a character of age-old ruggedness, thus preserving the spirit of the mountain. From the inception of the work on both map and plan, the designer was intrigued and thrilled by the possibility of here creating a massive work of utmost simplicity. There flashed in his mind a picture of old-world theatres carved in part from hills of rock, and adorned with marble, as in ancient Greece. They had a classic symmetry. But here on Mt. Tamalpais it was possible to secure solid, appropriate out-

croppings of rock of great variety in texture, color and beauty.

Sky Oaks Camp

The CCC Camp at Alpine Lake, known as Sky Oaks, was established in 1935. The first enrollees, young men from Pennsylvania and Maryland, mainly built firebreaks under the sponsorship of the MMWD. Altogether they built seven miles of firebreaks, nine miles of truck roads, and forty spring-fed water tanks for fire protection. They also built or improved five miles of foot trails. Sky Camp was closed sometime before Pearl Harbor and was taken over by the army.

By any standard, the CCC work on Mt. Tamalpais must be considered successful. The physical accomplishments in fire protection, erosion control and enhancement of recreation were outstanding and long-lasting. Just as important were the benefits to the men themselves: counteracting the devastating financial and spiritual effect of unemployment, fostering good work habits, and providing skilled training. And the men earned the highest respect from local citizens, as testified by Arthur Blake:

> At a time when public officials are generally condemned on all sides it is a pleasure to meet the men in charge of this work. One comes away from many a conference with them, impressed with the fact that their interest is as sincere as ours.

The projects succeeded because the jobs needed to be done; these were not make-work projects of the leaf-raking variety. And they would not otherwise have been done because no state or local agency could have afforded to do the work. Federal assistance was essential. And public support was generated by the accomplishments themselves. If there was any significant opposition it is not recorded. The program's popularity was both the effect and the cause of its success.

Finally, the success was due to community involvement. As soon as the Muir Woods CCC Camp was established, the Tamalpais Conservation Club appointed a committee to help plan the work, offering a list of trails that needed improvement. The CCC projects enjoyed the support and approval of conservationist groups, town councils and local government agencies.

The CCC camp at Alpine Lake, later used by the University of California as a camp for student surveyors in summer school. This picture was taken in the 1930s, when the CCC men occupied the barracks. The cars are all 1920s models, and probably belonged to CCC supervisors. (Courtesy of Nancy Skinner)

In 1983 the National Association of Civilian Conservation Corps Alumni (NACCCA) installed a simple plaque and planted a live oak tree in memory of the men who did the work at the theatre. The plaque reads: "In Tribute: Civilian Conservation Corps. This tree is dedicated to the Corps members whose toil enriched the lives of many. October 2, 1983." In 1985 a reunion of CCC alumni, arranged by Fred Rothschild, was held at the Mountain Theatre. Speakers pointed out that California has carried on the CCC tradition by establishing the California Conservation Corps, the Marin Conservation Corps, and other groups. The alumni endorsed congressional bills to create a modern national CCC.

Though the CCC was disbanded in 1942 it lives on in the Mountain Theatre and in other durable structures. But how many of the more than twenty thousand people who attended the 1985 production of *The Sound of Music* or 1986's *Peter Pan* know that the theatre as we see it today was the work of men who were a part of a huge national experiment, men whose desperation had driven them to the brink of revolution before the CCC provided them with honest work and a salary of $30 a month? The CCC, like Joe Hill, "ain't never died." It lives on in the memories of those still living who did the hard work. The theatre, the lookout station, the bridges and trails on Mt. Tamalpais are visible reminders of a turbulent period in our history, when the skill, patience, and monumental toil of the CCC Boys showed us the stuff this country was made of.

CHAPTER NOTES

History of the formation of the CCC and of President Roosevelt's deep interest in it is available from many sources. A useful overall volume is *The Civilian Conservation Corps, 1933-1942* by John A. Salmond. See also Raymond Moley's *The First New Deal* and *The Public Papers and Addresses of Franklin D. Roosevelt,* by Samuel I. Rosenman (several volumes).

Scattered reports of CCC activities on Mt. Tamalpais may be found in issues of *California Out of Doors,* the periodical publication of the Tamalpais Conservation Club. A complete file is available in the Mill Valley Library, but nowhere else.

The main source for this chapter is the U.S. National Archives, a source unfortunately not easily tapped. The Archives supplied copies of weekly reports by the project superintendent, giving details of the camp's activities. Most of the illustrations for this chapter are official CCC photographs from the same source.

The *Mill Valley Record* for January 27, 1934, praises the CCC work in fire prevention.

*T*HE AGE OF THE AUTOMOBILE *arrived more gradually than the railroad era, but its effects were even more profound. The invention of pneumatic tires and closed cars made motoring on Mountain roads more comfortable, if not always safer. Opposite, above: Congressman William Kent, giving a barbecue at Muir Woods for fellow members of the U.S. Congress in 1910, was driving some of them over the Mountain in his beautiful new car. There were no injuries. Kent, looking puzzled, is at right. (Courtesy of the Mill Valley Library)*

Opposite, below: Rock Spring Junction, around 1929, shows Panoramic going straight and Pantoll Road turning to the left. The roads are well-maintained and well traveled. (Courtesy of Nancy Skinner)

Above: A sleek coupe with rumble seat approaches Alpine Toll Gate in the late 1920s. Ridgecrest was still a private road; admission prices were "$1.00 per car with 2 pass., .25 each add. pass., .75 Motorcycle & owner." (Courtesy of Nancy Skinner)

110

Top: The first Mountain Play, Abraham and Isaac, *drew an audience of 1200 in 1913. Below: Crashers watch one of the early plays from atop Pohli Rock. (Courtesy of Nancy Skinner)*

CHAPTER EIGHT

The Mountain Plays

A poignant inscription in memory of Garnet Holme is to be found on Pohli Rock just above the Mountain Theatre: "I lingered on the hill where we had played." The words are from one of his own plays. Holme was the talented and much beloved director of the earliest of the Mountain plays, from 1913 to 1926, as well as the author of *Drake,* the 1925 production. He was a member of the drama department at the University of California, Berkeley, where he served as drama coach. At the same time he was Pageant Master for the National Park Service, and wrote shows for production in the parks.

The Mountain plays have been presented annually, usually on the third Sunday in May, beginning in 1913 and continuing to the present with the exception of 1924 when an epidemic of hoof and mouth disease forced an interruption, and the years 1942-45 during World War II, when the Army commandeered the site. Can any other volunteer outdoor theatre company, anywhere in the country, match this seventy-year record?

The significant word here is "volunteer." No salaries were paid until relatively recently, except to the play director. Even the lead players have usually donated their services. Members of the board of directors of the Mountain Play Association, some of whom served for many years, were not only not

paid, but were forbidden by the by-laws to have any pecuniary interest in the plays. Yet the board handled all the multitude of details involved in any production, a most meticulous and demanding assignment.

Marion Hayes Cain, a frequent performer who served both as president of the Mountain Play Association and as producer of the plays from 1959 to 1971, has explained that the success of the volunteer system is based on "caring": caring for the arts, caring for the Mountain, and caring for the friends made while working on the plays. The productions were a labor of love which survived financial set-backs and the temper tantrums not unknown among players and directors.

The First Mountain Play

On Sunday, May 4, 1913, the first play was produced, a 13th Century miracle play, *Abraham and Isaac.* As an added attraction, Malvolio's scenes from *Twelfth Night* were included, and an orchestra assembled for the occasion. Holme, who directed, brought over many of the cast from the University drama department, many of them young people eager for a chance to act. This first production was considered a great success, with an audience of

1,200, most of whom arrived on foot. The majority came from San Francisco by ferry and train to Mill Valley. From there the hardier people climbed the eight miles to the site, a gain of 2,000 feet, while others rode up to West Point Inn on the Mt. Tamalpais & Muir Woods Railway and walked the last mile.

One might think such a climb would be a deterrent. Actually the play was welcomed by many as a good excuse for a hike. But for those who had to transport the props, the distance from wheeled transport meant considerable hardship. Elaborate stage sets were out of the question for all the early plays, so they were more pageants than plays. The natural surroundings served as scenery.

One episode which occurred on that pioneer occasion illustrates what Mrs. Cain means by "caring." John J. Mazza, an enthusiastic hiker, knowing that climbers to the play would arrive thirsty, walked up early so he could bring pail after pail of drinking water from Rock Spring.

The remarkable success of the first production must be attributed to Holme's ability as a director and to the eager cooperation of the Tamalpais Conservation Club — made up mostly of hikers — and of hikers' organizations such as the Sierra Club and the Tourist Club. After the California Alpine Club was formed the next year it too became an active supporter of the Mountain plays, supplying not only spectators but also dozens of bit players.

Trails (1921) expressed the CAC's pleasure in supporting the productions: "The Club is proud of the privilege offered to its members. . . . The fifty-seven Alpiners who appeared as Indians and Spirits in *Tamalpa* felt the inspiration of being an integral part in something immensely worthwhile." The TCC shared this view. This symbiotic relationship between hikers and the plays was for many years a major reason for the success of the venture.

A tragedy occurred only a few days after the first production of *Abraham and Isaac.* Holme had selected a young man from the UC drama department, Austin Ramon Pohli, to be the general manager of this first play. Shortly afterward, while climbing in Yosemite, Pohli fell and was killed. A plaque in his memory was placed on a big rock, known ever since as Pohli Rock, directly behind the theatre site: "To Austin Ramon Pohli, A Lover of This Mountain, Who Died May 20, 1913, Aged 20 years, This Rock is Dedicated."

In the early days Pohli Rock was visible from the amphitheatre and was often used as a staging area from which players descended to the stage. It was used, too, for dramatic effect. Robin Hood shot his arrows from there, and in *Tamalpa,* the white-clad spirit of the Mountain stood on the rock. Then for years it was hidden by a dense growth of trees and shrubs. Now, since 1985, a vista has been cut through so that the Rock is again visible.

Garnet Holme and a lawyer-hiker, John C. Catlin, are quoted as having conceived the idea for the plays. The story goes that they were walking one morning with "Dad" O'Rourke, one of the best-known hikers on the Mountain, from West Point to Rock Spring. They stopped near a great rock to admire the fine view. Looking down at the slope in front of them, Holme remarked, "What a perfect setting for an outdoor theater." Catlin and O'Rourke agreed, and got right to work; *Abraham and Isaac* was the result.

Catlin was so enamored of the new scheme that he drafted a foreword for the program of that first play. This explosion of lyricism was a plea, in effect, to make the Mountain a public preserve:

> In the Mountain Play there is a message, a message and a prayer. They are from the Mountain to the People.
> 'Come unto me, O People. Ascend my lofty peaks, drink from my purling streams, rest in my shaded canyons. In the winds rushing through my trees, in the thunder of my cataracts and in the song of my waters, listen to the voice of my Creator.
> This is my prayer: 'Take me, O People, for of right I am thine. Set into motion your laws and purchase my freedom from the bondage into which I have been sold. Break my chains, that I may again be thine.
> 'From this spot where you now hold festival, I have been witness of many a world drama. I saw Sir Francis Drake, storm-tossed and sinking, driven blindly by the long-sought haven that lies at my feet. I watched the devoted Franciscans and weary soldiers come to the Golden Gate and stand spellbound by the glory of their discovery. I saw the pioneers come to their golden land and build a city. I saw that city sink to ashes and I saw it rise again.
> 'Now I wait for dreams greater and yet more glorious from my children. So to you I offer up my

prayer. Take me, O People, unto thyself. Dedicate me to the ages. Amen.'

John Catlin and Garnet Holme had earlier hatched a plan to put on a play at Rock Spring. Another lawyer, Augustin C. Keane, described a picnic at Rock Spring, probably in 1912, which he refers to as "an orgie of beer and red wine, which inspired the idea for a mountain play." Among the joyous participants were Holme, Catlin, Keane and his wife Lucie, Sophie Treadwell, Bill MacGeohan, Walter Anthony, and John Galpin.

Keane recalls that Catlin "burst out with a wild idea that the meadow and slope by Rock Spring would be a marvelous location to produce *Shenandoah* with dramatic opportunity for a stirring cavalry charge out from under the oak trees. . .and we were resolved for the full space of a week to prepare for the production." But their enthusiasm did not survive learning that such a cavalry charge would cost at least $30,000.

"Nevertheless," Keane continued, "the idea of a mountain play had been sown. During the autumn and next spring we nurtured it. The site of the theatre was selected in a more modest location."

The Mountain Play Association

Encouraged by the widespread acclaim which greeted their first production, the sponsors set up an organization to make the plays an annual event. At their first meeting in February, 1914, the Mountain Play Association was launched. John Catlin was chosen president, and R.F. "Dad" O'Rourke as first vice-president. Mrs. D.F. (Effie) Easton became Secretary Manager, a position she held for many years, earning the reputation of being "The mother of the Mountain Play." Congressman William Kent was elected second vice-president.

When the theatre was dedicated on April 6, 1915, Kent insisted that it be known as the Sidney B. Cushing Amphitheatre. Cushing from boyhood had enjoyed walking on the Mountain. In part in order to make the Mountain accessible, he had been instrumental in building the Mill Valley and Mt. Tamalpais Scenic Railway, of which he was president. Kent paid him this tribute: "He is the man who first taught me the lesson that this mountain is too good a thing to be reserved in the hands of a few." In this spirit, the following resolution was adopted by the new association:

Whereas the Mountain Play at Rock Spring, Mt. Tamalpais, Marin Co. has become permanently established as one of the great outdoor dramatic events of California, and *Whereas* the Mountain Theatre, the scene of the annual performance, is unrivaled in beauty and scenic grandeur, and peculiarly adapted for a mountain play, it should therefore be preserved for all times as a public park for the diversion and inspiration of all the people of California and especially the bay cities, *Now Therefore, be it Resolved* that it is one of the main objects of the Mountain Play Association to acquire and dedicate to the public this magnificent Mountain Theatre. *Be it Resolved Further* that the net proceeds of the Mountain Play, over and above such reserve as the Board of Directors may deem necessary to maintain for financing future performances, shall be placed in a permanent fund for improving the mountain theatre and eventually acquiring and dedicating it to the public, perpetually, or at least until it shall be included in a State or National Park.

In June 1914 Kent deeded the land to the association with the proviso that plays be given annually for twenty-five years. Somehow this condition was met, even during the difficult construction period in the 1930s. In 1936, after long negotiations with the state, the theatre was deeded by the Association to the State Park, a necessary precondition for the CCC work.

The building of the present beautiful stone theatre, together with the long-sought achievement of its public ownership, can be considered as marking the end of the plays' first period, clearly one of great success. From 1913 to 1936, twenty-three different shows had been presented (see the list at the end of this chapter).

Attendance fluctuated around 3,000, going above 4,000 in 1935. Receipts averaged around $1,500, sometimes more than $2,000. A small "profit" was set aside in good years to pay for theatre improvements. During the Depression it was nip and tuck whether the plays could be continued. But the board members rose to the occasion, stretching the dwindling income by all possible means. Some even made personal contributions. Without the steady dedication of Effie Easton the enterprise might have gone

Tamalpa, *sometimes spelled "Tamelpa," the story of the Sleeping Indian Maiden, was produced eight times between 1921 and 1970. (Courtesy of Nancy Skinner)*

under. She was one of the two keys to the success of the plays: she and Garnet Holme supplied the necessary technical knowledge of theatre and production. The members of the board were almost all men, hikers and lovers of the Mountain who, though devoted to the Mountain Theatre, were no experts in producing plays. Mrs. Easton also handled most of the publicity.

The ending of this first period saw a marked turnover in the group leading the enterprise. Most of the founders had died or retired, to be succeeded by a new and equally dedicated group. Garnet Holme died in 1929 as a result of a fall on a steep trail near his house in Larkspur. John Catlin (board president 1913-1916) resigned in 1932. "Dad" O'Rourke (president 1917-1934) died in 1937, as did Mrs. Easton.

William Kent, the Association's constant benefactor, died in 1928. His widow, Elizabeth, became a board member in 1929, and their son Albert followed in 1933. Their benefactions continued for many years.

O'Rourke's successor as president was Al Pinther, another hiker, active in both the TCC and the CAC. Reginald Travers, director from 1937-1948, brought with him the valuable support of San Francisco State College.

Dan Totheroh

By this time a new star had appeared: Dan Totheroh, later to take Holme's place as the director of many plays. His first appearance was as the author of *Tamalpa*, the play-pageant which eventually became the "official" play of the Mountain Theatre. In all, it was given in eight years, to great acclaim.

Tamalpa was first presented in 1921, when Holme was still the director. Indeed, it had been written at Holme's request, while Totheroh was living and working in New York as a playwright. Mrs. Easton wrote, after the 1921 production,

> The imagination of Totheroh peopled the sloping hillside with the spirits of the Mountain and the legend of Tamalpa, an Indian maiden. The play, offered in the natural setting of the out-of-doors, appeared to be unfolded from the atmosphere itself, and left me with a sense of having participated in a reincarnated dream.

The play's name, *Tamalpa*, is Totheroh's own. He wanted to base his play on the legend of the Sleeping Maiden, but his research turned up nothing about the legend and little about the Tamal Indians, simply that they considered the top of the Mountain to be mysterious and terrifying. So he created the legend himself. "It is the story of the purple maiden asleep forever on the slopes of the Mountain, her full length figure outlined against the sky."

William Duffy reports that when he was a classmate of Totheroh at San Rafael High School in 1912, he wrote a poem for the school paper, *The Searchlight,* entitled "The Sleeping Beauty." Duffy speculates that *Tamalpa* may have been inspired by this epic, which concludes:

> *After death of good old Quentin*
> *Spirits came down from the heavens,*
> *And at evening, while she slumbered*
> *Took the gentle Weh-Wah-he*
> *Placed her high upon the mountain*
> *And in memory of her people*
> *Called the Mountain Tamalpais.*

Totheroh's oral history, on file at Marin County Library, is a mine of information about the plays. One amusing incident occurred during the production of *Tallyho* in 1919; though Holme was still directing, Totheroh was present. The play was by Joaquin Miller, "the so-called 'poet of the Sierra'." Totheroh thought the play was awful. To make matters worse, Miller had specified that in lieu of a royalty his young daughter, Juanita, must be given the star role, despite the fact that no one at the theatre had ever seen her act. Once on stage, Juanita "over-acted all over the place, despite Holme's coaching," perhaps because her mother, backstage, was providing her with frequent gulps from a flask.

Her first line, calling to the hero from behind the trees, was "Hen-ree! Oooh, Hen-ree!" in what Totheroh called her "fruity" voice. The audience went wild, thinking it the funniest thing they had ever heard. At the end, Juanita rushed backstage crying, "Garnet, Garnet! It turned out to be a *comedy,* didn't it?" That was her last performance on the Mountain.

After the wartime hiatus (1942-1945) and even before the Army had completely moved out, plays were resumed much as before. The first play, in 1946, a new production of *Tamalpa,* was hailed by an enthusiastic audience who came in record-breaking numbers. But the automobiles brought a somewhat changed audience, with fewer hikers and more riders, many of them families with small children. Recognizing the change, the Association put on *Alice in Wonderland* in 1947; school buses brought 1,100 children, and total attendance exceeded 4,000.

The next decade had its ups and downs. Shakespeare's *The Tempest* (1954) and Aristophanes' *The Birds* (1956) proved difficult to adapt to the Mountain stage. Attendance fell below 2,000, and there was talk of abandoning the plays entirely.There had been earlier signs that the tradition was becoming difficult to maintain. Volunteer players were harder to find. Reginald Travers bowed out in 1948, and no regular director was in sight. Totheroh's return in 1949 to direct his play *Rough and Ready* eased matters temporarily, but for most of the 1950s continuation of the plays was a struggle. In 1950 expenses jumped to $5,388, more than double the average for pre-war years. In 1951 bad weather caused a record loss of more than $1,000. But the ticket price was never raised above $1.25. By 1955 the board had to make a decision. After much debate and a call for "new blood," they voted to continue the plays for ten more years.

The situation improved in 1957, when Dan Totheroh became the regular director, starting with another production of *Tamalpa*. He directed all the plays through 1968, and returned in 1970 for a final production of *Tamalpa*. Totheroh wrote two other plays himself: *Flamenca* (1928) and *Rough and Ready* (1949), and adapted a number of others from the original: *Alice in Wonderland* (1947), *Robin Hood* (1961), *Rip Van Winkle* (1962), *Peer Gynt* (1966), *Kismet* (1967), and *Alice Through the Looking Glass* (1968).

Totheroh was ably supported in his work by Marion Hayes Cain, who produced the plays he directed, and who served as president of the Association from 1959 to 1971. Mrs. Cain enjoyed a close relationship with College of Marin, which supplied all sorts of talent for the shows. She was indispensable to the success of the shows, as Mrs. Easton had been earlier.

Still discussion of the plays' future continued. In 1958 Totheroh told the directors, "If we are to be satisfied with a 'poor man's spectacle,' then continue giving the type of play we have been producing for one performance; otherwise start over with big money, big promotion and festival type of production." But the board was not yet ready for radical changes. These did not come until two decades later.

By 1961 attendance had improved so that *Robin Hood* was shown on two successive Sundays, breaking the tradition of one show each year. Two performances continued through 1972. By the late 1960s the Theatre was experiencing a new type of problem. The influx of hippies had its impact there as it did everywhere on the Mountain. Uprooted young people thronged to Tamalpais, many of them camping out for weeks or months on end. Their fires became a serious threat. Remnants of their stay are still being found in secluded spots.

As Dan Totheroh said in his oral history, in the late 1960s the hippies had "sort of taken over and refused to pay admission. They say, 'Why should we pay admission? We can go right around the trail and come into the theatre from above.' Shows have played to full houses, and yet we lost money." Yet the hippies did not seriously affect the plays themselves, which continued much as before.

Considerably more serious was the parking problem. Greyhound buses brought patrons up on play days, but they could handle relatively few people. Most people drove up and parked on the grass at Rock Spring, until conservationists persuaded the Water District to forbid parking there. Though car pools helped, the problem remained serious.

The early 1970s were lean years. Funds were short even though actors and other participants still received no payment. Expenses had risen sharply, and attendance was down, partly because hikers no longer came in large numbers. A picnic was substituted for the play in 1973. Musicals were tried in 1975 and 1976. Marion Hayes Cain, Association president (1958-1971), thought it might be time to give up the plays: "We are missing. . . really large groups of dedicated people," i.e. the members of the TCC and the California Alpine Club and other hikers who had once come to the play in droves.

The world had changed radically by 1970, mainly thanks to the automobile. Panoramic Highway was built in 1928; the Southside Road, from Pantoll to Rock Spring, was opened soon after and paved in 1938. And — the big change — the Golden Gate Bridge had opened in 1937. Thereafter, most of

Rob Roy, *the 1932 production, had resplendent and authentic costumes and the simplest back-drop. A note on the back identifies the photographer as Arthur Sheppard, and says "This place has the most wonderful acoustics." (Courtesy of Elizabeth S. Nash)*

The Mountain Play

MT. TAMALPAIS
MARIN COUNTY

"*Tamelpa*"

By
DAN W. TOTHEROH

Sunday, May 22, 1921
at 2:00 p. m.
[In case of inclement weather Sunday, May 29th]

—

Director, MR. GARNET HOLME
Management, MRS. D. E. F. EASTON

—

MOUNTAIN PLAY OFFICE:
RECREATION LEAGUE, 317 FLOOD BUILDING
TELEPHONE DOUGLAS 4293

Changing times are reflected in these two Mountain Play posters, from 1921 and 1977.

those who drove up to the Mountain Play were not so much lovers of the Mountain as visitors coming up for a good show.

As Dan Totheroh had suggested a decade earlier, the "poor man's spectacle" was out-of-date. He lived long enough to see the changes. He died in 1976, and is commemorated by a plaque at the Theatre, on a rock just above the stage. It reads: " 'My feet will mark the trail of stars.' *Tamalpa.* 1894-Dan Totheroh-1976."

Weather has been good to the Theatre. Rain fell on *Rip Van Winkle* (1915) but did not interrupt the performance or drive the audience away. John Catlin described "the wonderful cheerfulness and good nature of that devoted throng, who cheered and applauded when rivulets were trickling down their necks." Once, when *Thunder in Paradise* was being staged in 1937, the fog's coming and going actually enhanced the effect, according to a newspaper story: "The effect was at times breathtaking, and the entrance of Betty Hearst's girl dancers out of the fog was so beautiful it's still remembered and talked about."

A New Era

The current era of the Theatre, one of notable expansion and success, began in 1977 when Marilyn Smith took over as full-time executive director. Mrs. Smith, unlike her predecessors, is a promoter, skilled at raising money and putting on a popular spectacle. Unfortunately the play in 1977 ran into trouble of quite a new sort. Despite murmuring among board members, it was decided to branch out into something "modern." The play, *Clothes,* was based on Hans Christian Anderson's tale, "The Emperor's New Clothes." Many thought the theme was carried too far. A drawing on the program, though based on a classical model, showed the rear view of a nude man. Some language used in the show was criticized as "bawdy," not appropriate for family viewing, while others disliked the noisy music, including a 21-piece acid rock band.

Thereafter, the financial situation began to look up. The budget, a meager $13,000 in 1977, grew to $179,000 in 1984, after a money-raising campaign, sparked by Marilyn Smith, culminated in a three-year grant from the San Francisco Foundation.

Individuals and businesses have been generous. Another important assist has come from the drama department of College of Marin, which, beginning in 1981, was engaged to supply not only the director for the plays, but the scenic designers, as well as costumes and other equipment.

Income in recent years has more than met production costs. *Oklahoma* (1982) broke all attendance records, with five performances. *The Music Man* (1983) continued the upward trend, and *Fiddler On The Roof* (1984) with six performances, again broke attendance records. *The Sound of Music* (1985) was performed seven times and brought in even more money. *Peter Pan* (1986), in six performances, recorded the largest gate ever. The parking problem has been partially overcome by the use of shuttle buses.

Despite these successes and the fact that thousands of people obviously enjoy the current shows, some people regret the changes. Though the Association still operates as a non-profit corporation the now elaborate and expensive productions are providing sizable financial benefits to a growing number of people — necessary to the scale of the enterprise. Also, the large crowds strain the resources of the State Park and take rangers away from their regular duties. Because of the play's larger scale, both the Association and the State Park face difficult decisions in the future. Is it wise to attract huge crowds to such an inaccessible spot on the Mountain? If six performances a year sell out completely, should there be more? How much is too much?

The Mountain Play Association has been creative and flexible enough to adjust to new conditions and overcome some years of low attendance and money stringency. From a small beginning, supported mainly by hikers, and contending with the limitations of a natural amphitheatre, no matter how beautiful, the Association has acquired a handsome stone structure with many features that could last a thousand years, has adjusted, more or less, to the age of the automobile, and has learned how to raise money for more opulent productions. Most important, it has preserved its artistic integrity while pleasing a large and critical audience.

A plaque, recently afixed to a large rock near the entrance to the Mountain Theatre, honors three of the men who contributed so much to the Theatre and the plays. It reads:

Site of the First Mountain Play

Dedicated to our Associates who made our first years possible:

The Honorable William Kent, donor of Muir Woods National Monument to the public and of this theater to our Association

Sidney B. Cushing, Founder of Mt. Tamalpais Railroad, after whom the Theater is named

Alfred Pinther, their mutual friend, perennial leader of the Association and preserver of the mountain's natural state and trails.

The Mountain Plays 1913—1986

1913 *Abraham and Isaac,* a miracle play, and Malvolio's scenes from *Twelfth Night*

1914 *Shakuntala—Kalidasa,* translated from the Sanskrit by Dr. Arthur Ryder

1915 *Rip Van Winkle,* Washington Irving

1916 *William Tell,* Schiller

1917 *Jeppe-on-the-Hill,* Ludwig Holberg

1918 *Robin Hood,* Alfred Noyes

1919 *Tallyho,* Joaquin Miller

1920 *As You Like It,* William Shakespeare

1921 *Tamalpa,* Dan Totheroh

1922 *The Pied Piper* Peabody

1923 *Tamalpa,* Dan Totheroh

1924 (Area closed. Hoof & mouth disease epidemic)

1925 *Drake,* Garnet Holme

1926 *Rip Van Winkle,* Washington Irving

1927 *The Gods of the Mountain,* Lord Dunsany

1928 *Flamenca,* Dan Totheroh

1929 *Peer Gynt,* Henrik Ibsen

1930 *The Sunken Bell,* Hauptmann

1931 *The Trail of the Padres,* Frederic Stuart Smith

1932 *Rob Roy,* Sir Walter Scott

1933 *The Daughter of Jorio,* Gabriela D'Annunzio

1934 *The Girl of the Golden West,* David Belasco

1935 *The World We Live In,* Josef and Karel Capek

1936 *Androcles and the Lion,* George Bernard Shaw

1937 *Thunder in Paradise,* Cecil James Cook

1938 *Tamalpa,* Dan Totheroh

1939 *The Valiant Cossack,* Charles Caldwell Dobie

1940 *The World We Live In,* Josef and Karel Capek

1941 *A Thousand Years Ago,* Percy Mackaye

1942—1945 (Closed for World War II)

1946 *Tamalpa,* Dan Totheroh

1947 *Alice in Wonderland,* Lewis Carroll

1948 *If I Were King,* Justin Huntley McCarthy

1949 *Rough and Ready,* Dan Totheroh

1950 *Robin Hood,* Reginald de Koven

1951 *A Thousand Years Ago,* Percy Mackaye

1952 *Land of Oz,* L. Frank Baum

1953 *Tamalpa,* Dan Totheroh

1954 *The Tempest,* William Shakespeare

1955 *The World We Live In,* Josef & Karel Capek

1956 *The Birds,* Aristophanes

1957 *Tamalpa,* Dan Totheroh

1958 *Rough and Ready,* Dan Totheroh

1959 *The Pied Piper,* Peabody

1960 *Alice in Wonderland,* Lewis Carroll

1961 *Robin Hood,* Dan Totheroh

1962 *Rip of the Mountain,* Dan Totheroh

1963 *Tamalpa,* Dan Totheroh

1964 *Flamenca,* Dan Totheroh

1965 *Rough and Ready,* Dan Totheroh

1966 *Peer Gynt,* Henrik Ibsen

1967 *Kismet,* Edward Knoblock

1968 *Alice Through the Looking Glass,* Lewis Carroll

1969 *The World We Live In,* Josef & Karel Capek

1970 *Tamalpa,* Dan Totheroh

1971 *Playboy of the Western World,* J. M. Synge

1972 *Rough and Ready,* Dan Totheroh

1973 (Picnic substituted for play)

1974 *Rough and Ready,* Dan Totheroh

1975 (Music Festival)

1976 (Music Festival, Bicentennial)

1977 *Clothes,* George Leonard & Wm Hedgepeth

1978 *A Funny Thing Happened on the Way to the Forum,* Steven Sondheim, Shevelove/Gelbart

1979 *Indians,* Arthur Koppit

1980 *Carnival,* Bob Merrill & Michael Stewart

1981 *Annie Get Your Gun,* Irving Berlin

1982 *Oklahoma,* Rodgers & Hammerstein

1983 *The Music Man,* Meredith Wilson

1984 *Fiddler on the Roof,* Sholem Aleichem

1985 *The Sound of Music,* Rodgers & Hammerstein

1986 *Peter Pan,* J. M. Barrie

CHAPTER NOTES

Tamalpais, Enchanted Mountain, edited by Edgar M. Kahn and published in 1946 by the Roxburghe Club, contains a somewhat fanciful chapter by Henry Hart on the history of the Theatre up to that time.

The Mountain Theatre Association published an elaborate illustrated brochure in 1970, which contains a complete list of the plays 1913-1970, a description of each play, and many photographs. It has been drawn upon heavily in this chapter.

Emerson Knight wrote a descriptive article about the Theatre, "Mountain Theatre on Mt. Tamalpais,"

published in *Landscape Architecture,* October 1949.

The author was privileged to read the minutes of the Association's board of directors, 1913-1959.

Anna Coxe Toogood, in her study for the GGNRA, referred to earlier in these notes, includes an excellent account of the Mountain Theatre, Vol. I, pp. 25-33.

San Rafael High School kindly supplied a copy of *The Searchlight* (1912) in which William Duffy's poem appeared.

William Burch McMurtrie painted this serene watercolor of the Mountain as seen from San Quentin Point in 1855. It is exactly contemporary with the Edwin Moody drawings on pages 15 and 34. (Courtesy of the Bancroft Library)

CHAPTER NINE

Art and Literature on Mt. Tamalpais

For countless ages Mt. Tamalpais has inspired observers with the desire to capture its beauty and mystery and to preserve them in some comprehensible form. Marin Miwoks expressed their feelings of awe and reverence as legends passed down from one generation to the next. More recent visitors have tried to capture the Mountain's power in paintings, drawings, verse, prose, and photographs. There is nothing surprising about this. Even the most single-minded hiker, preoccupied with trails and landmarks, has come over a rise and seen a slant of hillside, a fall of light, which has made him stop, dumb-struck, and wish he could save this moment forever.

The first written account of a climb to the summit of the Mountain, by William H. Brewer, who was mapping for the California Geological Survey in 1862, shows us a scientist reaching for metaphor: "It was most grand, more like some views of the Alps than anything I have seen before — those glimpses of the landscape beneath through foggy curtains."

Visitors to art galleries, museums and auction rooms have seen paintings of Mt. Tamalpais which have managed to save such moments, which capture some aspect of light, color, mass, distance and perspective in a way that speaks at once to the eye and the heart. Some of these pictures are acknowledged masterpieces. Roy and Nancy Farrington Jones, who have assembled a magnificent collection of photographs of California paintings, have more than one hundred of Mt. Tamalpais.

But for every masterpiece by a William Keith or a Thaddeus Welch there are hundreds of works by Sunday painters which show how universal is the urge to capture the beauty and majesty of the Mountain in paint. No matter how naive the execution of such a picture may be, we recognize the artist's motive, and sympathize with his struggle to express his vision. Occasionally a really accomplished picture will stop the eye and jog one's memory of a similar view, a similar lightfall. From the rest we can learn something about the stubbornness of paint and the persistence of painters.

Captain George Vancouver, the British explorer, drew the first representation of the Mountain on his chart in 1792, but his motives were practical, not artistic. William Burch McMurtrie painted the Mountain's earliest surviving portrait in 1855, a fine water color now tucked away in the files of the Bancroft Library.

Among painters, Thaddeus Welch had the closest connections with the Mountain, having lived for several years (1898-1903 or 4) in a cabin he built himself in Steep Ravine, on the west slope of the Mountain. Many of his best-known paintings were done

William Keith made this engraving for the poem "Tamalpais," from Lyrics, *by Charles Warren Stoddard (1867). Keith later painted the Mountain several times, usually from the north side.*

at this time and in this vicinity, including one of his own cabin bedecked with flowers planted by his artist wife, Ludmilla Welch. A.L. Gump, dean of San Francisco art dealers, said of Welch's works:

> The Welch canvases will live. They are fairly well scattered over the country, but one — "Mt. Tamalpais" — hanging in the Family Club in San Francisco, I consider one of the finest naturalistic paintings ever made.

Unfortunately the Family Club is not open to the public.

One of California's best-known painters, William Keith (1838-1911), was a good friend of John Muir. Muir introduced Keith to mountain scenery and encouraged him to paint in the style for which he became famous, "in the tradition of grandiloquent realism," as the critic Jacob Foster put it. Keith, Foster added, "was able to translate Muir's attitudes to canvas." Reproductions of several of Keith's engravings and paintings were used by John Muir to illustrate the fabulous volumes he edited under the title *Picturesque California.*

One critic has said of Keith that "he has struck the key in art which Bret Harte struck in literature, when the latter devoted his nice talent to unique local themes the spirit of which he had absorbed by long residence and observation." One wonders whether Keith would have been flattered by the comparison.

Curiously enough, most of the pictures we have referred to were painted before 1910, suggesting that landscape painting may, until recently, have gone out of style. The growth of photography would explain this. Yet the Mountain has not lost its appeal for artists; it is depicted in etchings, woodcuts, engravings, and of course in thousands of photographs. And for every splendid, arresting photograph of the Mountain there must be tens of thousands which seem to their perpetrators vaguely disappointing, that fail to catch the sweep of landscape, the shimmering light, the sense of distance and vastness and volume which the Mountain displays.

Recently a distinguished young artist, Tom Killion, has published two books of woodcuts of the Mountain, *28 Views of Tamalpais* (1975) and *Fortress Marin* (1977), the latter dealing with the history of military emplacements around its shoreside fringe. The fine photographs of Jim Morley are dis-

played in his *Muir Woods* (1968), with an informative text. Richard Stortroen and Bud Fellon published *Tamalpais* (1978), consisting wholly of photographs. Hundreds of other photographers have been taking pictures of the Mountain for many years.

Literature, a more private art, rarely reaches the public eye unless its author is extremely gifted or famous, or unless he has connections or cash sufficient to secure publication. Furthermore, we read and pass judgment on literature in private. If we see a painting hung in a museum we are likely to admire it simply because it is being exhibited, or because it is old. Most readers today are intolerant of the florid or grandiloquent style in literature, although they may accept or even admire the same style in painting. Not everybody paints. But everybody speaks and writes and uses language, and the style of our time is terse, bare, understated, ironic, factual. So 19th century writing, especially verse, may seem to us overdone, too ornate, too exclamatory or rhetorical. Yet the poets and novelists, like the painters of the 19th century, followed a style which was valid for their work and their time. Literature must be understood in its historic framework. Some of the examples which follow will make this clear.

The first writer known to have climbed Mt. Tamalpais was Edward Rowland Sill (1841-1887), whose long poem *The Hermitage* was inspired by his camping on the Mountain in the spring of 1862. Harold French, an early hiker, wrote about Sill:

> First of the Tamalpais pioneers who opened the eyes of the world to the Sleeping Lady's ineffable fascination, was a young poet of but twenty-two, Edward Rowland Sill. In the summer of sixty-two, he camped for a month under a great oak above Laurel Dell, hard by the lone dogwood tree. Five years later, his first book of poems, *The Hermitage,* heralded Mount Tamalpais as one of the newly-discovered pleasure places of California.

As *The Hermitage* tells the story, Sill built himself a hut and lived there alone. The poem is much too long to quote in full (forty pages), but a few lines follow (the poet is addressing the Mountain):

> *See: I am come to live alone with thee.*
> *But I come with my life almost untried*
> *Teach me thy wisdom; let me learn the flowers,*
> *And know the rocks and trees.*

*Above: Edward R. Sill, the poet who camped on
the Mountain and wrote about it, in 1861.
(Courtesy of Nancy Skinner) Right: Ina
Coolbrith, one of the San Francisco Bohemians,
became California's Poet Laureate. (Courtesy of
the Bancroft Library)*

Against the huge trunk of a storm snapped tree,
I've built of saplings and long limbs a hut.
Thatched with thick-spreading palms of pine,
And tangled over by a wandering vine.

The big old oak against which Sill built his hut is still standing and is still enveloped by a "wandering vine." True, the lines are labored; the awkward postponement of "a hut," the trite "Teach me thy wisdom," and the badly confused image of a hut "Thatched with thick-spreading palms of pine," all tell us that the poet has much to learn. But he disarms us in advance by saying, "I come with my life almost untried." Somehow the idea of an idealistic twenty-one-year-old living in a hut on the Mountain and writing poetry is distinctly appealing. Later in the poem he manages to build a striking and original image:

I sat last night on yonder ridge of rocks
To see the sun set over Tamalpais,
Whose tinted peak, suffused with rosy mist,
Blended the colors of the sea and sky
And made the mountain one great amethyst
Hanging against the sunset.

Sill was among the first of a coterie of writers who contributed to the burst of literary activity which Franklin Walker describes in *San Francisco's Literary Frontier.* These included Mark Twain, Bret Harte and Ambrose Bierce. Poets, besides Sill, were Charles Warren Stoddard (1843-1909) Ina Coolbrith (1841-1928), and Daniel O'Connell (1848-1899). At a time when poetry was more widely read than it is today, they had a large following, but few know their work now.

Most of these writers have left some record that they were touched by the Mountain's beauty. In Stoddard's first book of poems, published in 1867, was one called "Tamalpais," with an engraved illustration by William Keith. Stoddard later wrote another "Tamalpais" that catches some of the aura of the Mountain. This is the concluding stanza:

Broad banners of mist thread through the gate,
*   And gather about him cold as a shroud;*
But little he cares, for his bare hoary pate
*   Is capped with the sunlight over the cloud.*
Brave Tamalpais! He looks so grand,
*   Bluffing the oceans off, guarding the land.*

The poetry of Ina Coolbrith, Stoddard's close friend, made the greatest impression on their contemporaries. Though few today remember her or her poetry, she lived to achieve recognition as Poet Laureate of California. The laurel crown was conferred by University of California President Benjamin Ide Wheeler in 1915, toward the end of her long life.

Coolbrith, Stoddard and Bret Harte together were known as the "Golden Gate Trinity," or, in less elevated language, "The Bohemians." Samuel Dickson, in *Tales of San Francisco,* wrote of them:

At almost any hour of the day or night you were likely to find the three of them seated on the floor of Ina's little Russian Hill house, drinking coffee and reading poetry, especially the poetry of the one poet that Ina adored above all the others — Lord Byron. . . . Day after day they were seen hiking the trails of Mount Tamalpais and Muir Woods, or drinking wine in little shops in Sausalito.

Bret Harte left no poems about the Mountain, but Ina Coolbrith wrote several. Best known is "California" (1871), later published in *Songs from the Golden Gate* (1895). In it she recalls the "faint smell of laurel up the slopes of Tamalpais," and then in the last stanza:

Was it wind, or the soft sigh of leaves,
Or sound of singing waters? Lo, I looked
And saw the silvery ripples of the brook,
The fruit upon the hills, the waving trees,
And mellow fields of harvest; saw the Gate
Burn in the sunset; the thin thread of mist
Creep white across the Saucelito hills;
Till the day darkened down the ocean rim,
The sunset purple slipped from Tamalpais.
And bay and sky were bright with sudden stars.

Bailey Millard, newspaper editor and poet, characterized Coolbrith as "that facile writer of fragrant verse." But even the brief samples included here show her to be considerably more accomplished than either Stoddard or Sill.

Out of Ina Coolbrith's love of Tamalpais and her reverence for Byron's poetry grew a charming episode. Coolbrith and her friend Joaquin Miller (1841-1913), also an admirer of Byron, were outraged to hear that Byron's grave at the old Norman church at Hucknall Torkard in England was neglected and overgrown with weeds. Miller, who had not yet made his mark as a writer, was planning a trip to England. The day before he left, they decided to do something to honor Byron. Together they took the ferry to Sausalito, climbed up the slope of Mt. Tamalpais, and brought back some laurel boughs. That evening Ina Coolbrith wove a wreath out of the laurel and wrote a poem. These she entrusted to Miller, who took them with him to England in August 1874. As she wrote much later:

> I wrote my "With a Wreath of Laurel" and made a wreath of laurel which I sent by Joaquin to the poet's grave in Hucknall Torkard Church. Joaquin faithfully deposited it there, but some enemies of Byron objected; his friends took it up and the dispute grew violent. The King of Greece took up the fight, added *another* wreath, and placed both under glass to preserve them — and attention being called to the ruinous condition of the church which was almost falling down, Byron's adherents caused it to be *restored,* and it is now in splendid condition. A fund is being raised to keep it so. All this from my little wreath.

Ina Coolbrith and her friends, in their style of living as well as in their devotion to art and poetry, were establishing a tradition of unconventionality and free thinking which continued in San Francisco up to the present.

Ambrose Bierce, another of Ina Coolbrith's friends, suffered from asthma attacks in San Francisco, and moved to San Rafael in 1875. His biographer, Carey McWilliams, reports, "He would tramp the brown hillsides with their. . .green, umbrella-like trees. He took long walks up Mt. Tamalpais where the sun burned down upon the slanting hillsides with warming indolence."

Charles Urmy (1858-1923), a member of the same coterie, left a poem, "As I Came Down Mt. Tamalpais," which has been called "the most famous of the lyrics inspired by its mighty crest." The last stanza follows:

> *As I came down Mount Tamalpais,*
> *To West Heaven's gateway opened wide,*
> *And through it, freighted with day-cares,*
> *The cloud-ships floated with the tide;*
> *Then silently through stilly air,*
> *Starlight flew down from Paradise,*
> *Folded her silver wings and slept*
> *Upon the slopes of Tamalpais.*

Many other literary figures of the 19th and early 20th centuries have connections with Mt. Tamalpais. A plaque in memory of Ralph Waldo Emerson, honoring his hundredth birthday, was installed in Muir Woods in 1903, five years before the National Monument was established. Robert Louis Stevenson (1850-1894) was much impressed with the Mountain's romantic beauty. In *Amateur Immigrant* he describes the view from an Oakland-San Francisco ferryboat at sunrise:

> A spot of cloudy gold lit first upon the head of Tamalpais, and then widened downward on its shapely shoulder; the air seemed to awaken, and began to sparkle; and suddenly "The tall hills Titan discovered," and the city of San Francisco, and the bay of gold and corn, were lit from end to end with summer daylight.

In *Silverado Squatters,* after living for a time on Mt. Saint Helena, Stevenson wrote of seeing Mt. Tamalpais from a Vallejo hill:

> More of the bay became apparent, and soon the blue peak of Tamalpais rose above the green level of the island opposite. . . . For Tamalpais stands sentry, like a lighthouse, over the Golden Gate, between the bay and the open ocean, and looks down indifferently on both.

Elsewhere he pays the Mountain his finest compliment, comparing it to a scene in his beloved homeland: "And the fine bulk of Tamalpais looking down on San Francisco, like Arthur's Seat in Edinburgh." No other natural feature of the Bay Area made such an impression on Stevenson during his brief visits here.

Jack London (1876-1916) visited Mt. Tamalpais and Muir Woods many times. According to Russ Kingman, an eminent scholar of London's life, one of "the highlights of Jack's early years was to go with Mable Applegarth and his first wife Bessie Maddeeron across the bay by ferry with their bicycles and head for Mt. Tamalpais or Muir Woods."

Sir Arthur Conan Doyle, who rode the railway to the summit and down to Muir Woods in 1924, expressed his delight:

> There is Tamalpais, the one and only Tamalpais, which should be ascended by the traveller if he has only a single clear day in the city of the Golden Gate. Our whole party went up it on the day after our arrival, and we were agreed that in all our wanderings we had never had a more glorious experience.

Ludmilla Welch lived with her painter husband (she too was a painter) in this picturesque but uncomfortable cottage on the Mountain, where she tried to grow their food in her garden. In 1905, unable to stand the poverty, chilly fogs and ocean breezes, they moved to San Geronimo Valley. Thaddeus Welch is famous for his paintings of cows on the slopes of Tamalpais. (Courtesy of Nancy Skinner) Right: The Lone Dogwood, where Edward Rowland Sill camped near Laurel Dell, is shown here in 1936; it was later shaded to death by a Douglas fir. (Courtesy of Nancy Skinner)

This beautiful photograph of Tamalpais from Sausalito was taken around 1884. The trestle for the narrow-gauge North Pacific Coast Railroad crosses Richardson Bay to Strawberry; a new line is being built northward to skirt the bay on the left side. The tiny churchyard has a picket fence and a privy at the back corner. But such a picture, with its superb composition and proportion, offers far more to the viewer than mere historical or topographical information; it aspires to the condition of art, and clearly succeeds. (Courtesy of the Bancroft Library)

John Masefield, visiting Muir Woods in 1937, felt the power of nature:

> Sometimes in cathedrals one feels the awe and majesty of columns. These columns were more impressive than anything of stone; these columns were alive. They were more like gods than anything I have ever seen.

Although the National Monument is named for him, John Muir (1838-1914) visited the Mountain only briefly. When he came down from the Sierra for brief periods of work on manuscripts in San Francisco, he occasionally went hiking to relieve the tedium of desk work. The following account is probably circa 1888, immediately following Muir's climbs of Mt. Shasta and Mt. Rainier with his friend, the painter William Keith:

> After I had lived many years in the mountains, I spent my first winter in San Francisco, writing up notes. I used to run out on short excursions to Mount Tamalpais, and I always brought back a lot of flowers — as many as I could carry — and it was most touching to see the quick natural enthusiasm in the hearts of the ragged, neglected, defrauded, dirty little wretches of the Tar Flat water-front of the city I used to pass through on my way home.... "Please, mister, give me a flower..." And when I stopped and distributed the treasures, giving each a lily or daisy or calochortus, anemone, gilia, flowering dogwood, spray of ceanothus, manzanita, or a branch of redwood, the dirty faces glowed with enthusiasm... It was a hopeful sign, and made me say: "No matter into what depths of degradation humanity may sink, I will never despair while the lowest love the pure and the beautiful and know it when they see it.

Today, of course, Muir would be arrested for despoiling nature. The passage shows the Olympian heights on which the naturalist saw himself, perhaps as a result of his years on mountaintops.

In 1909, five years before his death, Muir visited Muir Woods with his friends, the Newton family; he may have stayed in the Ben Johnson cabin, sometimes erroneously called the Muir cabin. He wrote a tribute to the Mountain in a letter dated Sptember 23, 1909: "The whole Tamalpais region is delightful and many times more interesting and instructive than is generally known by those living within an hour or two of it."

The San Francisco author Gertrude Atherton (1857-1948) is the only novelist known to have done some of her writing on Mt. Tamalpais. The following is from her own account of writing a portion of *Tower of Ivory* while staying at the Tavern at the East Peak terminus of the railway, probably in 1908:

> Few had ever spent more than a night there, and as I announced my intention of remaining throughout the winter they gave me the one room with a private bath and a stove, as there was no central heating. The winter storms set in immediately. It stormed for fifty days and fifty nights. I wrote to the accompaniment of a tremendous orchestration of the elements.... But winter turned abruptly into summer... It was so hot that the rattlesnakes woke up from their winter sleep among the rocks and came out into the sun. One even invaded the bar. And people came up every afternoon on the little mountain train to witness the sunrise next morning. I was awakened by "Oh's" and "Ah's" as they hung out of their windows at four a.m. watching a blood-red sun rise above an imponderable sea of white fog that blotted out the valleys, the Bay, and even San Francisco on its hills.

Kathleen Norris (nee Thompson) (1880-1966), one of the most prolific and financially successful of California novelists, was intimately connected with Mill Valley and Mt. Tamalpais. She is remembered by many old-time Mill Valley residents, and a number of her family, the Thompsons and their descendants, still live there. A small park in Mill Valley is named for her, on the corner of Molina and Wildomar.

In her autobiographical *Family Gathering,* Mrs. Norris writes of her childhood:

> It was a great adventure, in 1891, for my mother and father to move us all (from San Francisco) to Mill Valley, once the great Throckmorton Ranch, recently plotted into building lots scattered on the steep slopes of Tamalpais mountain and on the mountain chain stretching to the east and west to enclose the valley.

The whole area, she writes, "was all ours, we ranged free, riding on the milk wagons that came down from the Portuguese ranch on the ridge." Late in life she recalled these experiences: "Here for exquisite years, we ran wild." Mill Valley she described as "a two-pronged canyon running up against the flanks of Mount Tamalpais, heavily and beautifully wooded; one of the exquisite places in the world. In Sicily, in all the beauty spots of the Riviera, I have seen nothing more naturally lovely."

Her father, James A. Thompson, was always "ready with Sunday plans for long walks — of 10, 12 or even 14 miles," sometimes involving picnics in Muir Woods. The family moved back to San Francisco a few years later, buying a house on Hyde Street between Union and Filbert, not far from the house Stevenson's widow was building on the corner of Hyde and Lombard. From their rear windows they could see "the glorious, ever changing waters of the Bay, with Tamalpais rearing her familiar outline on the north." Very much later, as a widow in her eighties, she lived on the slope of Twin Peaks: "From my windows . . . I can see the Bay, and the arch of Golden Gate Bridge, and the dear familiar silhouette of Tamalpais mountain for a background against a dove-gray sky."

In the late 1950s and into the 1970s, a new generation of writers, many of them San Franciscans, burst upon the literary scene. Like those who had clustered around Ina Coolbrith a century earlier, they were "Bohemians" in their life-style, though their style of writing was vastly different. Allen Ginsberg and Lawrence Ferlinghetti were at the center of a group of "Beat" writers who, for one reason or another, were outraged by the complacency of established American culture. One member of the group, Jack Kerouac, used the phrase "Dharma Bums" to describe himself and his fellow adherents of Zen Buddhism.

Kerouac, in his novel *The Dharma Bums* (1958), described vividly and ecstatically a two-day hike on Mt. Tamalpais with his friend Japhy Ryder. They started from a friend's cabin, apparently near the top of Corte Madera Ridge. As the Mountain loomed up above them, Japhy remarked, "See up there ahead, as beautiful a mountain as you'll see anywhere in the world, a beautiful shape to it, I really love Tamalpais. We'll sleep tonight around the back side of it." And so they did, at Potrero Meadows, having meanwhile passed a "mountain lodge," probably West Point Inn, and having visited Muir Woods and the Mountain Theatre. The next day they hiked to Laurel Dell, and from there across Bolinas Ridge to Stinson Beach for a swim, finally returning on the south side all the way back to their cabin.

The cabin they were using became known as the Dharma Bums' camp; it belonged to Sean Monahan, who lived just down the hill. Another cabin, on a slope west of Mill Valley, belonged to Gary Snyder, the best known poet of the group. Snyder, too, had close associations with the Mountain, but seems to have written little about it. One brief poem, describing the life-style of the Beats, suggests that Tamalpais had meaning for him; it appears in his book *The Back Country* (1957):

> *North Beach Alba*
> *waking half-drunk in a strange pad*
> *making it out to the cool gray*
> *   San Francisco dawn —*
> *white gulls over white houses,*
> *   fog down to the bay*
> *Tamalpais a fresh green hill in the new sun*
> *driving across the bridge in a beat old car*
> *   to work.*

For Lew Welch (1926-1971), another of the Beat poets, Snyder's cabin on Tamalpais was a refuge to which he escaped from time to time when the world was too much with him, or when he was suffering from one of his recurrent bouts of depression. He stayed there often when Snyder was in Japan, becoming quite enchanted with the Mountain. He often mentioned it in letters to friends, and he published a slim volume of poetry entitled *The Song Tamalpais Sings*. The title poem ends with these strophes:

> *This is the last place. There is nowhere else to go.*
> *   This is why*
> *   once again we celebrate the*
> *   Headland's huge, cairn-studded, fall*
> *   into the Sea.*

> *This is the last place. There is nowhere else to go.*
> *   For we have walked the jeweled beaches*
> *   at the feet of the final cliffs*
> *   of all Man's wanderings.*

> *This is the last place.*
> *There is nowhere else we need to go.*

Another poem, "Song of the Turkey Buzzard," seems gentler and less desperate:

> *Praises Gentle Tamalpais*
> *Perfect in Wisdom and Beauty of the*
> *   sweetest water*
> *   and the soaring birds.*

John Muir is usually thought of as a naturalist, but he was also a gifted writer with a poet's sensitivity to nature. This superb portrait, a work of art itself, was made about 1893. (Courtesy of the John Muir National Historic Site)

Welch's use of capital letters here suggests that he saw Nature in the same way as earlier peoples did, attaching animistic meaning to birds, rocks and water. Indeed, in one letter he refers to himself and his friends as "white Indians."

Reverence for Nature shines through another poem, "Prayer to a Mountain Spring":

> *Gentle Goddess*
> *Who never asks for anything at all,*
> *and gives us everything we have,*
> *thank you for this sweet water,*
> *and your fragrance.*

Any wanderer on the Mountain who has stopped to drink at a spring has felt the same gratitude.
Lew Welch took his own life in 1971.

Ballet, too, has been enriched by the Mountain. In 1974 New York's Joffrey Ballet presented *Sacred Grove on Mount Tamalpais,* staged not on the Mountain, but at the San Francisco Opera House. Three years earlier Gerald Arpino, chief choreographer, and his associate James Howell, drove up Mt. Tamalpais and climbed to the top. "I went to the farthest edge of a great rock and stayed there until the sun set, and the vision became lost in the swirling fog," Arpino said. "It was the quietest time I have ever known, a very beautiful experience." The experience, surprisingly similar to those reported by visitors a hundred years ago, was the inspiration for the ballet.

Pablo Casals (1876-1973), for decades hailed as the world's greatest cellist, had a quite different experience when he was climbing down the Mountain in 1901. With him on the outing were Leon Moreau, "a bit of a daredevil, always ready for some new adventure," and Theresa Hermann, who "played the piano, and her sister was a violinist." They had hiked to the top and were coming down, probably on the Throckmorton Trail, then as now steep and hazardous. Albert E. Kahn, Casals' biographer, quotes:

> In San Francisco I had an experience which not only brought my first American tour to a sudden end but almost ended my career as a cellist. I was

enchanted by the city and by the surrounding countryside. And when several young, newly made friends invited me to join them on an expedition across the Bay to climb Mount Tamalpais, I was delighted. I have always loved mountain climbing. We crossed on a ferryboat which was, I think, the most ornate vessel I'd ever seen — a veritable floating castle.

> It was when we were making our descent on Mount Tamalpais that the accident occurred. Suddenly one of my companions shouted, "Watch out, Pablo!" I looked up and saw a boulder hurtling down the mountainside directly toward me. I jerked my head aside and was lucky not to be killed. As it was, the boulder hit and smashed my left hand — my fingering hand. My friends were aghast. But when I looked at my mangled bloody fingers, I had a strangely different reaction. My first thought was, "Thank God, I'll never have to play the cello again!" No doubt, a psychoanalyst would give some profound explanation. But the fact is that dedication to one's art does involve a sort of enslavement, and then too, of course, I have always felt such dreadful anxiety before performances.

> I remained in San Francisco while Emma Nevada and Moreau continued the tour. The doctors predicted I'd never regain the full use of my hand. But doctors sometimes make mistakes. With constant treatments and exercise, my hand healed completely, after four months, and I started practicing again. I fell in love with San Francisco — who does not?

When Casals returned to San Francisco nearly sixty years later, in 1960, he recalled:

> Thirty-five years had then elapsed since my last visit to California and sixty years since my first. When Martita and I arrived in Berkeley my mind was full of memories. One of the most vivid was the day on Mount Tamalpais which had almost ended my musical career at the age of twenty-four.

Of the many gods resident on Mt. Tamalpais, did one detest the sound of the cello and send the boulder hurtling down? Or did a god or goddess intervene to save the young musician's life and give us seventy more years of his inspired music?

CHAPTER NOTES

Among well-known artists whose Tamalpais paintings can be seen in nearby museums are Norton Bush (California Historical Society, San Francisco), Carol Christian Dahlgren (Kent Gallery, San Anselmo), Marius Dahlgren (Wortsman Gallery, San Francisco), William Keith (de Young Museum, San Francisco, and Robert Louis Stevenson Museum, St. Helena), Julian Walbridge Rix (California Historical Society), Jules Tavernier (Oakland Museum), Thaddeus Welch (Oakland Museum), and Raymond Dabb Yelland (California Historical Society).

J. Foster Jacob's article, "Artists and Illustrators of California," in *Pacific Historian,* Vol. 19, 1975, is useful; so is *California Art Research,* WPA Project pamphlet. Thad Welch and his cabin are discussed in "Story of Two California Artists," by Eufena C. Thompkins, in *Sunset,* June 1904. A new directory of California artists, by Edan Hughes, was widely praised on publication in 1986.

The best source for the writers is, of course, their own works. Stevenson's work on the Bay Area is collected in *From Scotland to Silverado,* James Hart, editor. Many of the poets discussed here are dealt with by Franklin Walker in *San Francisco's Literary Frontier.* Sir Arthur Conan Doyle's enthusiastic response to Tamalpais is reported in *Our Second American Adventure.* Russ Kingman wrote about Jack London in a letter to Fred Sandrock, August 22, 1985.

Lew Welch's poetry has been assembled in a volume titled *Lew Welch, Selected Poems,* with a preface by Gary Snyder. His philosophy and his troubled life are revealed in a two-volume collection of his letters, *I Remain, The Letters of Lew Welch and the Correspondence of His Friends,* both edited by his friend Donald Allen.

The "lone dogwood" near which Edward Rowland Sill camped was indeed lone. It was believed to be the only one of its species, *Cornus nuttallii,* growing on the Mountain. When it died in the 1950s it was replaced, as a tribute to botanist Alice Eastwood, by two others. These, however, turned out to be a different species, *C. capitata,* and unfortunately were not native. Other dogwoods, not uncommon on the Mountain, are Creek Dogwoods, *C. californica.*

An earlier version of this chapter appeared originally in *California History,* journal of the California Historical Society, Summer 1982. Revisions and additions were made by James Heig, editor of this volume.

*M*OUNT TAMALPAIS AND THE VALLEYS *tucked along its base are home to tens of thousands of people today, many of whom take for granted the way their town looks now, or the way it looked when they first saw it. Yet only a little more than a hundred years ago the grassy slopes, the stands of oak, laurel and redwood, looked much as they did in the time of the Coast Miwok people. Ranchers, farmers and lumbermen began changing the landscape from the 1840s onward, but the greatest single force for change was the railroad, which made the valleys accessible to all.*

Seven photographs of San Anselmo and Mill Valley show dramatically how rapidly those towns took form after the arrival of the railroad. Above: San Anselmo in the early 1880s is a sylvan valley, with the tiny train station and fenced-off track the only visible sign of the approaching deluge. (Courtesy of the Marin County Historical Society) Opposite top: Stores and houses have clustered along the railroad track, eucalyptus compete with native trees, and the magnificent stone buildings of the theological seminary adorn their gentle hill, circa 1907. (Courtesy of Charles Ford) Below: After the 1906 earthquake and fire, many people moved from San Francisco to outlying areas. By 1909 San Anselmo has spread out toward the hillside, and the valley has become something quite new. (Courtesy of the Marin County Historical Society)

*No. 404. Panorama of San Anselmo,
showing Mt. Tamalpais,
Marin County, California.*

Top: In 1891 the Thomas Kelly house (center) is the focal point of Mill Valley. Large-scale steps lead up from Lovell Avenue to Summit, a dirt track just scraped out of the hillside where cows still graze. (Courtesy of Nancy Skinner) Below: Two years later the town has a school (with privy), a church, and imposing houses, including the Alonzo Coffin house, which looks like a steamboat. (Courtesy of the Mill Valley Library)

By 1900 the school has been enlarged, another church has gone up, and many houses have been built, including the Queen Anne with tower (lower left). The Kelly house is dwarfed by the new scale. (Courtesy of Joseph A. Baird, Jr.) Below: This 1913 view shows a settled town, with mature eucalyptus and cypress windbreaks. The Kelly house, painted a dark color, has a barn behind it. (Courtesy of Elizabeth S. Nash)

Top: Engine #4, painted a deep, polished red, is shown at the summit about 1907. In the cab are Joe Paganini, fireman, and Frank Clark, engineer; below are Howard Folker, conductor, and H.C. Graves. (Courtesy of the Mill Valley Library) Below: From 1896 to 1904 passengers rode in a San Francisco cable car which the railway bought used from the Omnibus cable line. (Courtesy of Charles Ford)

CHAPTER TEN

The Mt. Tamalpais & Muir Woods Railway

For more than thirty years, from 1896 to 1930, the Mount Tamalpais Railway provided one of the most popular excursions for visitors to San Francisco, and a continuing source of pleasure and excitement for local residents. For tourists it was a must, much as the cable cars are today. It took them not only to the East Peak for the view, but after the extension was opened to Muir Woods in 1907, it served as a sort of Gray Line Tour to the redwoods. Travel agents booked their patrons for a ride up the Mountain and railroad brochures advertised it. Mill Valley teen-agers rode up for an evening dance at the Tavern and shot back down late at night by gravity car. It was the rage to go up in the evening, spend the night, and be up early to see the sunrise. At the time of the Panama Pacific International Exposition in 1915, 700 passengers rode the train daily; a total of 102,000 travelled up it that year.

It is difficult today, more than fifty years after the railroad closed down, to imagine the excitement that tourists experienced when they rode to the top or down to Muir Woods. The great violinist Yehudi Menuhin recalls childhood visits to Mt. Tamalpais which must have taken place around 1920. Speaking in 1980, he says:

I remember what I liked about San Francisco was the light, the air, the climate, the vigor, the whole-someness. The beauty of Mount Tamalpais, where my parents used to take us. They'd go hiking up there, and we'd take the little train.

Charles Francis Saunders wrote in 1916 about riding up on the railway:

The ascent of the mountain is by a queer little railway with a queer little engine, and it twists and winds and loops itself into bowknots, then unties itself and does it all over again, to your great amazement and delight.... It finally comes to a complete stop at a nice little hotel with a marvelous, unobstructed view to the four corners of the earth.

Louis Janes, secretary of the Tamalpais Land and Water Co., is credited with the idea of building a railway up the Mountain, with a hotel on top. And it was Augustus D. Avery, a surveyor hired by the Land and Water Co., who made the survey for the railroad. As built in 1896, the Mill Valley and Mt. Tamalpais Scenic Railway ran from the center of Mill Valley, sharing its terminus with that of the narrow gauge from Sausalito, to the East Peak, close to the eastern end of the present parking lot. It took an hour and ten minutes to cover the 8.19 continually twisting miles up the 2,200-foot climb.

The original idea for the railway was more ambitious. William Graves, President of the North

141

Top: From left are Charles Runyan, (?), Sidney Cushing, William Kent, and Louis Janes, the founders of the Scenic Railway. (Courtesy of the Mill Valley Library) Below: Two of the track layers rest near a trestle built around tree trunks. (Courtesy of Charles Ford)

Pacific Coast Railroad, announced in 1892 that he had the financial backing of eastern capitalists to build a railway from Mill Valley over a spur of the Mountain all the way to Bolinas where, when "the large hotels are erected. . . . Bolinas will be one of the most popular watering places on the coast." Though the 1893 depression killed the whole plan at this time, the vision of extending the railway over the Mountain to the ocean was revived later and came closer to fruition.

Among the chief backers of the railway in 1896 were Louis Janes, the Kents, Albert Emmett and his son William, and Sidney B. Cushing. Albert Kent not only subscribed $25,000 of the $200,000 in capital stock, but donated a right-of-way through his land in upper Corte Madera Canyon. The Tamalpais Land and Water Co. put in $20,000, and Cushing, who subscribed $25,000, became president of the corporation.

Each of these backers had a substantial financial interest in the success of the proposed railway. The Tamalpais Land and Water Co. owned large sections of Mill Valley, which they had acquired from the Throckmorton estate, and development was just beginning. Albert Kent owned nearly 1,000 acres of Kentfield, as well as a large section of the Mountain itself. Both figured that land values would rise after the railroad went in. At his death in 1901, Albert Kent's estate was appraised at $1,256,000, tax free at that time. Much of his property was inherited by his son William.

Sidney Cushing owned the Blithedale Hotel, which was near the proposed right of way and stood to gain patronage. Indeed, the ceremonial opening of the railroad, on August 26, 1896, attended by 75 newspapermen from San Francisco and by important dignitaries, was held at Cushing's hotel. In view of his later prominence as a leading conservationist, whose donations of land were crucial to the preservation of the Mountain for public use, it is interesting that William Kent's motives may have been partly commercial. Of course, the conservationist movement was then scarcely underway. Yosemite National Park was not established until 1890. Kent himself did not become a conservationist until some ten years later, and the movement did not affect Mt. Tamalpais in any way until around 1912. As Ted Wurm, author of *The Crookedest Railroad in the World,* says, the railroad was the product of "men

of imagination in a time of speculation and expansion."

During its construction, the railway ran into difficulties, both with the construction crew and with Mill Valley residents. Some workers walked off the job, complaining of overwork and poor food. They were being paid $1.75 a day for ten hours, had to pay $5.25 a week for board, and had to do their shopping at the company store, since nothing else was available in the small community of Mill Valley. Their action had a good deal of public support because railroads at that time were not in very good repute.

A good many people in Mill Valley bought $100 shares in the railroad, but some opposed it vigorously, principally those whose land would be encroached upon by the right of way along Corte Madera Creek. The most vociferous opponent was J. H. McInnes, one of the wealthiest men in the valley. He stopped work at the edge of his property by threatening the construction men with a six-shooter, and his wife personally overturned a six-team plow that was about to dig into their driveway. Other landowners were upset over the prospect of noisy steam locomotives ruining the peace of the valley. Meetings were held, the Mill Valley Property Owners' Association was formed, suits were filed and injunctions issued. Mrs. James ("Dolly") Jenkins, daughter of Sidney Cushing, related in her oral history: "When the mountain train went up the canyon it would hit a certain point and my house would shake like an earthquake."

After prolonged legal wrangling, the court decided in favor of the railway. Meanwhile, McInnes had become a convert, having sold two corner lots to the company, plus a right-of-way through some of his property. He had even become an owner of the railroad by taking part payment in stock.

Perhaps to mollify this early opposition, the railroad instituted another service in 1905 which proved very popular. During commute hours a local train shuttled more than a mile up and down the canyon of Corte Madera Creek between Lee Street and the depot downtown, where it connected with trains for Sausalito and the ferries. It was known fondly by Mill Valley residents as "the Lee Street local," "the little train," or the "Dinky." The 5 cent fare no doubt contributed to its popularity.

A "place in the sun" on the summit of Tamalpais reveals a map of marvelous beauty beside the Golden Gate. Uncle Sam says there's more sunshine per day on Tamalpais than at any other recording station in the United States—seventy-six per cent being the mean for the past two years.

A "place in the shade" of Muir Woods' magnificent sequoias is one without a peer in the world.

Air-line distances from the summit of Mt. Tamalpais:

	Miles		Miles
San Francisco	12	Mare Island	21
Cliff House	11	Mt. St. Helena	50
Twin Peaks	14	Sacramento	73
City Hall, Oakland	19	Mt. Lassen	183
The Campanile, U.C.	18	Mt. Shasta	237
Winehaven	10	Mt. Hamilton	66
Mt. Diablo	37	Farallone Islands	28

©1917 BY MT. TAMALPAIS & MUIR WOODS R.R.

Here is a map of the Pacific Coast in the vicinity of San Francisco and embracing a view of the Bay Country as seen

This map, published by the Mountain Railway in 1917, extolls the views from the Mountain in extravagant terms.

Tamalpais. There is more geography in evidence from this particular vantage point than anywhere else in the world

The brochure doesn't actually say that one can see Mt. Shasta or the erupting Mt. Lassen. (Courtesy of Ann Astill)

Top: Engine #7 emerges from the arch at the tavern in a picture taken by Mabel Fuller around 1900. (Courtesy of Joseph A. Baird Jr.) Below: Ladies in resplendent hats take the air on the Tavern porch. (Courtesy of the Mill Valley Library)

But most commuters walked to and from the Sausalito train on narrow boardwalks alongside the dirt roads. In winter, since they came and went in the dark, they carried candle lanterns, hanging them on their designated pegs in the railway station in the morning and picking them up in the evening for the walk up the hill.

The First Train

The first passenger train went up the Mountain on August 22, 1896, only six months after work had commenced in February. This was a remarkably speedy achievement, especially considering that there were no bulldozers or other power equipment. The cost, too, by present-day standards, was minuscule: $55,000 for building the track and $80,000 for the equipment.

The fare was originally $1.40 for the round trip from San Francisco, including ferry to Sausalito and train to Mill Valley, but was later increased. One brochure, later but undated, gives the fare as $1.90, and another, also undated, quotes it up to $3.69, but this latter probably included the round trip down to Muir Woods, on the spur added in 1907. Even though these prices to us seem low, they were an effective discouragement to most hikers; patrons were mainly out-of-town tourists.

The railroad was of sufficient technical interest at the time of its opening for the *Scientific American* to run a photo-spread, with pictures of one of the geared locomotives, of the Bow Knot, and of a typical curve and trestle. For San Franciscans, it is of special interest that the first car was a converted cable car. In its handbills the railroad claimed that "trains run every day of the year," but they probably had to close down during the winter months. The number of scheduled trains was reduced after 1917 because auto competition was reducing the number of riders.

Accidents were very infrequent, though safety provisions were reportedly inadequate. Two fatalities occurred: Chester Thomas, an engineer, died of severe burns after his engine overturned coming down the Mountain in 1900; and General H. Warfield, lessee and manager of the Mt. Tamalpais Tavern, was killed in a head-on collision with the Lee Street local in 1906.

In his oral history, William Provines, who worked as a brakeman and in other capacities for some years, tells us what the railroad workers were paid for the years 1925-1929. He says that engineers were paid $5 a day; conductors, $4; firemen, $3.75; brakemen, $3.50; and gravitymen, $3. The less skilled jobs were popular for college students during summer vacations. A gravityman handled the brake on the popular gravity cars that were introduced when an extension was opened in 1907 to Muir Woods.

This extension, suggested by Kent, sparked a big increase in the railroad's patronage. A new company was formed, the Mt. Tamalpais and Muir Woods Railway, and proved an immediate success. The most common trip was to ride up from Mill Valley to the Tavern for lunch, then coast down the six or seven miles by gravity car (no locomotive) to Muir Woods, and then go back to Mill Valley by way of Mesa Junction. The ride in the gravity car was not as fast as a roller coaster, but nevertheless provided a genuine thrill as it twisted around the many curves.

Subsequently, gravity cars were also used on the trip down to Mill Valley. One old-time Mill Valley resident tells of coming down by gravity car: "What a thrill that was, what a thrill!" The rulebook specified a maximum speed of 12 miles per hour but at some straight stretches they ran faster. Another long-time resident of Mill Valley recalls that as a teenager he and his friends on more than one occasion chartered a locomotive and a car to ride up to dances at the Tavern. They returned by gravity car, and sometimes were allowed to act as gravitymen.

He and his group appear to have been well-behaved, but the trains provided irresistible opportunities for pranks by many of the young fry. Men who grew up in Mill Valley recall that in the early days of the train, when there were a number of trestles over canyons, some of the boys would climb under the trestle and hang on the ties when they knew a train was coming. As the train approached, with a row of unsuspecting riders in the front seats (the locomotive was almost always in the rear), the boys would pull themselves up so their faces could be seen from the train. This, of course, caused a sensation, but the only retaliation by the train crews was sometimes to dump sand on the pranksters. The sand, of course, was carried to promote traction on the way up. Maybe the boys' game was one reason the railroad later eliminated most of the trestles by filling in the canyons.

The Tavern

Unlike the early climbers who reached the summit complaining bitterly and in vain about their thirst, riders on the Scenic Railway found refreshments at the Tavern near the top of East Peak. Built at the same time as the railroad itself, the Tavern served meals and provided sleeping accommodations. The typical tourist rode up in the morning, had lunch at the Tavern, and then either returned to Mill Valley or, after 1907, made the round-trip excursion to Muir Woods. In summer many people stayed overnight at the Tavern or lingered to sample the dinners; the most expensive item on the menu was filet mignon with mushrooms, for $1.35.

The Tavern had two encounters with fires. It was damaged in the big forest fire of 1913, and then, ten years later, burned to the ground in a fire that started inside, presumably in the kitchen. Melanie Kliewe, who worked for some years at the railroad's West Point Inn, tells in her oral history that at the time of the 1923 fire the chef was roasting chickens. He rescued them along with himself and after the fire was out the weary fire fighters enjoyed a freshly roasted chicken.

The Tavern was rebuilt, in a different architectural style, and saw its liveliest period during Prohibition in the 1920s. Its relative inaccessibility made it a popular spot for dining, dancing, and sipping the illegal products which came at night into Marin's west coast ports from ships docked outside the three-mile limit. Revelers, bringing their own hooch, would ride up on the train for the evening. The descent, late at night by gravity car, must have been exhilarating. New Year's Eve parties were especially memorable.

The rebuilt Tavern survived the dreadful 1929 fire and outlasted the railroad itself. The cuisine became limited to short orders, with beer and wine but no hard liquor. Postcards, souvenirs, candies and cigars continued to be sold in the lobby. In 1942 the Tavern, by this time owned by the Marin Municipal Water District, was leased to the U. S. Army for use as a barracks. The Army left the building a shambles, and by 1950 it had fallen into such extreme disrepair owing to vandalism and more natural causes that the Water District burned it down. The foundation can still be seen and will be preserved. ·

The Muir Woods Terminal

As part of the planning at the time of the railroad's extension to Muir Woods, William Kent proposed to build a "fine, modern" hotel which he would rent to the railroad for twenty years. He also proposed to allow the railroad full use of his 600 acres for a period of five years, after which he anticipated using portions to the north and east for subdivisions. This was land which, in 1908, he deeded to the federal government for Muir Woods National Monument. Kent was also to receive ten percent of the fares generated by the extension, for a limited period.

But this arrangement never came to fruition; plans were changed because of the opening of the Monument. Instead, Kent sold the railroad 192 acres on which it built its own hotel, the Muir Woods Inn, opened in June 1907. It was located close to where Alice Eastwood Camp is now, a good mile from Park headquarters. The access road to the park was extended up the canyon to the inn. This building burned down in 1913, but was replaced the next year at a site considerably further downstream, with the railroad extended to that point. The 1929 fire ended the railroad's operations in Muir Woods and in 1931 the railway property (50 acres) was added to the Monument. The inn was torn down in 1932.

West Point Inn

Another inn, the West Point Inn, was built by the railroad in 1904 at the point where the train reached the westernmost point in its gyrations, hence its name. The building is still standing but has gone through many changes. Henry Masjon (or Masyon) was the first innkeeper. Then, in 1919, it was leased to Mr. and Mrs. Kliewe. Mrs. Kliewe says they were very busy weekends with hikers, while most of the railroad passengers stayed up at the Tavern. At that time the inn had six sleeping rooms and four cottages, two of them dormitories, one for "boys" and one for "girls," each with eight bunks. The cottages were often filled by boys or girls from the Sierra Club or the California Alpine Club. Rooms rented for $1 a night, less for bunks; dinner was $1.25, breakfast, 75 cents. Supplies were brought up by the railroad, except on winter days when the train was not running; then Mr. Kliewe would ride horseback down

Top left: West Point Inn shortly after its completion, 1904. Top right: Muir Woods Inn, built in 1913, is shown here in the 1920s. (Courtesy of Nancy Skinner) Left: A postcard depicts the first flight over the Mountain, by Weldon Cooke in 1911, only seven years after Kitty Hawk. The flight was actual, but the plane is almost certainly drawn into this photo, since no camera could have stopped a plane in flight in 1911. (Courtesy of Charmaine Burdell and Louise Teather) Below: After a fire in 1923 the Tavern was rebuilt in the newest "Spanish" design. It was a very lively spot during Prohibition because federal agents could hardly make surprise visits. Trashed by the army during WWII, it was burned by the fire department in 1950. (Courtesy of Nancy Skinner).

Carpenters who built the original Tavern of Tamalpais pose on the steps in 1896.
(Courtesy of the Mill Valley Library)

the right of way to Mill Valley. Mrs. Kliewe says that in the big snowstorm of January, 1922, four feet of snow fell at the inn. This might seem exaggerated, but other accounts of the snow that year are consistent with it.

The West Point Inn continued to operate after the railroad stopped running in 1930. As of 1937 it was reported that the inn was open the year round, with sleeping accommodations, hot meals "and the usual service of a rustic hotel." At that time, the charge for dinner, room and breakfast was $2.50, dinner, $1 and breakfast, 50 cents. The innkeeper then was Johann E. Knecht, a naturalized German, who served in that capacity from 1932 to 1939. During that period, registers of guests were maintained, one of which may be seen at the Marin County Historical Society. Unlike the East Peak registers of the 1880s, these contain no comments or drawings, just signatures and addresses. For a number of these years the cast of the Mountain Plays stayed at the inn for the week preceding the play, walking the mile or so to the Theatre each day for rehearsals. Visitors who signed the register came from most of the states of the United States, from the territories of Alaska and Hawaii and, among other countries, from Austria, Belgium, Canada, China, Denmark, England, Germany, Greece, Holland, India, Ireland, Italy, Norway, Poland, South Africa, Sweden and Switzerland. The crew of a round-the-world yacht from Kiel were also there and, among dignitaries, H.I.H. Prince Phillip of Saxe-Coburg and Gotha.

Knecht was followed as innkeeper by the Deans, who gave it up in 1943 because patronage had fallen off as a result of the war and because the Marin Municipal Water District, which now owned it, was planning to burn it as a fire hazard. But, at this point, to keep it available for hikers, the Tamalpais Conservation Club organized the West Point Club and sold $10 memberships to join, with annual dues at $4 single and $7 for a couple. The club leased the inn from the Water District. As of January 1951, TCC reported a club membership of 187. The inn is now operated by the West Point Inn Association and is no longer connected with the TCC.

For a time in the 1960s and 1970s, the Club was quite exclusive; only members could use the overnight accommodations, though lemonade was served to hikers during the day. In 1977, the Water District made it a condition of a new lease that mem-

berships be open to anyone on a reasonable basis; that there be public access to the grounds, the porch, and the main room from 9 a.m. to 6 p.m.; and that sleeping accommodations be made available to nonmembers.

The Road to Stinson Beach

The purpose of the inn, when built by the railroad in 1904, was to serve clients who rode up from Mill Valley and wanted to transfer to the stage that went down daily from West Point to the Dipsea Inn at Willow Camp (later Stinson Beach). The stage, drawn by four or six horses, went down from West Point in the morning and came back in the afternoon, and was run by Mr. Nunes, who owned a dairy farm between Stinson Beach and Pantoll.

The stage road had been built in 1902, by Charles Dowd of Mill Valley, for more elegant purposes. William Kent and his friend Sidney Cushing, president of the railroad, had conceived an ambitious plan to extend the railroad down Steep Ravine to Stinson Beach, across to Bolinas on a drawbridge, and on up to Olema. In anticipation, Kent, always the enterpriser in those days, had purchased practically the whole Stinson Beach sandspit and all the land in Steep Ravine necessary for the right of way. As Jack Mason says, "It was possible now to walk from Kentfield to the ocean without leaving Kent Property." Kent gave Cushing half the sandspit and sold ten acres near its midpoint to William Newman, who used the land to build the Dipsea Inn in 1904. But their plans were stymied by the 1906 earthquake and by suits over title to the Stinson Beach properties; finally the whole railroad extension project was permanently derailed.

This was not the only plan that failed. In 1910, the Muir Woods and Lagoon Electric Railroad was formed to run a line from the Locust station (in Mill Valley) on the Northwestern Pacific to Muir Woods, then on to Big Lagoon (Muir Beach) and terminating at Willow Camp. D. C. Braid, the organizing director, had lyrical expectations of the many people who would ride the railway and enjoy the scenery. The idea was to connect at Stinson Beach with Kent's railway, though by this time the Kent-Cushing plans had collapsed.

A particularly charming account of impressions

Top: Passengers boarded the open cars at Mill Valley depot, shown here after 1913. From the top they could ride down to Muir Woods in a gravity car, a trip which must have been one of the greatest thrills available for travelers anywhere. This group was a special party from Chicago & Northwestern Railroad; their sedate expressions suggest they don't realize what is in store. The young brakeman looks confident. (Courtesy of Nancy Skinner)

Coasting down the mountain to Muir Woods in a gravity car is a safe and frolicsome adventure.

Muir Woods—A National Monument
The gem of America's National Parks

Leaving the main line at the famous "Double Bow Knot," a branch road runs into the Muir Woods, and, crossing the face of the mountain to the southwest, passing through a deep cut, enters the east fork of Sequoia Canyon. By easy grades the railroad winds along the sides of the canyon, through groves of laurel, fir, oak, redwoods, madrone, and numerous other varieties of trees, terminating at Muir Inn overlooking the Muir Woods, a virgin forest of giant redwoods thousands of years old. Paths have been constructed into the heart of the canyon where the mammoth redwood trees rear their perpendicular trunks to a height of 200 to 300 feet. The journey through the forest is delightful. The roadway follows the mountain stream which flows through the canyon; the paths are carpeted with fallen leaves; the banks are one mass of ferns; and the soft air is impregnated with perfumes of the forest.

Above: A railway brochure from 1917 describes the gravity car ride as "a safe and frolicsome adventure." (Courtesy of Ann Astill) Right: The cover of an early brochure was based on a photograph but was considerably changed by an artist, who has the sun rising in a improbable place, and a woman who would have to be a giantess if proportion were exact, waving a handkerchief.

of trips by railroad from Mill Valley to the summit, down into Muir Woods, and by stage from West Point to Bolinas (crossing the lagoon by steam launch) is contained in Helen Bingham's book *In Tamal Land,* published in 1906. She writes in the fullblown style of the time:

> It requires many trips to fully appreciate and comprehend the marvelous diversity of views spread before one, while the variety of superb effects to be witnessed from this mountain cannot be found in a single visit. To watch the wonderful radiance of sunrise when Apollo mounts in his chariot of fire above the Berkeley hills, or to see a billowy floor of fog, outspread before one, obscuring the lower world and leaving naught save this mountain peak unwrapped by the fog-mantle; and then witness the pale light of the moon marking a silver pathway in the Bay, and casting grotesque shadows on the landscape, and these are but a few of the beauties garnered here.

Profits and Losses

In its heyday the railroad fully justified the hopes of its founders and backers; it was very profitable, "probably the biggest dividend paying road in the State," as one report proclaims. While enthusiastic accounts of the trip by the riders were the best advertisement, the railroad itself undertook a big promotional job with help from travel agencies catering to Bay Area visitors. As one of its publicity stunts, the railway sponsored the first over-flight of the mountain. The story was headlined in the *Mill Valley Record Enterprise* for December 11, 1911: "Fearless Aviator Circles Peak of Mt. Tamalpais." Weldon B. Cooke, an '07 University of California man, flew over the Mountain at a height of 3,000 feet in a Curtiss type biplane built in Pittsburg. The engine failed after he had made his circle, but he was able to land near the Locust Avenue station of the Northwestern Pacific.

Finally, after a prosperous lifetime of thirty-four years, the railroad was displaced by the auto, with the devastating fire of July 1929 administering the *coup de grace.* The fire destroyed one engine and miles of ties. While the damage was temporarily repaired, the railroad was finally abandoned in the summer of 1930.

What the present-day hiker sees of the old railway are the foundations of the Tavern, the concrete platform of the junction station at the Mesa, West Point Inn, and the right of way, now a dirt road except for a short paved section above Mill Valley where it becomes Fern Canyon Road. The old stage road still goes from West Point as far as Pantoll, but its lower portion, through Steep Ravine and on to Stinson Beach, leads down to Highway 1.

Despite the railroad's popularity in its time, it is almost inconceivable that public opinion today would permit it to be rebuilt. Indeed, there have been at least two proposals for commercial transport to the top of the mountain, both of which have been defeated by conservationists. The first plan was for an aerial tramway to go up from Baltimore Canyon to the Summit, with a possible extension to Muir Woods. Suggested in 1957, the plan survived a year and then died. The second proposal, originally made in 1965, was defeated in a campaign directed by the Marin Conservation League. The promoters' idea was to start at Mountain Home and run tracks up the old right of way to the top, where a lavish inn would be built. Three men were active in promoting the plans: Frank C. Allen, a San Anselmo swimming pool contractor, Chester F. Gilbert of Kent Woodlands, a retired credit company executive, and Andrew Gladney of Kentfield, a railroad construction engineer. The developers were quoted as saying that their railroad would be a "restoration of something that was a colorful part of Marin County's history."

The Conservation League, for its part, feared that the door would be opened to commercial exploitation of the mountain. Even though the old Scenic Railway was popular in its day and older people look back upon it with nostalgia, times have changed. Not only has the conservation movement grown, but competition by autos would probably make any such plan as unprofitable as the Scenic Railway became in its later years. Some argue, however, that many people would park their cars at Mountain Home and ride the train, rather than drive all the way to the summit.

Above are two halves of a panoramic photograph taken at the double bow knot in 1915. The right half (top) and the left half overlap slightly; the woman in a light-colored, two-tiered costume and hat appears in both halves. (Courtesy of the Bancroft Library)

Top: The San Francisco Sightseeing Company began carrying passengers up the Mountain in the early 1920's, in buses equipped with solid rubber tires, leaf springs, and radiators elaborately designed to prevent overheating. (Courtesy of the Mill Valley Library) Below left: A view of the Tavern, the dance pavilion, and the weather station from the summit in 1904. Right: Almost the same view in the late 1920s. The Tavern has been rebuilt after the fire, and a parking lot, still in use today, has replaced the other buildings. The triumph of the automobile is complete, and the railway is in its last days. (Courtesy of Nancy Skinner)

CHAPTER NOTES

The Crookedest Railroad in the World, by Theodore G. Wurm and Alvin C. Graves, is far and away the best single source about the railroad. Originally published in 1954 by Howell-North, Berkeley, it has been republished in several editions, the latest revised and enlarged, published in 1983 by Trans-Anglo Books, Glendale.

Again, the oral histories supply some interesting accounts.

Two of Jack Mason's books, *The Making of Marin* and *Last Stage to Bolinas,* contain useful information and are readily available.

Anna Coxe Toogood, in her unpublished Historic Resource Study, prepared for the Golden Gate National Recreation Area, entitled *A Civil History of Golden Gate National Recreation Agency and Point Reyes National Seashore, California,* Vol. I, pp. 22-23, has a brief account of the railroad.

158

A record snowfall in January, 1922, provided a field day for photographers. The Mountain already had served for decades as a weather observation point. (Courtesy of Nancy Skinner)

CHAPTER ELEVEN

The Many Uses of Three Peaks

For well over a century the peaks of Mt. Tamalpais have been crowned, or as some would say, desecrated, by structures of many different sizes and shapes serving a great variety of uses. Because the Tamalpais range overlooks the Pacific and the Golden Gate, military authorities have built fortifications, including the radar station still lingering on West Peak, and during World War II occupied large areas, shutting them off from civilian use. Because the Mountain stands alone and overlooks a large area, it has provided fire spotting protection, has been used to report incoming ships, has served as a triangulation base for making maps, and has been very useful for weather prediction. Private agencies, too, have found the Mountain useful, especially for telecommunication.

West Peak

Of the three, West Peak was the one most used in the old days, for two reasons: until 1951, when the Air Force built the radar station there, it was the highest of the three peaks at 2604 feet; it was then bulldozed down to 2560 feet, below East Peak's elevation of 2571 feet. Also, until there were roads on the mountain, West Peak was the most accessible for hikers or for pack animals bringing supplies and equipment.

The U. S. Coast Survey, directed by George Davidson, used West Peak as a triangulation point in the 1850s, but there is no record of whether any buildings were erected for the surveyors' use. W. H. Brewer, who climbed the Mountain in 1862, refers to a Coast Survey Station, but details are lacking. Brewer's own agency, the California Geological Survey, used West Peak as a surveying point.

Two decades later, the *Marin Journal* for June 26, 1881, reported that the Coast Survey was soon to rendezvous on the "highest point" of the Mountain, and that lumber had gone up the day before for a building. Whatever structure had been there earlier must have been abandoned by this time.

In its issue of January 3, 1884, the *Marin Journal* said that Professor Davidson of the Coast Survey had recommended that the government erect a signal station on West Peak "for the protection of travel and commerce of the port of San Francisco." Davidson explained that this was not only the greatest altitude with the best outlook for commanding the approaches to the Golden Gate, but that being above the fog line it gave the observer every opportunity to observe the fog's formation and dissipation, as well as to check on the condition of the bar. (This was before the semi-circular bar outside

A stagecoach, complete with rolled canvas curtains, carried passengers from West Point, on the Mt. Tamalpais Railway, to Willow Camp (Stinson Beach) and McKennan's dock on Bolinas Lagoon, where they could take a launch to Bolinas. This was the most expeditious way to get to Stinson and Bolinas; the trip from San Francisco took between four and five hours. Round trip fare on the stagecoach was $1.75. West Point Inn is visible on the middle ridge, and the Tavern barely visible at the peak, in this 1906 photograph. (Courtesy of Charles Ford)

the Golden Gate was regularly dredged and buoyed for navigational purposes.)

From the earliest years of hiking in the 1880s until the military closed the higher parts of the Mountain at the outset of World War II, the West Peak was used by hikers perhaps even more than the East Peak. There is an unconfirmed report that a register was maintained on the West Peak in the 1870s even before those on the East Peak. But we know for certain that the California Alpine Club placed visitor registers there beginning in 1918, using a small stone stand to facilitate signing. However, only one of these books, for the years 1936 to 1938, has been found.

Right after the end of World War I, members of the club built a substantial stone monument on West Peak as a memorial to its 74 members who had seen service in the war. None of the men had been killed in action, though 36 percent of the club's membership had been in uniform. The plaque read: "Erected by the California Alpine Club and Dedicated to Those Members Who Gave Their Service to Our Country During the Great War—A.D. 1919."

World War II brought to a halt most of the usual activities on the Mountain. In July 1941, even before Pearl Harbor, the Army Corps of Engineers sought permission from the Water District for the Air Corps Warning Service to use a portion of West Peak as a detector site. Then, that November, the Army requested two sites, one for equipment and another for a camp. They selected Rock Spring as the camp site but, on being informed that this was extensively used by hikers, settled for a site near their equipment site. Both areas were fenced off. When the war came, the Army quickly occupied some areas and closed a large section at the top of the Mountain.

The prohibited areas were leased to the government by the Water District. One of the leases, consisting of 49 acres along Ridgecrest Boulevard from Rock Spring to the road to Laurel Dell, was designated Radar Site B78 and was manned by the 411 AAF Base Unit. A second lease was for an area on top of West Peak, including the Mountain Theatre, for another radar site and barracks. On the East Peak, a third lease turned over the old unused railroad tavern to serve as a barracks for a communications group. The lease included the restaurant equipment, pump, water, etc., for $60 per month.

Still a fourth lease, signed early in 1943, covered four acres for another radar installation near the old CCC Camp on the road into Lake Lagunitas. This area had been occupied during 1942 by the California State Guard which had been called in to protect the lakes. In 1945, the area was again taken over by the Army, even though the lease had expired the year before.

The Army also maintained a rifle range below Rock Spring, and was granted occasional use of watershed lands for map reading, maneuvers, night problems, etc., always with the understanding that care would be taken to protect the watershed. But one investigation of a small fire revealed that the Army had been using machine guns and bazookas in some of their exercises. The District protested that such use had not been authorized.

As a result of the Army's occupation of large portions of the Mountain, hiking was necessarily curtailed. Most of the popular hiking areas were officially closed, including Rock Spring, Barth's Retreat, Potrero Meadows, Rifle Camp, Colier Spring, Mountain Theatre and Bootjack Camp. Nevertheless, hikers continued to roam the rest of the Mountain and were often permitted into the closed areas, as the Army's guards became acquainted with the regular hikers. The atmosphere was apparently quite relaxed.

The worst air disaster in the Mountain's history occurred in November 1944, when a Navy PB4M, heading for Honolulu from Treasure Island in the fog, crashed into the East Peak below the tavern and near the Telephone Trail. Eight men were killed. A special trail had to be cut in order to remove the bodies.

Another crash occurred in 1945, shortly after the war ended, when two army planes collided over the Rock Spring area. Both pilots parachuted to safety. Today's hikers can see one engine still lodged in Cataract Creek between Rock Spring and Laurel Dell; what is left of the fuselage lies a quarter mile up on the hill above.

When the war ended, most people assumed that the Army, whose leases were for the duration, would relinquish its control, and restrictions would end. But President Truman delayed a declaration that the emergency had ended, and the TCC and the hiking organizations had to mount a campaign to end restrictions. While in practice these were no longer

Hiking was more than just an arduous pursuit for members of the Touristen Verein—Naturfreunde, *who liked to carry their music with them. Ben Schmidt, the boy standing by the donkey, is just to the right of the accordionist in the top picture, taken in the early 1920s. (Courtesy of Ben Schmidt)*

seriously enforced, the Army continued to assert its jurisdiction.

In 1948, the Army notified the Water District of plans for a permanent radar station on the West Peak as part of the SAGE network under the Air Defense Command. The District was reluctant to grant a lease, in part to protect the radio lessees on Middle Peak from electronic interference and also because there was no guarantee that the Army would remove its structures when the lease terminated (a concern that later proved sound). Eventually, however, a lease was signed for about 82 acres for $4,400 per year.

The radar station, operated by the Mill Valley Air Force Station, was built and occupied in 1951. As of 1976, it housed units of the 14th Missile Warning Squadron, based in Arizona, and was linked to two other coastal radar surveillance units, at Point Arena and at Almaden, near San Jose. Its primary mission was to track missile launches from air, land and sea. It had quarters for 80, including nine families.

For the most part the radar station site, with its high chain link fence, was off limits to hikers. When the station was built in 1951, the two connecting trails over the ridge, the Eastwood trail from West Point to the top, and the Arturo trail down on the north side to Rifle Camp, were blocked off by the fence. Not until 1983 did the Air Force conclude that the radar station had become obsolete, though the domes have been retained for use by the Federal Aviation Agency. The bulk of the property, however, declared surplus by the military, was taken over by Golden Gate National Recreation Area. The military refused to honor its obligation to remove its buildings, claiming that the money to do so was needed elsewhere.

The GGNRA, after extensive consultation with all interested parties, and under heavy pressure by most segments of Marin County, announced in 1985 its decision to tear down all the old barracks and other buildings with the intent of returning the area insofar as possible to its natural state. As a first step, in response to a request from the Tamalpais History Project, GGNRA has built a small section of trail through its property to reconnect the Arturo and Eastwood trails, and has cut an opening in the fence. West Peak is gradually being restored to hikers. The plan, so far as it is known in 1986, is to use the California Youth Corps to tear down the buildings,

using one temporarily as their barracks. The major demolition has not yet begun (1986), but a few buildings have been torn down by volunteers.

East Peak

The East Peak, as we have seen earlier, was used by many hikers in the 1880s, and was the mecca for thousands of tourists who rode up on the train. But it has had other distinctions. Two years after the railroad arrived at the summit, a weather station was built just west of the Tavern. When it was officially opened on September 21, 1898, W. H. Hammond, forecaster for the United States Weather Bureau, anticipated that the station would be of great value:

It will be of the greatest importance, not only to this Coast of the U. S., but (to) meteorologists throughout the world as a valuable observation point, and the results we shall obtain from it will greatly enhance the efficiency and change the policy of our bureau. I have gathered more valuable information during a stay of one month on Mt. Tamalpais than I have ever acquired during the same period of my life. . . . Mt. Tamalpais is different (from the other two "elevated" stations, on Pike's Peak and Mt. Washington, both of which had to be abandoned on account of inaccessibility). It occupies a very unique position . . . . an isolated peak, directly over the ocean. I have no doubt it will furnish the best observing point on the whole coast.

Dr. Marsden Manson, writing in *Popular Science Monthly* (May 1900), listed the special advantages of the weather station:

1. It is close to the coast line, and is so elevated that it is not seriously affected by the local indraught of air through the Golden Gate.

2. No station in the United States has so full and free a projection into the lower third of the vapor-bearing stratum.

3. In studying the phenomena connected with the occurrence of fog, this station furnished highly valuable data that could be obtained from no other.

4. (In the study of) the physics of the atmosphere, Mount Tamalpais is of further importance, as it stands near the easterly limits of the great area of high pressure which, during the

summer, lies over the North Pacific and which dominates the climatic phenomena of California for the greater portion of the year.

Satellites have long since blown away these advantages, along with Dr. Manson's ponderous sentence structure.

Official records were kept from 1898 through May 1921, when the station was closed for lack of funds. By this time, the building was so ramshackle that it had become an eyesore and worthless for its purpose. However, some records apparently continued to be kept, because daily predictions of Mt. Tamalpais weather continued to be published on the front pages of San Francisco newspapers through 1922.

The station reported a wind velocity of 94 m.p.h. in April 1920; a brilliant aurora borealis on May 14, 1922; and a low temperature of 19 degrees on January 19, 1922, the year of the big snow storm.

A different kind of record was made in 1908 when Mrs. Ray C. Fisher gave birth to an eleven-pound baby at the weather station, the first baby born on the Mountain. Mrs. Fisher lived at the station all year round to keep her husband company.

In 1924, the San Francisco Chamber of Commerce urged Congress to appropriate $25,000 to re-establish the weather station. The next year, officials of the Mt. Tamalpais and Muir Woods Railway announced that construction would start soon on a "$10,000 home for the U. S. Weather Station," to include quarters for railway officials and trainmen.

Overlapping with the weather station was the marine observatory erected by the San Francisco *Examiner* in 1901 on the very top of the peak. Its purpose of sighting and reporting incoming ships was rendered obsolete by ship-to-shore wireless communication in 1919. On May 1, 1921, the Tamalpais Fire District took it over as a fire lookout station.

Middle Peak

At what must have been enormous expense, two 300-foot wooden towers were erected on Middle Peak by the Pacific Wireless Telegraph Company in 1905, just four years after Marconi had sent his first transatlantic message. A lease from the Water District for a circular piece of land 1,200 feet in diameter was signed by Charles Watt Howard, the O. L. Shafter Estate, and Leland Stanford University. The towers were intended to communicate with Hawaii and possibly Japan, but it is not clear that they were ever used successfully.

The towers were built in Oakland, disassembled and erected on the site. The materials were brought up the Mountain by the Mt. Tamalpais Railroad to the gap between Middle and East Peaks. From there they were taken to Middle Peak by a funicular constructed for the purpose. The towers were built of oak and fir, the only metal being the bolts and braces. They were reputed to be "the highest in the world," as a postcard of the time proclaimed. A big wind blew the towers down on December 10, 1906, and they were not replaced. Only the two concrete platforms and a tangle of wire were left.

Thereafter Middle Peak was untenanted for many years. In the 1940s, Fox-West Coast signed a thirty-year lease for two acres for a TV station, and Don Lee Radio Broadcasting was negotiating for another, but nothing came of it. The Water District foresaw the coming age of television and planned to reserve East Peak for future TV installations. Fortunately these were never built.

In 1954 the Civil Aeronautics Administration leased space for a transmitter, remotely controlled from the Oakland Airport. And the Water District has since granted leases to several government and private companies for micowave transmission: Federal Aviation Agency, Pacific Gas and Electric Company, U. S. Department of Justice, Roman Catholic Welfare Corporation, County of Marin and Golden Gate Bridge Highway and Transportation District.

Early in 1979, the Water District concluded that the array of radio towers, albeit much smaller than the early wireless towers, were responsible for "visual degradation" which had reached a "point that the community is asking for solutions." In response, the district's board of directors decided to build a single new communications facility, which was opened in 1981; it has indeed improved the looks of the Middle Peak. But a new source of "physical degradation" has appeared in the form of sizable "dishes" which now fringe the area at the top.

The Water District's worry over the "visual impact" of the structures on the Middle Peak, and the GGNRA's decision to tear down the eyesore barracks on West Peak, reflect the growing public concern over the looks of the Mountain. Yet the issues are still not finally settled. In late 1986 new proposals were being advanced for the construction of broadcasting towers on the Mountain.

CHAPTER NOTES

Much of the material for this chapter is from MMWD records which are not readily available. Worth looking at, however, are:

Old Marin With Love, Marin County American Revolution Bicentennial Commission, 1976.

Mt. Tamalpais State Park, *General Plan.*

Tom Killion's handsome book of woodcuts, *Fortress Marin,* an interesting sidelight on military uses of the coastal fringes of the Mountain.

These preposterous wooden towers, three hundred feet high, were built in Oakland and assembled on Middle Peak in 1905, for radio communication with Hawaii and Japan. They blew down in December, 1906. In September 1986 the Army Corps of Engineers proposed to erect a 70-foot tower near the peak, on land leased from MMWD. The plan met opposition from many conservation groups, but the Corps of Engineers "is a long way from giving up," said the Chronicle.

A pathway through Muir Woods in the days before paving. (Courtesy of the Mill Valley Library)

CHAPTER TWELVE

Muir Woods National Monument

The ancient trees stand to support Heaven
Lest heaven should fall.
—Chiang Lee

Long before its establishment as a National Monument, Redwood (or Sequoia) Canyon had been an objective for hikers and horseback riders. Beginning in the 1870s or perhaps even earlier, they had climbed over the ridge from Mill Valley. Then as now, the canyon was a place of great beauty and majesty. Helen Bingham wrote in appreciation in 1906:

Bending low over the little stream . . . . huge sprays of azaleas filled the air with their delicate perfume; on the banks lacy wood warriors (woodwardia ferns) and the hardy sword ferns mingle in graceful profusion, while the flickering sunlight filtering aslant through the tree tops fell on the transparent hazel leaves, lending a soft, green glint to a neighboring pool.

The creation of Muir Woods National Monument in 1908 was the first step in making the whole of Mt. Tamalpais a public preserve. Subsequently, the Marin Municipal Water District (1912), the Mt. Tamalpais State Park (1927-30) and, most recently, Marin County Open Space District (1972), have vastly increased the protected area. Together they comprise some 40 square miles.

The casual hiker, who begins his walk in Muir Woods, climbs the Ben Johnson and Staplevelt Trails to Pantoll, circles around the southern face of the Mountain on the Matt Davis Trail, drops down to the Mountain Home Inn and so back to Muir Woods, is unaware that he has gone through three separate public jurisdictions.

Redwood Canyon, before it became Muir Woods, had been acquired by the Tamalpais Land and Water Company from Samuel Throckmorton. They planned to develop it as a water supply, but before launching that venture leased the Canyon to the Tamalpais Sportsmen's Club, a very exclusive hunting club.

According to Ida Johnson Allen's oral history, the club's members dammed Redwood Creek to make a big pond where they fished for trout, steelhead and salmon. They also hunted deer "all the way to Stinson Beach." Redwood Creek is still noted for its winter run of steelhead coming up to spawn.

Ida Allen is Ben Johnson's daughter. She reports that Ben, who built and gave his name to the Ben Johnson trail, had worked as superintendent of Samuel Throckmorton's dairy ranches, but became gamekeeper of the Sportsman's Club in the 1890s. He lived in what is now known as the Ben Johnson cabin(demolished in 1928; sometimes mistakenly called the John Muir cabin.) near the confluence of Redwood and Fern Creeks, an area reputed to have been an Indian campground.

The Ben Johnson Trail climbs up from this point

Above: The largest redwood in Muir Woods in the 1950s. (Courtesy of the Mill Valley Library) Right: William Kent in 1913. Kent's gift of Muir Woods to the federal government in 1908 was only one of his many gifts of land for public use on the Mountain. (Courtesy of Nancy Skinner)

and comes out in the grassy area near what was then the Lone Tree trail, now the Dipsea. It was probably built to provide members of the Sportsman's Club a direct route from Redwood Canyon to Stinson Beach.

After William Kent purchased the land in 1903, Johnson worked for him as caretaker and ranger. He died in 1906, his death perhaps hastened by his problems as caretaker. His daughter says: "People used to get in there on Saturday nights and they'd raise Cain. So he'd be up all night, on horseback, watching crowds of people to see they didn't tear things down."

The Ben Johnson cabin was actually built by Jonathan Bickerstaff in 1884 or 1886, according to an oral history by a Bickerstaff descendant. Bickerstaff trapped coyotes, bobcats, skunks and raccoons and sold their skins, some of them to Liebes department store. He got $3.00 for a skunk skin and $8.00 for a good coon skin. He had the distinction of catching the last black bear caught in Marin County.

After World War I, Bickerstaff's son, Joe, built and operated "Joe's Place," a popular convivial gathering spot where hikers and patrons of the railway danced and bought refreshments. Located on the road close to the entrance to the Monument, it was a familiar landmark for forty years. Joe served hamburgers, hotdogs, coffee and lemonade. His son, Thomas A. Bickerstaff, lets us into one of the secrets of the lemonade: "He'd buy a case of lemons, and the rinds would stay in the same batch all day. He'd just add a little more water and sugar—15 cents a glass! He made good there!" Since these were prohibition days, more may have been served than lemonade. The place is said to have had a racy reputation, and is remembered fondly by old-time hikers.

On September 3, 1892, the Bohemian Club had its summer encampment, "High Jinks," in an area of Muir Woods which is now labeled Bohemian Grove. They decided against purchasing the tract for $15,000, saying the nights were "cold enough to freeze the male evidence off a brass monkey." The Bohemian Club erected a massive statue of the Buddha which later had to be torn down. The club later bought property on the Russian River, where the nights are warmer.

The only road into the canyon in these early days was over the ridge from Mill Valley, along much the same route followed by the present road. Harold French, an inveterate hiker writing in 1904, described the winding wagon road:

> It ascends a densely wooded north slope, emerges on a grassy divide and undulates downward around many a wooded tributary and jutting point. Only one house is visible in four miles. . . . the lodge of Ranger Johnson, warden of Tamalpais Sportsman's Club preserves. . . . The wagon road now becomes a bridle path. . . . this in turn becomes a foot trail. . . . The footpath merges into an indistinct deer-trail which. . . . has an uncertain tendency to diminish to a squirrel track, which eventually runs up a tree.

Ten years later, in 1914, *Tamalpais Magazine* reported that a party drove over the road from Sausalito to Muir Woods in a Studebaker six, perhaps the first auto to negotiate the dirt road. The account adds that Kent (who had built or rebuilt the road) was being urged to secure an appropriation from Congress to improve it.

Though Muir Woods National Monument was not created until 1908, it was the culmination of a dream that goes back at least to 1902, when Morrison Pixley wrote:

> There is in Marin County, an opportunity for San Francisco to obtain a seaside park with giant redwoods and Mount Tamalpais in one enclosure and within an hour's travel time from the foot of Market St. . . . . . . A few thousand acres of this tract which is now being sold to Portuguese milkmen at milk ranch prices, would include, besides the peak of the mountain, several miles of sea coast, pleasantly varied with cliffs, sheltered sand coves and pebble strands, the big redwoods, and a salmon stream. The whole could be purchased for no more than some Californians have paid for a single horse.

The next year, on September 2, 1903, a meeting was held at the Lagunitas Country Club in Ross to consider a proposal for a 12,000 acre park to include Redwood Canyon. William Kent presided. Among those present were Gifford Pinchot, Chief U. S. Bureau of Forestry; Dr. C. Hart Merriam, Chief, U. S. Biological Survey; and David Starr Jordan, President of Stanford (The University owned a large area in the Carson watershed).

Although the plan failed, this meeting spurred William Kent's decision to purchase a portion of

Above: John Muir was photographed at Muir Woods with Mr. & Mrs. William Newton and children Mary and William on August 21, 1909. (Courtesy of Maribeth Patrick) Left: John Muir, William Kent, and J.H. Cutter, first president of the Tamalpais Conservation Club, in front of the Muir Woods Inn. (Courtesy of Lincoln Fairley)

Redwood Canyon the very next year. As Kent says, his friend Morrison Pixley "urged upon my attention the necessity of saving these trees. This must have been in 1890. I had never seen the Woods and had no idea of taking the matter up, although greatly interested in the general conservation of Tamalpais and its dedication as a public park." In the face of an immediate threat of logging, he was moved to act. His purchase made possible the creation of Muir Woods National Monument. Redwood Canyon, because of its isolation, had escaped the earlier logging on the Mountain. But new techniques and better transportation had now rendered the operation profitable.

Kent himself writes:

I got to thinking about it, and soon visited the property with Mr. S. B. Cushing, who had recently built the Mt. Tamalpais Railroad. The beauty of the place attracted me and got on my mind, and I could not forget the situation. Finally, I requested Mr. Cushing to get the lowest possible price from Mr. White, it being understood that the purchase was for preservation, and not for exploitation. He succeeded in obtaining a figure I could reach, $45,000.

Lovell White, president of the Tamalpais Land and Water Company, was offered $100,000 by someone else, "but knowing my intention of keeping it intact and desire to have it a national park, he let me have it." When Kent's wife Elizabeth, demurred at going further into debt, he silenced her by saying, "If we lost all the money we have and saved the trees it would be worthwhile, wouldn't it?"

Once Kent owned the land, it soon became clear that more action was needed to save the trees. In 1907 the North Coast Water Company, successor to the Tamalpais Land and Water Co., instituted condemnation proceedings, involving 47 of Kent's 611 acres, in order to construct a reservoir in Frank Valley which would have flooded Redwood Canyon. At the last minute, Kent's attention was called to the recently adopted Act for the Preservation of American Antiquities, under which private individuals could deed property to the federal government if it possessed historic or other great interest. He applied to Gifford Pinchot, then U. S. Forester, who took the matter up with President Theodore Roosevelt. Roosevelt agreed to accept the gift of 298 acres and formally created Muir Woods National Monument on January 9, 1908.

In an exchange of letters, Kent, James R. Garfield, Secretary of the Interior, and President Roosevelt agreed on the name to be given the Monument. Kent, sending Secretary Garfield the deed, wrote:

After having traveled over a large part of the open country in the United States, I consider this tract, with its beautiful trees, ferns, wildflowers and shrubs, as the most attractive bit of wilderness I have ever seen. In tendering it I request that it be known as Muir Woods, in honor of John Muir.

Roosevelt, after thanking him for "this singularly generous and public-spirited action," wrote, "I have every admiration for John Muir; but after all, my dear sir, this is your gift. . . . I should like to name the Monument the Kent Monument if you will permit it." Kent replied:

Your kind suggestion of a change of name is not one that I can accept. . . . I have five good husky boys that I am trying to bring up to a knowledge of democracy and to a realizing sense of the rights of the 'other fellow,' doctrines which you, sir, have taught with more vigor and effect than any other man in my time. If these boys cannot keep the name of Kent alive, I am willing it should be forgotten.

He enclosed some photographs of the Woods. To this the President replied:

By George! You are right. It is enough to do the deed and not to desire, as you say to 'stencil one's name on the benefaction.' Good for you and for the five boys who are to keep the name of Kent alive! I have four who I hope will do the same thing by the name of Roosevelt. Those are awfully good photos.

John Muir, on learning that the grove was to be named for him, wrote in his characteristic style:

Saving these woods from the axe and saw, from the money changers and water changers is in many ways the most notable service to God and man I have heard of since my forest wanderings began, a much needed lesson to saint and sinner alike, and a credit and encouragement to God.

Subsequently, Kent made additional donations totalling 132 acres, plus a further 50 acres given by the railroad in which Kent had a major interest, thus nearly doubling the size of the Monument.

Though it is the redwoods which everyone thinks of in Muir Woods, William Kent's own favorite tree was not a redwood but a Douglas Fir. This tree, the largest fir on the mountain, was dedicated to his memory on May 5, 1929. The plaque may be seen attached to a rock next to the tree near the start of the Fern Canyon Trail. The rock, weighing three and a half tons, was brought from Fern Canyon by flat car on the Mountain Railway to the end of the line and loaded on a wagon, but fell off into the creek 200 yards short of the site. Park employees, aided by Tamalpais Conservation Club members, succeeded in rescuing it.

William Horsefall of the TCC installed the plaque, which was accepted by William Kent's oldest son, William E. Kent. (William Kent had died March 13, 1928.) At the ceremony, singing was provided by a male chorus from the Sierra and California Alpine Clubs; instrumental music was offered by the Tourist Club; and bird calls were given by Bert Harwell. The project was financed by ten-cent contributions (a total of $60) by hiking club members.

Though Mt. Tamalpais certainly was not as dear to John Muir's heart as were the Sierra and Alaska, he is appropriately honored by a plaque. When a Liberty ship, the *John Muir,* was launched in Sausalito in 1942, a plaque was placed on what was called the "Victory Tree" — perhaps not exactly what Muir would have chosen as a memorial. Portraits of both Muir and Kent, painted by Herbert A. Collins, Sr., were presented to the Monument in 1937; they hang in the Monument cafeteria today.

A redwood known as the "Pinchot Tree" stands in Bohemian Grove, with a plaque, dedicated May 1, 1910. There is a considerable irony in this. Gifford Pinchot, who as U. S. Forester had been active in founding the Monument, was outraged that President William Howard Taft, who had succeeded Teddy Roosevelt in 1909, had made it a part of the National Park Service rather than the Forest Service. Because of the open split, Pinchot was dismissed. Pinchot had also feuded with John Muir, though both were dedicated conservationists. As a consequence there was a split in the conservationist movement over erecting a plaque to Pinchot in a park named for Muir.

Finally, on an occasion typical of him, the sculptor Beniamino Bufano erected one of his statues of

St. Francis in Cathedral Grove in honor of the United Nations. The ceremony was held on October 25, 1969, but only a handful of people attended. Marvin Hershey, Chief Ranger, says that Bufano arrived one day unannounced with his tremendous statue on a truck. After some hasty communication with Park Service headquarters in Washington, it was decided that the statue could remain, but only for a short period. Bufano, however, had it erected so substantially that the Park had great difficulty in taking it down.

Located so near to a large metropolitan area, Muir Woods has attracted throngs of visitors, now more than a million annually. Even on a rainy winter weekday, the parking lot is often crowded. Besides craning their necks to see the tops of the redwoods, visitors gather around the redwood cross-section to marvel at the 1021 rings. But few know that this was not cut from a Muir Woods tree; it was donated in 1930 by the Union Lumber Company.

Other visitors are drawn to the Nature Walk, while some come to see the steelhead spawn. A few consider the Woods in the early spring one of the best places to find the rare purple and white trilliums, fritillarias and fetid adder's tongues. Later in the season, the azalea is an attraction for all and, in winter, those who wander away from the Monument headquarters may find one of the several swarms of lady-bugs which return each year to the same locations.

Among the visitors have been a great many distinguished public figures from here and abroad — heads of state, cabinet ministers, ambassadors, scientists, musicians, writers. The Monument has furnished what must be a very incomplete list containing some mysterious incongruities:

1934, October. 500 delegates to the AFL convention; 18 Gray Line stages

1937, October. 1400 postmasters; 34 buses and 81 cars

1928, June. 1600 from Rotary International; 281 cars; 10 buses

1941, October. "Most elaborate luncheon ever held in Muir Woods." 150 delegates to convention of National Association of Waste Material Dealers. Orchestra, Singer, Play: "Snow White."

1943, October. H.R.H Prince Faisal and H.R.H Prince Khalid, sons of King Saud of Saudi Arabia, accompanied by two seven-foot Nubian bodyguards, swords, jewel-studded daggers, in Arab dress. "Caused quite a stir."

1945, May. 500 delegates from Organizing Conference of the United Nations, a memorial service for F.D.R. Speakers included Edward Stettinius, U. S. Secretary of State; V. M. Molotov, Foreign Minister, U.S.S.R.; Field Marshall Jan Christian Smuts, Prime Minister, South Africa; and Alger Hiss, U. S. State Department, organizer of the Conference.

1949, October. Jawaharlal Nehru, former Prime Minister, India, and his daughter Indira Ghandi, future Prime Minister. They hiked to the F.D.R. memorial, and bought burls, a carved redwood horse, and postcards.

1953, August. 8,732 Boy Scouts over an 8-day period

1955, June. 6,000 teen-aged delegates from Convention of the Lutheran League and Choral Union, in 152 buses. Produced a record of 9,277 visitors for one day.

1956, August. Many party leaders from Republican National Convention, including V.P. Richard Nixon.

1959, June. Large group from the Bolshoi Ballet.

1960, March. Many members of foreign Olympic Teams at close of Squaw Valley Winter Olympics.

1962, August. 150 delegates from National Shade Tree Convention. Held session in Cathedral Grove.

1962, August. 2,000 American Bar Association delegates. 43 busses. Champagne.

1967, April. Warner Bros. filmed a portion of "Petulia," starring George Scott and Julie Christy.

With these massive invasions, the Monument over the years has had to impose severe restrictions on its visitors. The rules specify: no pets, no picnicking, no picking plants, and no straying from paths (main ones are now hard surfaced). Most of these restrictions date back to the 1930s when visitors multiplied as the number of autos proliferated, especially after the opening of the Golden Gate Bridge. So many lovely five-finger ferns were uprooted and carried away in the 1930s that someone donated 500 ferns to replenish the supply. At present, five-finger ferns are rare, but a few can be found along Redwood Creek and along streams elsewhere on the Mountain.

Though the Monument, like all the national parks which have to contend with a million or more visitors annually, is sorely tried, it continues to please all comers. Walking along Redwood Creek among the stream of visitors, one hears again and again voices tinged with excitement and awe at the magnificence of the redwoods. The reaction is clear even when the language is foreign. The place is incomparable.

CHAPTER NOTES

The best single source about Muir Woods is Jim Morley's *Muir Woods, The History, Sights and Seasons of the Famous Redwood Forest Near San Francisco; A Pictorial Guide.* Copies are available at Monument headquarters.

William Kent's widow, Elizabeth T. Kent, left in manuscript form a *Biography of William Kent,* available in some libraries.

The correspondence between Kent and President Roosevelt may be found in an article in the *Sierra Club Bulletin,* June 1908, by E. T. Parsons, entitled "William Kent's Gift."

Fishing at Lake Lagunitas in the 1930s. Exercising control over large areas of the Mountain, Marin Municipal Water District provides recreation and protects open space as well as collecting and distributing water to county residents. (Courtesy of the Marin County Historical Society)

CHAPTER THIRTEEN

Marin Municipal Water District

For more than a hundred years the history of Mt. Tamalpais has been inseparable from the needs of county residents for water. Marin County's water supply system began in 1871 as an adjunct to a real estate project of William T. Coleman, of San Francisco vigilante fame. Coleman had purchased the 100-acre Irwin Ranch in San Rafael, and needed water to supply the houses he was building. He formed the Marin County Water Company, which then constructed a dam on Lagunitas Creek, designed and built under the direction of Herman Schussler, Chief Engineer of the Spring Valley Water Company in San Francisco, and completed November 9, 1873. The work was done by Chinese coolies who were paid $20 a month. Besides serving Coleman's subdivision, the water supplied the village of San Rafael and the State Prison at San Quentin.

During the thirty-two years following completion of Lagunitas Dam, until Phoenix Gulch Dam was build in 1905, Lagunitas Lake was the only storage reservoir of the company, though several other sources of supply were developed to meet the increasing demands of the growing community: Worn Springs (located above today's Ross Reservoir), purchased in 1881; Bill Williams Gulch Dam, built in 1886, a small diversion dam at an elevation of 455 feet, the remnants of which are still visible; and lastly, a small dam on SwedeGeorge Creek. These sup-

plementary sources were subsequently abandoned, Swede George not until 1956.

As demand for water continued to grow, the Marin County Water Company was forced to seek additional storage capacity. The first attempt, to build the Tamalpais Dam, proved abortive. Though construction was started in 1903 not far below Lagunitas Lake, the County Board of Supervisors halted the work, refusing permission to flood out a portion of the Bolinas-Fairfax road. The company appealed to the State Supreme Court, which over-ruled the County, but a new location for the road aroused controversy, and not until 1910 was the road relocated through Liberty Gulch. By 1916, when the Marin Municipal Water District came into the picture, all the company had done at the site was to clear it, excavate for the foundation and pour a concrete cutoff wall across the creek. This wall can still be seen opposite the Alpine-Bon Tempe pump when the lake is low.

Because of all these difficulties with the proposed Tamalpais dam, the Marin County Water Company, out of desperation, announced in August of 1905 that it would build a dam in Phoenix Gulch which would double the company's storage capacity. A contract was awarded to C. M. Erickson of Fresno for construction of the dam, and work was commenced in September and completed the following

July. The work force consisted of 43 men and 120 horses. When completed, the earthen dam stored about 100 million gallons. Later, in 1908, the dam was raised 15 feet, increasing its capacity to 172 million gallons.

During the earthquake of April 1906, the dam suffered minor damage to the upstream face. Laborers on the job quit to get work in San Francisco but, according to newspaper reports, "soon came back because of the high cost of living and probably nothing to drink." In the 1960s, State authorities found the dam did not meet earthquake standards. The lake was drained and rehabilitated in 1968, under an agreement with the Wildlife Conservation Bureau for a fishing and recreation project toward which the State contributed $89,000. Since then it has not been used as a reservoir except during the drought years of 1976 and 1977. Though the State authorities later approved the dam when it was rehabilitated in 1968, they later decided that the wooden spillway did not meet current earthquake standards; it was replaced with concrete in 1985.

On the south side of the Mountain, the water systems were quite different. Prior to the establishment of the Marin Municipal Water District, there were no large storage facilities; small diversion dams or intakes delivered water from the creeks directly into the system. As at Lake Lagunitas, this supply was developed as part of a real estate venture, which began as the Tamalpais Land and Water Company. Incorporated September 5, 1889, the company subdivided and sold its first lands at public auction, May 31, 1890, the beginning of Mill Valley. In order to provide water for the development, the company first tapped the waters of Lagoon (Fern) Creek to supplement the Mill Creek supply. The water was stored behind a small dam on Cascade Creek.

In the early 1900s the Tamalpais Land and Water Company, in order to separate its land interests from its water interests, set up the Mill Valley Water Company to handle its water business. But this company was shortlived; its interests were sold in 1904 to the North Coast Water Company, which after entering into an agreement with the Belvedere Land Company to supply it with water, built Belvedere Dam (now Mill Valley Reservoir) in 1905 and expanded the intake system from Lagoon Creek. The pipe was laid westerly along what became the famous "Pipeline Trail."

Two years later, in 1907, the North Coast Water Company, responding to the growing demand for water, instituted condemnation proceedings against William Kent's property in Frank Valley, which led Kent to deed the land to the Federal government for Muir Woods National Monument. Blocked on this front, the company, the same year, installed a number of additional intake systems in creeks above Mill Valley, each delivering varying and unpredictable amounts of water, depending on the rainfall each season. For this reason, and because they created possible health hazards, they were abandoned in September, 1967, long after the Marin Municipal Water District had been established and long after southern Marin was receiving MMWD water.

The Marin Municipal Water District, strongly backed by William Kent, was created by referendum in 1912, the first such district in the state. The plan overcame strong opposition from the existing private companies and their utility affiliates in San Francisco. As Elizabeth Kent says in her biography of William Kent, "A precedent was being set repugnant to the ideas of private capital."

Once the corporation was established, the new Water District succeeded in getting on the ballot a $3,000,000 bond issue to build Alpine Dam. Realizing that the campaign for the bond issue would be a tough one, Marin County leaders sought William Kent's assistance. At the time, Kent was serving as Congressman for Marin and was reluctant to leave Washington.

Sufficient pressure was exerted, however, to bring him out as the featured speaker at a big pro-bond picnic held on the site of the proposed Alpine dam. His widow has written that his address was "not only a revelation of the fashion in which private utilities of that period were looting the people, but also of the speaker's concept of the relation which should exist between wealth and public obligation."

Congressman Kent said, in part:

It so happened that about thirty-five years back my father became the possessor of three hundred and five shares of the capital stock of the old Marin County Water Company. . . .which represents a very definite proportion of the property of the Marin Water & Power Company. That stock has paid six per cent ever since I have known anything about it; that property has been practically a protected monopoly and the people in their water

Above: Phoenix Lake, frequented by hundreds of joggers and hikers each month, is the smallest reservoir of the MMWD. Left: Bon Tempe Dam, built in 1949 above Fairfax. (Courtesy of the Marin Municipal Water District)

Looking upstream from the junction of Big Carson Canyon and Lagunitas Creek in September 1952, when land was being cleared for construction of Big Carson Dam (1954) and Kent Lake, largest of the MMWD reservoirs. (Courtesy of the Marin County Municipal Water District)

rates have paid for it. I feel that I have had enough out of that property and I am going to put the stock in trust to be given to the Water District in the event of the bonds' passing. That will be a little help.

I hope to be of assistance in aiding the campaign for the adoption of these bonds. . . . I have such absolute confidence in the engineers and the men who have worked this thing out and fought it out that I stand here ready to back their recommendations, and I go into this campaign with more enthusiasm than I could possibly go into any other movement in the County.

As Elizabeth Kent reports: "At the election on August 28, 1915, the bond issue was carried by a vote of three and a half to one. There were, however, threats of litigationn by the minority, and obstructions barred the way to selling the bonds." The Congressman and his friends again took a hand, appealing to the Eastern tax authorities and bond houses. They succeeded. The company was able to sell the bonds at a small discount of $165,000, the money was received in October, 1916, the properties of the private companies were promptly taken over, and the Water District was in business.

Proceeds from the bond issue were used to purchase 5500 acres of land and to plan and build Alpine dam, completed on January 7, 1919, and to build also the Pine Mountain tunnel (now no longer used as part of the water transmission system) and the concrete pipe lines which hikers still follow. The new dam greatly increased water storage capacity, being designed to deliver five million gallons per day, compared to a maximum of two million from the preceding private companies. Enthusiastic supporters claimed that the dam "can easily be filled six times on the average rainfall of a single winter."

The dam has been raised twice since it was built: first, in 1924, by eight feet, so that the District could supply two million gallons a day for the California and Hawaiian Sugar Company refinery at Crockett. Water for the C & H went by pipeline, which became known as the "Sugar Line," to the Marin Rod and Gun Club pier at Point San Quentin and from there by barge to the refinery. This contract service was discontinued in 1931. Then, in 1939, the District decided to raise the dam another 30 feet, bringing it to its present height of 140 feet, flooding 219 acres and storing a total of 2,900 million gallons.

The work was completed just before the outbreak of war. This was fortunate not only because population was increasing and along with it the demand for more water, but also because the military began its buildup in 1940: at Hamilton Field, at the Naval Net Depot in Tiburon, and at Forts Barry, Baker and Cronkite near Sausalito. Then, in 1942, the Maritime Commission announced it would build a shipyard in Sausalito and this, along with the housing in Marin City, added even more demand for water.

With the end of the war, the shipyard closed and military personnel was reduced throughout the County. Nevertheless, the District knew that additional storage would be needed and began looking for still another dam site. This was found in the area of Bon Tempe ranch. The Water District had acquired the land in 1916 from the Marin County Water Company and had torn down the ranch buildings as part of the Alpine Dam Project in 1918.

Bon Tempe Dam was constructed in 1948-1949. The water is used primarily to supply the southern part of the District through the Southern Marin line, built shortly after the dam was completed. The Southern Marin line road today is a favorite of runners; it is esentially level and is precisely three miles long.

In the late 1940s and early 1950s, during the Korean War, the number of consumers increased steadily and again additional storage was sought. Once again it was found on Lagunitas Creek, at a point eight miles below Alpine dam, where a new dam was completed in 1954. Peters dam was named in honor of James S. Peters, then General Manager, who had been with the District for 41 years. At the same time, the lake was named Kent Lake, for Thomas T. Kent, one of William Kent's five sons, then President of the MMWD Board, who had served as a director for 32 years.

Recently, in 1982, Peters dam was raised 45 feet, increasing the storage to slightly over ten billion gallons. Together with the other dams on Lagunitas Creek, storage capacity is now almost 15 billion gallons, stored behind Peters, Alpine, Bon Tempe and Lagunitas Dams. The Table at the end of this chapter supplies more detail on the several reservoirs within the Tamalpais area.

Kent Lake is far less readily accessible to hikers than the other reservoirs but is well worth the effort. Water District "protection roads" lead to it from several points, but to reach it is a considerable hike. Because of its inaccessibility, it is used as a nesting area by ospreys who have taken over the tops of a number of dead trees. Much of their fishing is done on the other side of Bolinas Ridge in Bolinas Lagoon.

Immediately at its inception and much to its credit, the Water District adopted a policy of fostering recreational use of its large property so long as such use does not interfere with the primary purpose of supplying uncontaminated water. As soon as the District became operational, the 3,500 acres of Marin Water & Power Company lands, as well as the 5,500 acres of Lagunitas Water Company lands on the north side of the Mountain, were opened to the public. While in private ownership, these lands had been posted and patrolled, and trespassers were warned or arrested. The 1,300 acres of the North Coast Water Company on the southern side of th Mountain were already open to the public.

The lakes were originally opened to fishing and later to boating. These uses were suspended during World War II when the lakes, as well as the top of the Mountain, were closed to the public. After the war boating was permanently discontinued, but fishing was opened up again and, for many years,

the lakes have been regularly stocked by the California Fish and Game Department.

Over the years, hikers, horsemen, and more recently runners and cyclists have made happy use of the vast watershed and, through the several hiking clubs, have contributed to the maintenance of old trails and the construction of new ones. The clubs helped, also, to develop and improve picnic and camp sites, though overnight camping had to be discontinued in the late 1960s because of the public's disregard of health hazards and fire dangers. Yeoman work was also done, as earlier described, between 1933 and 1942 by the Civilian Conservation Corps, operating out of their Alpine Lake camp. The CCC built new roads and many miles of fire breaks, developed trails, improved picnic grounds and did much to control erosion. Today, similar though less extensive work is being done by the State CCC.

All in all, the District's record on recreational use of the watershed lands is one of unique cooperation among the District itself, other governmental agencies and the hiking clubs. A long-standing dispute between hikers and horseback riders over which trails would be available for the use of horsemen, was finally settled in 1985 by the Water District; trail signs now indicate which trails may be used by horses.

Marin Municipal Water District
Reservoirs in Mount Tamalpais Area

Name	Year Completed	Capacity (Millions of gallons)	Watershed (acres	Water Surface Elevation (feet)
Lagunitas	1873	127	1,094	784
Phoenix	1905	89	N.A.	165
Raised 15'	1908	172	N.A.	180
Alpine	1919	947	4,774	598
Raised 8'	1924	1,246	—	606
Raised 30'	1941	2,900	—	636
Bon Tempe	1949	1,309	640	718
Kent	1954	5,400	7,360	355
Raised 45'	1982	10,000	—	400

Source: Marin Municipal Water District

CHAPTER NOTES

An early draft of this chapter was written at my request by Robert Lethbridge, of the staff of the MMWD, now retired.

The Water District has itself published two well illustrated and very informative reports: *Land Use and Management Report,* 1968, prepared by Paul B. Neese, and *Environmental Planning Study,* up-dated, prepared by Thomas G. Dickert and Robert H. Twiss, under the direction of Clerin Zumwalt.

A third, less general report, issued in 1978, is en-titled *Raising Kent Lake.*

Elizabeth Kent's typewritten account of her husband William Kent's life is recommended. (Marin County Library)

The oldest reservoir in the MMWD system is Lake Lagunitas, built in 1873 by William T. Coleman to supply water for his San Rafael real estate development, and shown here in an engraving from Harper's Weekly, *1875.*

LAGUNITOS LAKE

*T*HREE VIEWS FROM TELEGRAPH HILL *show the Mountain's importance to city photographers. Above: Eadward Muybridge stood in a cowpasture in the early 1860s to take this
view of the Bay, published under the* nom de camera *"Helios." Meiggs' Wharf juts out from
North Beach at left. (Courtesy of Charles Ford) Opposite top: Carleton E. Watkins photographed
the Mountain and the Bay about twenty years later, in the 1880s. Several houses from the earlier picture have survived, and statelier ones have been built. A big chunk of the Bay has been
filled, partly with rock taken from the east slope of Telegraph Hill. (Courtesy of the Bancroft
Library) Below: Almost the same view in 1927, before Coit Tower was built; photographer
unknown. (Courtesy of the Mill Valley Library)*

R.F. "Dad" O'Rourke, shown here with his wife at the dedication of the O'Rourke Bench near Rock Spring in 1927, was a familiar figure on the Mountain trails for decades. The plaque reads, "Give me these hills and the friends I love. I ask no other heaven." (Courtesy of Nancy Skinner)

CHAPTER FOURTEEN

Mt. Tamalpais State Park

Though Mt. Tamalpais State Park at first consisted of only 531 acres, considerably less than a square mile, its establishment forestalled a threatening real estate development in the heart of the hiking area, and became the capstone which safeguarded the whole area for recreational use. With Muir Woods on the south side of the Mountain and the Water District on the north, the State Park fitted in between. Since its establishment in 1927-1929, it has expanded rapidly to the south and west, its western boundary now abutting Golden Gate National Recreation Area, which wanted to gobble it up. Local conservationists saw to it that Mount Tamalpais remained part of the state park system so that they could continue to influence its policies.

The park's existence is a tribute to the enthusiasm of hikers, coordinated for the purpose by the Tamalpais Conservation Club as early as 1918. What finally galvanized the Club into an all out campaign was a 1926 county plan to build a highway from Mountain Home to Stinson Beach, via Pantoll. Hikers were up in arms, fearing that James Newlands and William A. Magee, the owners of the property below the Pipeline Trail and between Mountain Home and Bootjack, would move at once to subdivide and develop their holdings, thus effectively splitting the most popular hiking area on the Moun-

tain and cutting off the Pipeline Trail. Hikers had already seen H. M. Ballou construct William Kent's toll road from the Bolinas-Fairfax Road to the top of the Mountain (Ridgecrest Boulevard, completed in January 1926), and now it appeared that more roads and unlimited development were imminent.

Charles F. Reindollar, a Marin Assemblyman, spearheaded a bill in 1927 which allowed the road to go through, but provided a way to stop any further development. It challenged the sponsors to come up with two-thirds of the purchase price of the Newlands-Magee property for a state park; for every $2 raised by the sponsors, the state would contribute $1, and an appropriation of $20,000 was authorized for the purpose. If the legislature was to "interfere with progress," the TCC and its friends would have to back up the plan with donations.

The TCC immediately solicited contributions from members of hiking clubs, the money to be paid into a trust fund. Trustees were B. F. Schlesinger, a prominent San Francisco business man and ardent hiker, Mortimer Fleishhacker, and Selah Chamberlain. Many organizations helped, including the Sierra Club, The California Alpine Club, the Contra Costa Hills Club, the California Camera Club, the San Rafael Improvement Club, and the Marin Conservation League, under Mrs. Livermore's leadership.

When Newlands-Magee refused to negotiate a

sales price, condemnation proceedings established a price of $52,000 for the 531.48 acres. Since the legislature had appropriated $20,000, the sponsors needed to raise $32,000. To supplement the $22,000 already subscribed, Mr. Schlesinger and his friends contributed the additional $10,000 necessary. The Newlands-Magee property was finally acquired on May 18, 1928, and the park became fully operational in 1930.

Mt. Tamalpais State Park became the first of the state's 250 state parks which today total more than a million acres. The new park began at once to grow. William Kent ceded 204.30 acres in Steep Ravine to the park on condition that the road when built would not mar the scenery of the ravine. Kent also turned over to the park his share of a 138 acre tract which had belonged to the Mt. Tamalpais and Muir Woods Railway, and lay between the former Newlands-Magee property and Muir Woods. Then until World War II, only 200 acres were added to the park, for the emphasis now was not on land acquisition but on building trails and waterlines and improving the Mountain Theatre. In 1930, a dirt road was cleared from Pantoll to Rock Spring. Most of the work was done by the Civilian Conservation Corps, Tamalpais Conservation Club members and other volunteers.

In the early 1950s park development quickened. Three new residences, the shop building and the Pantoll Ranger Station were built. Camp Alice Eastwood, built on the site of the old CCC camp at the original terminus of the Mountain Railroad, was dedicated on the botanist's 90th birthday. The park staff was increased to five, and the number of visitors began to climb rapidly — from 150,000 in 1950 to 313,000 in 1951 — because of improved roads, cheap gas, more cars and rapidly growing population. On "good" Sundays, from 250 to 800 cars visited East Peak.

The park also grew larger in the 1950s, adding the eleven miles of Ridgecrest Boulevard along Bolinas Ridge and up to the summit, together with a narrow strip on each side. The state also purchased the land where the Railroad Tavern still stood at East Peak, but the building had been so badly vandalized in the years since the army gave it up that it was demolished as a fire hazard. Still another acquisition was the Scott property, a 265-acre tract on the west side of Bolinas Ridge which included

O'Rourke's Bench. Nearly half the matching funds were put up by William Kent, Jr., with $1,000 each from the TCC and the Sierra Club. The TCC contribution came from a bequest of John I. Miller, for whom Miller Trail is named. This purchase of the Scott property, largely made possible by the William Kent estate, was not the last of the Kent contributions. In 1960, the estate turned over another 240 acres, comprising the lower part of Steep Ravine down to the ocean, including several cabins that were soon to become controversial. They belonged to friends of the Kents, all wealthy people who, after the state's acquisition, leased them from the state for quite nominal rentals. The cabins, a target for conservationists for a number of years, were finally vacated, and today after being renovated, are available to the public. All in all, over the years 1928 to 1960, Kent and his heirs were responsible, directly or indirectly, for the park's acquisition of almost 1000 acres, half of the total acquired up to 1960.

In the late 1960s and early 1970s, the park faced serious problems arising from what was often called the "hippie invasion." The "love-in" and "happenings" of this time, plus anti-war sentiment over Vietnam (perceived as a threat to the Air Force Radar Station on West Peak) created an uncomfortable situation for park management. The largest event in park history, the "Fantasy Fair," occurred in June, 1967. During this two-day rock concert some 50,000 people devastated the Rock Spring-Mountain Theatre area. The event was promoted as "A benefit for the Hunter's Point Child Care Center" and "A Thousand Wonders and a Two-Day Collage of Beautiful Music." Some of the most popular rock groups of that era appeared — Jefferson Airplane, the Byrds, and many others. As if this were not enough, the Hell's Angels escorted the Fifth Dimension group into the Theatre area, and a helicopter brought one performer to Rock Spring meadow. Drugs and alcohol were used freely. Rangers, county sheriffs, and the Highway Patrol could do little to control the throngs.

Park Superintendent Robert Hatch vividly described the aftermath:

It is virtually impossible to describe the impact that this crowd has had upon the area. There was considerable green grass on the slope, throughout the seats and on the floor of the stage area before the performance. There is now practically no grass anywhere, and late Sunday afternoon there was so much dust, it reminded one of a corral during roundup time.

Park authorities recommended that an affair of this kind be considered an improper use of the Mountain Theatre — no adequate clean-up, destruction of grass, and a horrendous traffic and parking problem were given as reasons.

In the same year, late evening parties and boisterous conduct at East Peak, Rock Spring, and Bolinas Ridge led to closure of the Park after sunset and stricter enforcement of camping and fire rules. Camping was henceforth allowed only at Pantoll and Camp Alice Eastwood. A guard station across from Pantoll permited only Air Force personnel to enter after hours. As a matter of historical interest, the station was built on the site of the toll house which gave name to Pantoll.

The park administration also strengthened the police power of its rangers. This was accomplished, first in 1970, by dividing the ranger staff into two groups: park rangers who were assigned to law enforcement as well as to handling visitor services; and maintenance workers who were to work on maintenance and construction. Then in 1975, new laws provided that all rangers have peace-officer training and authority, and be issued firearms. This change, sadly enough, did not prevent the shocking murders by the "trail-side killer" in 1980, but did help to allay the fears of some visitors to the Mountain.

On a brighter front, the reallocation of duties among the rangers resulted in more attention to visitor services, including the establishment in 1983 of a visitor center at the top of East Peak, manned by volunteers but overseen by rangers. The center provides up-to-date information about Mt. Tamalpais and its history. For the two and one-half years through December 1985, the center recorded more than 36,000 visitors.

The park more than tripled its acreage during these same years. Between 1960 and 1972, it acquired some 4,400 acres on the south and west, largely the result of a long campaign sparked by the Sierra Club, with help from the Marin Conservation League and the TCC. Soon after the end of World War II, Dr. Edgar Wayburn, a hiker on the Moun-

tain since the mid-1930s began urging the Sierra Club to increase the park's acreage. He early conceived the idea of acquiring the Diaz and Brazil ranches, very large tracts which included Frank Valley and Diaz Ridge, stretching from Highway 1 to Steep Ravine.

Several occurrences demonstrated the necessity of buying these properties quickly. Early in the 1950s, a small part of the Brazil Ranch, on a knoll near Pantoll, was purchased for a housing development, but the buyers were persuaded to return the land to the ranch. About the same time Carl Priest and Stanley Weigel (who later became a federal judge) bought the Diaz ranch, but on learning of the plan to acquire it for the State Park, agreed to delay its sale until the state could put through a bond issue for the purchase of park lands.

The bonds were finally authorized late in the decade, and it was not until 1960 that the state was able to buy 376 acres of the Diaz ranch. This did not include that part of the ranch north of Panoramic Highway at the junction with State Highway 1. This portion eventually became part of the Golden Gate National Recreation Area, having escaped several unsuccessful attempts at development. At one time conservationists were aroused by a plan to put up housing there, plus a shopping center, filling station and even a hotel. It is ironic that the park's current general plan calls for building an information center on Diaz ranch property: an area where conservationists prevented private development may now be developed by the park itself.

The toughest fight was to overcome the reluctance of the state park hierarchy to use the proceeds of a second (1964) bond issue to acquire the Brazil ranch. The ranch had already sold off a considerable amount of its timber when a much more serious threat developed. A majority of the acreage was sold to a realtor, John Fell Stevenson, (son of Adlai Stevenson) who, in 1965, sold it to the First Christian Church of America. The church announced plans for an "Institute for Advanced Studies in the Humanities," with town houses for the faculty, and with an expected student enrollment of up to 2,000. The church forestalled state purchase of the property when it persuaded the legislature to keep the purchase price of the ranch out of the 1966 state budget.

But the legislature reversed itself when the "church" was shown to be in fact a real estate development. Assemblyman William Bagley of San Rafael, one of the main supporters of the state purchase, called the "church" a "front for promoters and developers, masquerading as a church in order to gain tax exemption. The old game of ballooning the values of properties isn't wrong in itself," Bagley said, "But it's wrong when you masquerade in the name of the Lord." The evidence appeared to support Bagley's judgment. The church group, not established until 1964, shared an office address and a telephone number with Consolidated Financial Corporation, a profit-making land-acquisition and development firm, founded shortly before the church purchased the two ranches.

At the park commission hearing in October, 1966, the church representative expressed surprise that the state was interested in these properties and indicated a willingness to sell if the price was right. But the church was asking considerably more than the state was prepared to pay, and it was not until early 1968 that the acquisition was finally made, at a compromise price of just over $3 million for the 2,150 acres.

In 1971, a final tract of 1,311 acres was bought by the park — the George P. Leonard property west of Ridgecrest Boulevard and north from the Pantoll-Stinson Beach road almost to the Audubon Canyon Ranch. Working for this purchase, besides the Sierra Club, were the TCC, the Marin Conservation League, the Contra Costa Hills Club, the California Alpine Club, the Tourist Club and the Muir Woods Improvement Association. After the subsequent addition of a number of very small tracts, the total acreage of Mt. Tamalpais State Park reached 6,301. The hiking clubs and their conservationist allies had thus triumphed over both private interest and the inertia of the state bureaucracy.

The conservationist drive to protect Mt. Tamalpais from real estate development and commercial encroachment, which began in 1908 with the founding of Muir Woods National Monument, received a big assist when the Marin Municipal Water District was created and was finally capped with success in 1971 when the State Park reached its present dimensions. Since then a fourth agency has become active in acquiring undeveloped Marin land for preservation. This is the county Open Space District, which now has some 14 tracts on or directly adjacent to Mt. Tamalpais. When the Golden Gate National Recreation Area was being fought for in the early 1970s, the slogan was "Parks to the People." But Mt. Tamalpais had long ago demonstrated that an attractive wild area, maintained for public enjoyment, could flourish close to a large urban population. Today it attracts somewhere in excess of three million visitors each year.

But is it desirable that three million people visit the Mountain? One's immediate reaction is "Sure, the more the merrier." Surely "Parks to the People" means just that. But more people create more problems for the park authorities — highways, parking, pollution, to name only a few. Over-use of parks ruins them for visitors, too. Mt. Tamalpais is not an isolated case. Recreation areas throughout the country have to wrestle with such issues, wherever large numbers of people come to enjoy nature. It is a tragedy of our times that we, the people, tend to destroy what we love.

The next chapter looks at such issues.

CHAPTER NOTES

An early draft of this chapter was written at my request by Richard Gililland, at that time a ranger at Mt. Tamalpais State Park.

In the matching-funds campaign, Lilas Mugg, a TCC officer, raised an initial $100 of a sum which ultimately grew to $22,000. The campaign was conducted by a TCC committee charged with "saving the Mountain." Jesse K. Brown was chairman; James Wright, Sidney Van Wyck, Jr., Jonathan Webb, F. O. O'Brien, R. F. O'Rourke, Alice Eastwood, Harold French, W. F. Plevin and Al Pinther were members.

Sidney M. Van Wyck, Jr., the lawyer for the TCC in the condemnation proceedings against Newlands and Magee, served without fee. He was another enthusiastic hiker, for whom Van Wyck meadow (for-merly Lower Rattlesnake Camp) was later named.

Acreage figures in the text come from State Park documents labelled "Acquisitions," and may differ slightly from those stated in local documents.

Most of the documentary material relating to Mt. Tamalpais State Park is fragmentary and difficult to locate. There is one book, by H. Howe Wagner, *Mount Tamalpais State Park, Marin County.* A WPA project, it's one of the California Historical Survey Series, Historic Landmarks, Monuments and State Parks, 1941. Unfortunately, from an historical standpoint, it is primarily descriptive and not always 100 percent accurate. The best single source, though not indexed, is the TCC publication *California Out-Of-Doors,* passim.

This early aerial view, around 1920, shows us East Peak, the Tavern, and the winding course of the railroad from an unusual perspective.

Mt. Tamalpais from Greenbrae in the 1930s, when arks were lined up along the banks of Corte Madera Creek. The marshlands shown here are now packed with houses, condominia, and expensive shopping centers; housing developments have crept up the slopes from Larkspur and Escalle. Except for the Mountain itself, this picture would be unrecognizable to a contemporary reader. (Courtesy of the Marin County Historical Society)

CHAPTER FIFTEEN

Looking Ahead

Mt. Tamalpais must be free from fires, cans, old newspapers, and municipal cussedness, free from hounds and firearms, where people can enjoy ocean and forest and beast and bird.
    —Ross Valley citizens' group, 1902

No one would quarrel with the statement above; it is as true and pertinent today as it was 84 years ago. But there's a catch. People can't enjoy ocean and forest and beast and bird if they are sweltering in bumper-to-bumper traffic, breathing car exhaust fumes, or being elbowed aside at a scenic overlook.

William Kent, in his deed of Steep Ravine to the state park, said that the property should be "preserved for all time, as far as possible, in its natural and wild state." He was very wise to recognize that the "natural and wild state" could be preserved only "as far as possible." The very road through his land, from Pantoll to the coast, destroyed some of the "wild state." But the road makes the wilderness accessible to many more people. Therein lies the dilemma. All attempts to stop change on the Mountain would seem to be futile.

Yet the record so far is excellent. The entire Mountain is off limits for commercial development, it is open for recreational use, and wildlife is officially protected. All three of the public agencies which have had jurisdiction over the Mountain, beginning with the Muir Woods National Monument in 1908, have been dedicated to the Mountain's preservation while permitting recreational use.

Two agencies that have recently taken over areas of the Mountain can be depended upon to carry on the same tradition. The Golden Gate National Recreation Area, which assumed jurisdiction over the barracks area of West Peak after the Air Force declared it surplus, has an established policy of removing existing structures and restoring land to its previous natural condition. GGNRA was therefore quite agreeable to accepting the clear mandate of Marin residents, who voted ten to one in favor of tearing down the barracks and related buildings on West Peak. As of 1987, demolition has barely begun; the Park Service is dragging its feet. Many conservationists think the roadway and parking area should be torn up as well as the buildings. Meanwhile, GGNRA has been most helpful in restoring the Arturo Trail for hikers' use.

The second agency is the Marin County Open Space District. A substantial portion of its holdings are in the Northridge area, which includes major portions of Blithedale and Corte Madera Ridges. The District is a tax-supported agency, "dedicated to preserving and protecting strategic open space throughout Marin." Its adoption by county-wide popular vote in 1972 lends assurance that Marin County residents will continue to protect Mt. Tamalpais from further development.

The District's properties are open for recreation so long as such use is compatible with the "preservation of natural amenities." Though several rangers are employed, hiking trails and other amenities "must be financed by means other than the District's tax rate."

Despite such dedication on the part of all the public agencies, conservationists and hikers must be eternally vigilant. The conflict never ends. More visitors create pressure for more highways, more parking lots, more snack bars, souvenir shops, restrooms, garbage cans, paved footpaths, more campgrounds and RV hookups. Public outcry has stopped some threats, such as the 1966 proposal for a new railroad to the peak, but the agencies which now protect the Mountain are always vulnerable to the pressure for development. This is particularly true of Mt. Tamalpais State Park, but the others are not immune.

Because of its overriding obligation to protect its watershed, the interest of the Water District tends to coincide with that of wilderness lovers and conservationists. Nevertheless, like all public agencies, it faces periodic financial crises. When these occur, the District sometimes advances proposals that run counter to preservationist principles. A few years ago, the board considered a proposal to raise revenue by logging off the Bolinas Ridge watershed above Kent Lake. This would have been an ecological disaster, and would, in fact, have endangered the lake itself because the inevitable soil erosion would have filled it with silt. Such proposals can be defeated only by vigorous public lobbying.

The Muir Woods Dilemma

Muir Woods National Monument has had to resort to measures which tend to defeat its purpose of providing city dwellers with a taste of untrammeled nature. The rapidly growing number of visitors forced the early prohibition of camping and picnicking. More recently, fences had to be built to keep people on the walkways which themselves had to be paved. Enormous parking lots have been laid down to accommodate the dozens of buses and hundreds of cars arriving each day at peak season. The Monument, like all national parks, must welcome more and more visitors each year, yet is faced with severe funding restrictions. fortunately, current threats to other national parks will pass Muir Woods by; no mining or logging is likely here.

Mt. Tamalpais State Park is in a more difficult fix. It not only must struggle with wholly inadequate appropriations, but faces conflicts of interest among its constituents. Though law forbids commercial enterprises within the park, it is not so severely constrained to preserve wilderness. It sometimes feels obliged to satisfy people who would carry the city with them to the country. The attempt to satisfy divergent interests is reflected in the Mt. Tamalpais State Park General Plan, issued by the Park Department in 1979.

The plan proposed no further roads or trails, urged measures to counteract erosion, and called for elimination of that worst of all exotics, the Scotch broom. Pantoll, Bootjack, Mountain Theatre, Rock Spring, and East Peak were to remain essentially as they are now. But the plan proposed to add a number of facilities to benefit car-borne visitors: additional parking areas, a visitor center, and more overnight accommodations, primarily for backpackers. This emphasis on building worries many members of the TCC and their friends.

The plan was the subject of a hearing in October 1979, at which several recommendations were challenged. Conservationists were present from the Sierra Club, the TCC, People for the GGNRA, Nature Friends, and the League of Women Voters. They persuaded the Park Commission to delete a proposal for a hostel at Steep Ravine, on the grounds that a geologist's report showed the site was unsafe because of slippage. And they were able to block two of the four camp sites proposed for Frank Valley, on grounds that they would interfere with the salmon spawning in Redwood Creek. On the other hand, they couldn't persuade the Commission to eliminate the existing snack bar at East Peak, which the concessionaire claimed was needed by visitors, even though the California Code explicitly prohibits the commercial use of state lands. This hearing was a foretaste of the continuing battles to be fought by those who want to preserve the Mountain as a natural wonder.

Some issues are very clear. For example, testimony was given at this hearing by advocates of ORVs (off-the-road vehicles). These are motorcycles, whose tracks are visible as steep scars on hillsides all over the state. What these enthusiasts were seeking was "an ORV trail from Mexico to the Oregon border with overnight facilities." From the conservationists'

Six views of Mountain scenery, from a brochure published by the Mill Valley & Mt. Tamalpais Scenic Railway, circa 1900. (Courtesy of Joseph A. Baird, Jr.)

viewpoint there can be no argument about such obvious threats, or about the continuing creep of suburbs up the slopes of the Mountain. But proposals for other types of change produce conflict even among conservationists. The hostel in Frank Valley and campgrounds for backpackers were strenuously opposed by some, while others were not perturbed.

We must remember that a "natural area" is not a static concept; some change is inevitable. The Mountain's flora have changed significantly in two hundred years since the arrival of the Spanish. Animals — except for the recent plague of wild pigs — have become much scarcer. The coming of automobiles, together with hard-surfaced roads, has destroyed much natural acreage. The northside reservoirs are a development to which no one now objects. And the most familiar recreation spots such as Rock Spring and Bootjack are no longer "natural areas."

But a few enthusiastic conservationists appear to advocate seriously that all the roads — Ridgecrest Blvd., Panoramic Highway, perhaps even Route 1 — should be torn up. In 1986 a campaign was launched to remove all eucalyptus trees from the Mountain, on the ground that they were not native plants; a counter-movement immediately arose to protect the trees. At a 1985 hearing one person testified that the Mountain Theatre should be returned to nature, by pulling up the stone seats. What about hiking trails? Should they be obliterated? Banishing comfort stations would produce a conflict between "nature" and pollution.

Marin Conservation League

These extreme ideas suggest that conservationists may need to think through the concept of returning the Mountain to its "natural and wild state." Fortunately, such issues do get settled by discussion, but the conclusions are usually *ad hoc* and are rarely expressed in an agreed-upon general statement. The Marin Conservation League offers an exception. In 1966, at the height of the campaign for the state purchase of the Brazil ranch, the League published a pamphlet, "Criteria for Decisions on Uses of Mount Tamalpais," headed by the declaration that "Mt. Tamalpais shall be preserved and restored as a natural area," with the following definition:

A natural area is a wild or primarily undeveloped area where native plants and animals are protected and encouraged; where physical developments are limited to a few scenic roads, parking and overlook areas, hiking trails, and horseback riding trails for access, to essential public conveniences, such as comfort stations, drinking water, picnic tables and benches, camp sites, and to structures necessary for public safety and for maintenance and interpretation of the area.

This definition, of course, describes Mt. Tamalpais as it was in 1966, not as it was at some earlier time.

The League went a step farther by listing "the activities and physical developments that are recognized as compatible and incompatible with Mt. Tamalpais as a natural area."

COMPATIBLE ACTIVITIES:

Hiking	Horseback riding
Scenic driving	Picnicking
Camping	Fishing
Study of natural science	Painting and sketching
Photography	Outdoor plays and
Wildlife management	concerts

Minor concessions for daytime food service and for sale of souvenirs related to Mt. Tamalpais, photographic supplies, and literature concerning parks, recreation, natural sciences, conservation, and closely related subjects.

INCOMPATIBLE ACTIVITIES:

Driving unauthorized motor vehicles on hiking and horseback trails or over undeveloped terrain

Motor boating	Littering	Grazing

Commercial exploitation of natural resources

Unauthorized collection of specimens of animals, plants or other natural material

COMPATIBLE OR NECESSARY
PHYSICAL DEVELOPMENTS

Hiking trails	Horseback trails
Scenic roads	Overlooks
Parking areas	Drinking Water
Comfort stations	Picnic tables
Camp sites	and benches

Buildings required for protection, maintenance, and interpretation of Mt. Tamalpais as a natural area

Radio stations required for fire protection and public safety

Underground utilities and communications insofar as practicable

INCOMPATIBLE PHYSICAL DEVELOPMENTS:
High speed roads   Launching ramps
Railroads   Tramways
Aircraft landing fields Hotels, motels, boatels
                  Bars
Mercantile establishments, except minor concessions for public service
Radio and television towers and overhead power and communication facilities with the exceptions specified as necessary.

These criteria were welcomed and endorsed by virtually all the county's conservationist and hiking organizations, and by many public agencies, including the Marin Municipal Water District, which subsequently published its excellent *Environmental Planning Study* (1973) which supported the League's position in all essentials.

The Advisory Committee

Perhaps the criteria need to be reviewed now, twenty years after they were adopted. One occasion for review occurred in the summer of 1985 as a result of public concern over the State Park's decision to allow six concerts by a jazz group in the Mountain Theatre. At a public hearing set by State Senator Milton Marks, after testimony from all interested parties, an advisory committee was set up to establish guidelines to help Park authorities decide what should and should not be allowed at the Theatre.

The issues are formidable. Most people seem to agree that the Mountain Plays should be allowed to continue on the basis of grandfather rights, as lawyers call them. Musical groups present a difficult

problem. A court decision in southern California suggests that if the State Park allows *any* group to use the Theatre (except the Mountain Plays) it will be prohibited from stopping any others, whether because of noise, traffic, crowds or any other criteria.

Committee members differ over such relatively simple matters as the maximum capacity of the Theatre. The Park Service would like a limit of 3500; others want 4000. Most agree to a limit of six performances of the plays each year, though some would prefer fewer. Traffic and parking problems persist, as do the questions of who should pay for services of park rangers, and who should clean up debris after performances.

The issues involving the Mountain Theatre apply more generally to the whole Mountain. How much and what kind of "development" is to be permitted? To whose wishes should the State Park give priority? What is meant by "maintaining the Mountain in its natural condition"? These tough questions will never go away. They must be decided piecemeal, after widespread public discussion.

Despite the pressures created by a mechanized, affluent mass society seeking instant outdoor recreation without expenditure of effort (to take the pessimistic view), there may be some ground for optimism in the struggle to protect the Mountain from further encroachment. Marin County is lucky to have a lively, effective conservationist movement, and a long tradition of dealing with public issues in an orderly way. If our luck holds, visitors to the Mountain one hundred years from now will find it as beautiful, as inspiring, and as unspoiled as it is today.

Index

Lincoln Fairley was born in 1903, and grew up in Brooklyn, New York. He attended Amherst and Harvard Colleges as an undergraduate, and received a Ph. D. in economics at Harvard. He came to San Francisco in 1946, and spent the ensuing decades in research and study of labor relations, as a college teacher, federal government researcher, Congressional committee staff member, and labor arbitrator. For more than twenty years he was research director for the International Longshoremen's and Warehousemen's Union in San Francisco. He was the author of *Facing Mechanization: The West Coast Plan,* (U.C.L.A. Press, 1979). Mr. Fairley spent his retirement hiking on Mount Tamalpais and sailing on San Francisco Bay. He died in June, 1989, after two years of acclaim as the author of this history, originally published in 1987.

Born and raised on a farm in South Dakota, James Heig received an M.A. in English from UC Berkeley, and for 21 years taught writing at College of Marin, with one year as a Fulbright exchange teacher in Germany. His interest in California history grew out of restoring old houses in San Francisco, where he lives with his children, Morgan and Patrick. Since founding Scottwall Associates, Publishers in 1982 he has published 13 books by various authors, including histories of Petaluma, Tiburon, Palo Alto, San Mateo, Mount Tamalpais, the Farallon Islands, and the 1939 Golden Gate International Exposition on Treasure Island.

PREVIOUSLY PUBLISHED BY SCOTTWALL ASSOCIATES:

History of Petaluma, A California River Town
by Adair Lara Heig

Pictorial History of Tiburon, A California Railroad Town
by James Heig

Place Names of Marin
by Louise Teather

Both Sides of the Track
A Collection of Oral Histories from Tiburon and Belvedere
James Heig and Shirley Mitchell, Editors

Mount Tamalpais, A History
by Lincoln Fairley and James Heig

The San Francisco Fair: Treasure Island, 1939-1940
by Patricia Carpenter and Paul Totah

History of Palo Alto: The Early Years
by Pamela Gullard and Nancy Lund

Big Alma: San Francisco's Alma Spreckels
By Bernice Scharlach

Pioneers of California: True Stories of Early Settlers in the Golden State
By Donovan Lewis

California Heartland
A Pictorial History of Eight Northern California Counties
By Sandra Shepherd

San Mateo: A Centennial History
by Mitchell P. Postel

Hometown San Francisco: Sunny Jim, Phat Willie, and Dave
by Jerry Flamm

The Farallon Islands: Sentinels of the Golden Gate
by Peter White